GLOBAL JUSTICE

GLOBAL JUSTICE

THE POLITICS OF WAR CRIMES TRIALS

Kingsley Chiedu Moghalu

Foreword by Pierre-Richard Prosper

STANFORD SECURITY STUDIES
an imprint of Stanford University Press
Stanford, California
2008

To the memory of my father Isaac Moghalu, and to my
mother Vidah Moghalu, with love and gratitude

Contents

Foreword

As the world moved into the twenty-first century the issue of how best and, in some cases, of whether to prosecute war criminals grew as a lively and controversial debate in the halls of government throughout the international community. The academic, transatlantic, and global discourse centered on the inherent tension between States pursuing their national interest and the quest for the globalization and standardization of justice. Claims of sovereignty, universal jurisdiction, accountability, and immunity were bantered as diplomats and lawyers negotiated their respective positions. What started in the 1990s as a noble effort to use the law as a tool to combat breaches of international peace and stability became a political football with each side vying for possession.

In some quarters international justice was seen as an obstacle to diplomacy. In others a general intolerance for anything but accountability at the international level existed. With each side working to gain favorable public opinion, the debate often became less about the cause—achieving justice—and more about winning the argument. What became clear was that, regardless of motives, politics was at play.

With the lessons learned a new appreciation of the need for flexibility and nuance emerged. The time has come to take inventory of the state of war crimes prosecutions and their future. In this book Kingsley Chiedu Moghalu does just that—giving us an historical analysis of the evolution of war crimes trials. Kingsley articulates how the strict black-or-white approach that was evident at the end of the twentieth century is bending to the complexities of diplomacy. He examines how political interests are inherent to the process and why political will is necessary for international law enforcement to be successful.

Importantly, using concrete examples in different geographies, as well as the intersection between international law and international relations theory, he examines the conceptual tension between globalization and sovereignty as it concerns war crimes. This aspect of the subject, as well as the conceptual approach used in this book, has not received sufficient attention before now.

Kingsley is perfectly suited to write such a comprehensive book. He has dedicated his professional life to international law and relations after having studied in universities such as the London School of Economics and The Fletcher School of Law and Diplomacy. He served in numerous peacekeeping and human rights missions and on high-level panels with the United Nations, including the International Criminal Tribunal for Rwanda (ICTR) where he and I first met.

It was 1997 in Arusha, Tanzania. I was the prosecuting attorney in the matter of the *Prosecutor v. Jean-Paul Akayesu*—which became the first ever conviction for the crime of genocide by an international war crimes tribunal—and Kingsley had just become the legal advisor to the Tribunal's registrar. It was a time when international criminal prosecution was in its infancy. Literally everything was being developed from scratch. Courtrooms had to be built, rules were being drafted, and procedure was being established. It was all new. The goal was to build the day-to-day practice of international law with no room for error.

The political issues were equally high stake. The leadership of the Tribunal tackled difficult diplomatic negotiations and grappled to secure the cooperation of states. They were forced to navigate through both the geopolitical and cultural components of the work. They had to stay true to the mandate at a time when governmental leaders thought everything was negotiable, including justice. Kingsley Moghalu was at the center of this effort. As the ICTR tackled each challenge to the Tribunal's authority, Kingsley was instrumental in helping chart the course for success. He has written about the Rwanda genocide trials in an earlier book, *Rwanda's Genocide*.

In *Global Justice*, Kingsley approaches the topic of war crimes trials from a realist perspective and draws provocative conclusions. His insight illuminates questions that have heretofore been set aside or ignored. Kingsley Moghalu offers much needed clarity and perspective to a complex and fluid issue.

Pierre-Richard Prosper
Former U.S. Ambassador at Large for War Crimes Issues

Preface

This book is the outcome of a marriage of the insights of a practitioner, academic research, and intellectual reflection. But it is, one hopes, accessibly written. That is because the book's intended audience is a broad one—one not limited to the scholars or practitioners of its subject—as befits a subject of enduring importance for millions around the world. Just think of Saddam Hussein, Slobodan Milosevic, and Charles Taylor in the dock, and the passions that rage for and against their trials from the Baghdad street to those from Belgrade to Monrovia, Lagos and beyond. Barry Gewen was surely right when he noted in an essay in *The American Interest* that "whether we like it or not, war crimes trials have become a part of our lives; we are obliged to pay attention."

From 1997 to 2002, for 5 years of the nearly fifteen in which I have worked in the United Nations system, I was at the frontlines of the international law, policy, and diplomacy of war crimes trials and tribunals as a legal and policy adviser to the International Criminal Tribunal for Rwanda (the Arusha tribunal), one of two international war crimes created by the U.N. Security Council in the 1990s. During those years, my perspective on international justice was essentially a purist, legalist one.

With the benefit a more distanced and dispassionate hindsight, sharpened by subsequent research in which I explored the intersection between international law and international relations, I arrived at a more nuanced interpretation of war crimes justice. This understanding included an enhanced appreciation of the phenomenon's political and strategic context. If war crimes trials are emptied of this context, they would lack relevance and would, in all probability, not be such an important topic in international affairs. Thus the subject of war crimes trials should not be taken at face value; it is necessary to get beyond epiphenomena and examine their underlying causes and currents.

The task is not made easy by the fact that most books and commentary on this subject offer a crusading, advocacy-laden perspective—which often leads to a conflation of what the law on war crimes actually is with what it *ought* to be. This is not surprising, for the subject of war crimes and war criminals is one that, as noted earlier, excites passions. But a somewhat detached, clear-eyed exposition of the subject is needed. This book attempts to do just that. My hope is that, after you have read this book, the next time you see a "war criminal" on trial, you will see more clearly, which is to say not that these "bad guys" are not the nasty fellows the prosecutor describes in their indictment—indeed they often truly are—but why *they* happen to be on trial while the "good guys" define who the bad guys are, the treatment they get, *what* is or is not a war crime, and *who* prosecutes the accused war criminals—their own courts or the foreign agents of "global justice."

This combination of the insight of a practitioner with the conceptual clarity of the theoretical underpinnings of international relations and world politics as a backdrop led, first, to my earlier work, *Rwanda's Genocide: The Politics of Global Justice*. In that book, which I described therein as an "interpretative narrative" of a particular event—Rwanda's genocide and the politics surrounding international prosecutions for that crime—I interpreted the pursuit and trials of the masterminds of the Rwandan genocide from the standpoint of the tension between purist legal and political considerations.

This book is an exposition about war crimes justice as a *global* phenomenon. Here I widen the political aspect of the debate over war crimes justice by focusing on the clash between globalization and sovereignty in the arena of international justice for war crimes in post-conflict societies. This book may be the first to expound on the subject of war crimes trials from the specific perspective of a looser international *society* as opposed from the dominant one of a tightly knit international *community* as a conceptual background. But it is not a work of grand theory. Instead, it attempts to apply a conceptual perspective to real trials and controversies that have dogged war crimes justice. Much like the controversies over the death penalty in domestic national systems, the debate about war crimes justice is really one of worldviews.

The establishment of the two ad hoc international war crimes tribunals for former Yugoslavia and Rwanda by the U.N. Security Council in the 1990s and of the permanent International Criminal Court (ICC) by treaty shortly afterward led some observers, practitioners, and supporters of international justice to believe that we had arrived at some kind of "end of history," one in which the Westphalian system of sovereign states has submitted itself to a universal international jurisdiction for war crimes, and that international war crimes justice is in existence for its own sake, is informed mainly by a liberal commitment to legalism, or is otherwise devoid of political considerations.

This book seeks to establish that, contrary to conventional wisdom, these assumptions are wrong. War crimes trials serve inherently political ends determined mainly by states, especially by the great powers in the "international society," and while globalization is certainly a fact of life—even if a somewhat exaggerated one—the end of history predicted by supporters of international justice has failed to materialize. To avoid accusations of cherry-picking convenient sets of facts, I accept and demonstrate competing perspectives where they are indeed applicable to the subject matter.

The book is also ambitious in scope. It examines the trend toward globalization of justice—and how that trend has gone into decline—across the span of one full century, from the beginning of the twentieth to that of the twenty-first. It begins with a brief explanation of the book's conceptual framework and the implications of that framework for war crimes trials. In Chapter 2, the book undertakes a historical–conceptual review of why international justice for war crimes stirred in the imagination of statesmen after World War I but was stillborn, only to blossom at the Nuremberg and Tokyo trials after World War II even as the phenomenon's real nature was simultaneously on display at both trials.

Chapter 3 discusses how the legacy of Nuremberg was hesitantly established with the creation of the International Criminal Tribunal for the Former Yugoslavia (The Hague tribunal) and the eventual trial of Slobodan Milosevic. Encouraged by the trials of Balkan and Rwandan war criminals at the Hague and Arusha tribunals, advocates of international justice sought to globalize such trials through the controversial doctrine of universal jurisdiction. This doctrine and its limits are discussed in Chapter 4.

The response to the setbacks suffered by attempts to press forward with universal jurisdiction, and more generally the emerging limits of international justice as a result of challenges to its legitimacy, was to create a mixed national–international war crimes tribunal for Sierra Leone. This is discussed in Chapter 5, mainly in the context of its indictment and the eventual trial of former Liberian President Charles Taylor.

Nevertheless, as we shall see in Chapter 6, the forces of liberal legalism pressed on to the establishment of the ICC, but were denied the ultimate victory that they sought over sovereignty. In Chapter 7, the repercussions of these conceptual battles are exhibited when, after the United States invasion of Iraq, the defeated Iraqi leader Saddam Hussein was put on trial not by an international court or even a hybrid tribunal, but by a national war crimes court.

In Chapter 8, the concluding chapter, I examine why the globalization of war crimes justice lost steam and the implications of this conceptual reality, and make some prescriptions to address the imbalances in power relations in the international society that have given international justice its current character.

Acknowledgments

I might never have written *this* book if it were not, in the beginning, for Peter Wilson, my PhD supervisor at the London School of Economics and Political Science (LSE). Peter introduced me to the seminal writings of Hedley Bull and the English School approach to the study of international law and world politics. That perspective helped me connect, at a coherent, conceptual level, my day-to-day experience as a practitioner.

Peter's support for a constantly harried overseas research student who held down a busy day job, traveled globally and frequently on the job, and wrote and defended a doctoral dissertation in between, was phenomenal. Although this book in its present form is substantially different from the doctoral dissertation that is its origin, the English School and the interdisciplinary international relations/international law perspective it engendered remains its essential point of departure. For that I am grateful to Peter.

My thanks also go to Professor William Wallace (Lord Wallace of Saltaire), member of the British House of Lords and former director of the doctoral program in international relations at LSE, for his support, and as well to my PhD examiners Spyros Economides of LSE and Jason Ralph of the University of Leeds.

Agwu Ukiwe Okali, former United Nations Assistant Secretary-General and Registrar of the International Criminal Tribunal for Rwanda, provided me with a fortuitous professional opportunity that was to shape my career in many ways when he selected me to join the staff of the U.N. war crimes tribunal as a legal and policy advisor to the tribunal. That experience made possible whatever expertise I acquired on the subject of this book.

As always, my deep love and gratitude to my beloved wife Maryanne, who made useful comments on the manuscript and is a constant tower of support in all I do. Our sons Tobenna, Sochi, and Yagazie, and our daughter Chidera are always a source of inspiration.

My sister, Mrs. Nancy Ijeoma Ijemere is always there for me. During the work this book took, it was no different.

Angeline Djampou, chief librarian at the International Criminal Tribunal for Rwanda, helpfully and reliably supplied research material. Beatrix Heyward-Mills typed the manuscript with the impressive and personal dedication of a family friend.

I thank the anonymous and named reviewers who saw and commented on the earliest versions of this manuscript and so helped improve it. I remain, however, responsible for any errors or shortcomings.

Many things help make a book, some of them indirect and distant in past time from when it is written. For my time as the Joan Gillespie Fellow at the Fletcher School of Law and Diplomacy at Tufts University a decade and a half ago, I thank Professor Jeswald Salacuse, former Dean of the Fletcher School, Gerard Sheehan, Executive Associate Dean of the Fletcher School, and Professor Bolaji Akinyemi, former Minister of Foreign Affairs of Nigeria, for their support in different ways. Fletcher was and remains an unforgettable nurturing environment.

Similarly, I am grateful for the support of David Ellwanger, former President of the Center for American and International Law (formerly the Southwestern Legal Foundation) in Dallas, Texas, for the wonderful experience I had as a Southwestern Legal Foundation Fellow at the Academy of American and International Law in 1991 and, two years later, as the first Research Fellows Scholar in Residence at the Academy.

Finally, I acknowledge with humility the grace and the guidance of the Almighty.

KCM
New York, June 2006

War Crimes Justice in World Politics

> The sad duty of politics is to establish justice in a sinful world
> —Reinhold Niebuhr

In the spring of 2005, as countries seeking permanent seats in a potentially enlarged United Nations Security Council crisscrossed the globe lobbying for their favored outcome in the context of proposals to reform the organization,[1] Japan's bid for a permanent seat ran into a significant obstacle. Twenty-two million private Chinese citizens, with apparently tacit approval of their government, signed a petition seeking to have the Chinese government use its veto power in the Council to block Japan's bid for admission to the most elite club in world politics, one entrusted with the greatest responsibility for the maintenance of international peace and security. The campaign was soon followed by angry demonstrations in Beijing and other Chinese cities including Chengdu, Shenzhen, and Guangzhou. Japanese shops were vandalized and its embassy pelted with stones and eggs.[2] China's angst was fed by simmering tensions over war crimes committed by Japanese forces in China during World War II, for which Japan had declined to apologize and stood accused of historical revisionism.

As tensions rose in East Asia, some commentators argued that Japan, which has long sought increased political clout to match its economic one, had to come to terms with its past in the region if it wanted the region's cooperation in its quest for a permanent seat at the Security Council. A newspaper editorial in the Gulf state of the United Arab Emirates put the demand starkly: "Having mastered economics and technology, Japan is still having trouble with history. Admittedly, it is in a neighborhood where history is held hostage to the present. The North Koreans treat it as party propaganda, while the Chinese are extremely selective about what they teach schoolchildren. The trouble for Japan is that its inability to come up with a history syllabus that acknowledges the brutality it inflicted on its neighbors during the Second World War is tarnishing its future prospects. The latest attempt to rewrite its history textbooks brought a chorus of condemnation from both China and South Korea. That's bad enough but this is a pivotal year for Tokyo as it tries to press its case for a permanent United Nations Security Council seat. Its prospects of sitting at the highest table in world diplomacy are lessened by its constant refusal to teach its young about dark deeds that occurred generations ago. For Japan to secure its future, it must come to terms with its history."[3]

Some other commentators argued that enlarging the Security Council without Japan (states such as Germany, India, Brazil, Nigeria, South Africa, and Egypt have sought permanent membership on the strength of a case for a broad-based decision-making body) would "make nonsense of the whole exercise" and that Japan's membership was necessary to check China's rising influence in the region.[4] If anyone needed any demonstration of how war crimes—and questions of justice for them—affect world order, this was it. A reform proposal for a modification of the architecture of multilateral diplomacy in the twenty-first century had run into unresolved tensions with roots in violations of international humanitarian law committed early in the twentieth century.

The politics of war crimes trials are all around us. And it is major league. The United States Congress passed a law authorizing a military invasion of the International Criminal Court at The Hague if it indicted and put any American soldier on trial. Saddam Hussein, the former president of Iraq, was put on trial before an Iraqi war crimes tribunal for genocide and crimes against humanity, following his capture in a controversial American-led war that forced him from office. Slobodan Milosevic, erstwhile "butcher of the Balkans," who masterminded a notorious campaign of ethnic cleansing that followed the collapse of Yugoslavia, died at The Hague before a verdict could be reached in his trial at the International Criminal Tribunal for the former Yugoslavia (the Hague Tribunal). And Charles Taylor, former president of Liberia and a career warlord, is on trial at the Special Court for Sierra Leone for crimes against humanity and war crimes committed in that country's deadly, decade-long civil war in the 1990s.

Why should defeated leaders be tried as war criminals for genocidal crimes in their own countries when in centuries past such atrocities were "internal affairs" that would not lift neighborly eyebrows? Something is in the air in international law and world politics. Something *has* been in the air ever since the beginning of the twentieth century but, with the exception of international war crimes trials at Nuremberg and Tokyo after World War II, found expression only after the fall of communism in 1989 dramatically and fundamentally changed the arena of international politics.

This book is written to explain war crimes trials at a level that goes beneath the surface of what we take for granted as international law in action. It is an attempt to establish the political nature of legal justice for violations of international humanitarian law by analyzing *why* and *how* such justice is made possible and affected by politics. It will shed light on the limits strategic political considerations impose on the effort to establish a truly *global*—not just international—justice for war crimes that would have serious implications for sovereignty and the nature of international order.

There are few ideals that capture the popular imagination like the concept of justice—that crimes or violations of the rights of individuals and groups should be punished or otherwise rectified, and that wrongdoers get their just desserts. That is why trials for mass atrocities such as genocide, crimes against humanity, and war crimes are such flashpoints in national and international society. These crimes are often committed by powerful political leaders and armed forces, and target groups of people by reason of their ethnic, political, or religious affiliation, or, in the case of war crimes, target military personnel and civilians in ways not permitted by the laws and customs of war. Collectively, these crimes, whether committed in times of war or peace, constitute violations of international humanitarian law.

INTERNATIONAL HUMANITARIAN LAW

International humanitarian law has for several centuries referred to a set of standards to be observed by parties in armed conflict, and so has historically been largely applicable to soldiers. It was aimed at humanizing war—an oxymoron[5]—by protecting wounded and sick soldiers and prisoners of war, and delineating what methods and means may or may not be used in combat.[6] Following U.S. President Abraham Lincoln's promulgation of the "Lieber Code" (*Instructions for the Government of the United States Armies in Field*) that codified the customary law of war on land during the American Civil War, these humanitarian standards were codified in the Geneva Conventions of 1864, 1906, 1929, and 1949, and the two sets of treaties signed at The Hague in 1899 and 1907, widely known as the Hague Conventions. The Geneva Conventions aim to provide legal protection for victims of war, while the Hague Conventions regulate *how* and with what means war can be legitimately fought (*jus in bello*).

International humanitarian law was initially applicable only in international armed conflicts, and then only to soldiers and not civilians. But through the Geneva Conventions of 1929 and 1949 they were respectively extended to civilians and the noninternational conflicts that have constituted the bulk of contemporary wars. Within the wider framework of the protection of human rights, international humanitarian law has also become increasingly applicable in times of "peace" in which there may be no easily definable state of war between two or more parties. For example, genocide and crimes against humanity do not require a war in order to be committed; they can be perpetrated against civilians in peacetime for purely political or at least nonmilitary reasons. In practice, however, these crimes frequently are committed in the context of armed conflict. The nature of acts that constitute violations of international humanitarian law remains in constant evolution. With the establishment of a permanent International Criminal Court, the ambit of these crimes has expanded to include attacks against United Nations peacekeepers. In the war against terrorism, the status of captured terrorists under the Geneva Conventions has become a matter of legal and policy debate.[7]

The phrase "international criminal law" is now commonly used interchangeably with international humanitarian law. Although closely related, they are not, in a strict sense, the same thing. For one, international criminal law and justice includes legal responses to transnational crimes including drug trafficking, money laundering, and so on. It also refers to the institutions (international criminal tribunals) set up to enforce international humanitarian law. These courts are presided over by civilian judges (although the defendants before them may be civilians or military personnel), as opposed to the military courts that frequently try soldiers for war crimes.

International humanitarian law has long been part of mankind's recorded history, but became codified as such only from the nineteenth century. As Yves Beigbeder has observed, moral, philosophical, and religious considerations led to the setting of unilateral and bilateral agreements seeking to contain and limit the cruelty of war.[8] In *The Art of War*, the acclaimed Chinese classic on war and military strategy written by Sun Tzu in 500 BC, Tzu laid down the limits of what was permissible in war: the need to avoid excessive violence and a ban on the complete destruction of enemies.[9] In India, the Hindu code of Manu, developed around 200 BC, contained references to and prohibitions of war crimes such as the killing of an enemy with a concealed weapon, attacking a combatant who has surrendered, and attacking a wounded or fleeing enemy.[10] These standards were progressively adopted in Europe between the fourth and fifteenth centuries AD, including the issuance by the Swedish King Gustave II Adolphus of the *Articles of War* decree in 1621 in which rape in war was to be met with capital punishment.

Although violations of international humanitarian law are punishable under international law, and in some cases in domestic courts under national laws, there have been very few instances of enforcement of these prohibitions despite the historically loud abhorrence of such crimes by political and military leaders. Genocide, for example, has rarely been punished in history.

This is a central challenge that international humanitarian law continues to face for reasons that are precisely the subject of this inquiry.

JUSTICE—SOME DEFINITIONS

The popular fixation with the idea of justice actually springs from a certain duality in human nature. There is a strong instinct toward injustice because unjust acts frequently procure some advantage for the person who is unjust. But the evil that the victim of injustice suffers far outweighs the temporary benefits injustice confers on the person who commits it, and the instinct to be unjust has come to be checked by law and by moral precepts.[11] There is thus a certain tendency to see war crimes trials, somewhat romantically, as mechanisms for neutral, impartial justice meted out to the really nasty fellows who commit egregious violations of human rights—"ethnic cleansing," raping and pillaging war victims, and so on. That is undoubtedly the case. But it is an incomplete picture. This is so because war crimes justice is framed and carried on in a political context of sovereign states. War crimes are frequently committed to advance political agendas. The responses to them are necessarily political as well, whether expressed through a criminal trial or a negotiated pardon.

War crimes tribunals are created by political bodies and processes, be they decisions of the United Nations Security Council in the case of the ad hoc international criminal tribunals for the former Yugoslavia and Rwanda, agreements between sovereign states and international organizations such as the UN in the case of the Special Court for Sierra Leone, domestic war crimes tribunals such as the Iraq Special Tribunal, or multilateral treaties in the case of the permanent International Criminal Court. The political and strategic considerations of states are thus frequently factored into decisions and negotiations on the formation of international war crimes tribunals.

I use the term "justice" not in the general sense in which it is conflated with morality, but rather in a number of related senses. The first is justice as equality of rights and privileges, "equality in the distribution or in the application of rights as between the strong and the weak, the large and the small, the rich and the poor, the black and the white, the nuclear and the nonnuclear, or the victors and the vanquished."[12] The second is justice in the specific context of the equality of such rights and privileges before the law, referred to as formal justice.[13]

This book, then, explores the term in an institutional legal sense, one in which duly constituted courts mete out retribution and restitution for actions defined and accepted as crimes in international humanitarian law. One author has termed this "legalism."[14] My main object of examination is international war crimes justice as rendered by international tribunals, but national legal processes that have—or claim—jurisdiction to hand down justice for international war crimes will be reviewed where appropriate. Just as national jurisdictions may in some instances assert a role for themselves in international war crimes justice, the distinction between the international and the strictly national has been further blurred by a sharp rise in civil wars within states in which international humanitarian law issues are directly relevant. This is different from the conflicts *between* sovereign states that characterized war prior to the second half of the twentieth century. Indeed, "war" and "war crimes" are very limited concepts that are part of a wider spectrum of international humanitarian law that courtroom trials may seek to address. As noted earlier, violations of such laws can occur as well in times of "peace." I nevertheless use the phrases "war crimes," "war crimes tribunals," and "war crimes justice" in a general sense for simplicity, without prejudice to the specific discussions of war crimes in their technical sense.

In discussing war crimes justice and tribunals, another distinction is necessary for the sake of clarity. That distinction, aptly captured by Hedley Bull, is one between what he calls "international or interstate justice," "individual or human justice," and "cosmopolitan or world justice." International justice deals with the rights and duties of sovereign states in international relations on the basis of sovereign equality; individual justice encompasses the rights and duties of individuals as subjects, not just objects, of international law; and cosmopolitan justice embodies a radical *transnational* extension of individual justice. All three kinds of justice are, in fact, interlinked. Here again, in this book, I use the phrase "international justice" as encompassing human justice as well as justice between states, because the pursuit of human justice, and even cosmopolitan justice, frequently also involves the duties of sovereign states.

Regarding cosmopolitan justice Bull expounds: "These are ideas which seek to spell out what is right or good for the world as a whole, for an imagined *civitas maxima* or cosmopolitan society to which all individuals belong and to which their interests should be subordinate. This notion of justice as the promotion of the world common good is different from that of the assertion of the rights and duties of individual human beings all over the globe for it posits the idea that these individuals form or should form a society or community whose common interests or common good must qualify or even determine what their individual rights and duties are, just as the rights and duties of individuals within the state have in the past been qualified or determined by notions such as the good of the state, the greatest happiness of the greatest number of citizens, or the general will...."[15]

These distinctions generate certain tensions, with each form of justice seeking dominance through various agencies, be it governments, transnational civil society, or other actors.

INHERENT TENSIONS

The sponsors of war crimes tribunals often present them as designed to build or maintain international peace by bringing justice to situations where its absence is a major cause of conflict. In this sense law is brought into the service of what is essentially a political goal. A description of war crimes justice as "political justice" is thus an apt one.[16] It has been defined as "the use of legal institutions and processes to create, sustain and legitimate a particular order...."[17] But the assumed logic inherent in formal justice (that no one or no interest is above the law and that justice is completely impartial) frequently clashes with political considerations that are not so pure, and tensions develop between justice and these other interests. Judicial approaches to conflict resolution can also be either a fig leaf for political inaction, or part of a larger strategy that is not always altruistic, with "justice" serving as a means to that end.

These tensions operate at three levels. The first one is the internal and external selectivity of international justice. Internal selectivity applies to the definition of what is a crime in international humanitarian law. Genocide, crimes against humanity, and violations of the laws and customs of war are all grave crimes. But what about high-altitude "precision" bombing that produces immense collateral damage during warfare, or the targeting of electrical grids or other objects or spaces used by civilians? The legal status of the threat or use of nuclear weapons in international humanitarian law also remains hazy.[18] This internal selectivity is one of the more endogenous characteristics of international humanitarian law. These contradictions exist because, for example, the states most likely to engage in high-altitude bombing are the powerful states in the international society, which have the technology to fight air wars that expose their soldiers to an absolute minimum of risk. The external selectivity is that which puts limits on where and to whom accountability for violations of international humanitarian law can apply. Thus there are international war crimes tribunals for Rwanda and the former Yugoslavia, but not for Liberia, Sri Lanka, or East Timor.

The second level of tension is the occasional clash between cosmopolitan conceptions of justice and domestic order in its most basic form—stability. This tension is real because although justice helps order societies, it does not follow that there can be no tension between justice and societal stability. That tension is at its most glaring in the context of transitional justice in domestic societies emerging from conflicts. Here there are situations when insisting on legal justice for violations of international humanitarian law may threaten or hamper societal stability, as was the case in South Africa's transition out of apartheid.

A third level of tension, which follows naturally from the previous two, is one between the phenomenon of globalization and sovereignty. It is reflected in the clash between cosmopolitan notions of international justice and that of international order, defined by Hedley Bull as "a pattern of activity that sustains the elementary or primary goals of the society of states, or international society."[19] This tension is largely due to the sovereignty that asserts the primacy of states within their territories except when they give it up of their own volition, for example, in a bilateral or multilateral treaty. The tension is best reflected in the controversy over "universal jurisdiction"—justice *sans* frontiers for war crimes—by national or international courts.

THE "ENGLISH SCHOOL" OF WORLD POLITICS

Gary Jonathan Bass in his lucid book *Stay the Hand of Vengeance* has adopted the liberal paradigm in his study of such tribunals, arguing that the chief impetus for their creation is the urge to export to the international plane the liberal ideals of liberal states, in particular due process and the rule of law, or what he terms "due process across borders."[20] I argue in this book that, appearances notwithstanding, liberalism is *not* the dominant motivation for the establishment or support of international war crimes tribunals by states, liberal or illiberal. I will offer an alternative conceptual framework for what I believe would be a more accurate understanding of international war crimes justice and its institutions. That paradigm is that of an "international society" advanced by the "English School" of international relations, rather than an "international community" that is presupposed in the liberal ethical tradition or the cosmopolitan worldview.

The English School and international society together constitute a phenomenological and historical perspective of international relations that runs through the writings of a distinct group of scholars. These academics originally came together as the British Committee for the Theory of International Politics, founded in 1958 with a grant from the Ford Foundation. The Committee was a group with close professional and personal ties that included Herbert Butterfield, Hedley Bull, Adam Watson, Alan James, Martin Wight, C.A.W. Manning, and R.J. Vincent among others. They are known mostly for their rationalist or Grotian approach to international relations.[21]

Bull, the intellectual leading light of the English School, posited that the international order comprises a society of states that have established institutions of cooperation as a result of shared values, have no overall sovereign, and remain primarily self-interested.[22] It is this unpredictability of actors in the international realm, which stems from primordial self-interest, that is referred to as "anarchy." This anarchy coexists uncomfortably with the notions of cooperation in the international society.

I adopt the international society approach of the English School to this study of international war crimes justice for three main reasons. First, it embodies a pluralist approach to the study of world politics. In Robert H. Jackson's definition of pluralism, the term means that "human conduct, taken as a whole, discloses divergent and even contradictory ideas, values, and beliefs which must be recognized by our theories, and assimilated by them, if they are to be faithful to reality."[23] The international society approach is sensitive to the voices of disparate political and legal theorists such as Hugo Grotius (rationalist), Nicolo Machiavelli (realist), and Immanuel Kant (cosmopolitan/revolutionary).[24] As will become clearer in the chapters that follow, elements of all three voices will be heard in the politics of international justice for war crimes. Thus I recognize the influence of liberal assumptions, for example, in demanding political action—humanitarian intervention or legal accountability for violations of international humanitarian law—but question the assertion that those assumptions are a dominant factor when states actually create tribunals to judge war crimes.[25]

Second, the international society approach is the most accurate prism from which to examine the phenomenon that is international justice. It is a detached analytical perspective that is not laden with a social or political agenda, such as the activist agendas of liberalism, the static or inordinately self-engrossed worldview of realism, or the radical cosmopolitanism of critical theory.

The third reason for the choice of the international society theory is that Bull's *Anarchical Society*, when adapted to contemporary world politics, explains the apparent contradiction in which attempts at global justice for war crimes in an otherwise globalizing world have not been altogether successful.

Bass sets out five propositions to support his thesis of liberalism as the driving force in the creation of war crimes tribunals. First, it is only liberal states that support war crimes tribunals. Second, even liberal states will be reticent to press for war crimes tribunals if that course of action increases the risk to their own soldiers. Third, liberal states are more likely to be outraged by war crimes against their own citizens than by war crimes against foreigners. Fourth, such states are heavily influenced in their support for war crimes tribunals by domestic opinion. And fifth, nongovernmental organization (NGO) pressure groups frequently shame liberal states into action.

But, there are a number of contradictions in Bass's five points. Taken together, these contradictions actually suggest that the motivations of liberal states acting in international affairs on the question of war crimes justice are not all that liberal. First, it is not the case that it is only liberal states that create war crimes tribunals or that even where illiberal states support such trials, they are necessarily show trials, and that the motives of liberal states are purer. As is well known, Russia supported and participated in the International Military Tribunal at Nuremberg when it was not a "liberal" state and indeed was itself implicated in violations of international humanitarian law.[26] British Prime Minister Winston Churchill, the leader of a liberal state, argued strongly (together with Joseph Stalin) in favor of summary justice at Nuremberg. And, as I argue in Chapter 2, the motives of the Allied Powers at Nuremberg were not altruistic. Moreover, Ethiopia, the "liberal" credentials of which are debatable, has conducted national trials for genocide and crimes against humanity since 1994, with its former head of state Mengistu Haile Mariam (who is in exile in Zimbabwe) and several of the defendants tried in absentia—just as France had argued that the German Kaiser Wilhelm

II be tried in absentia after World War I.[27] The fact is that states, liberal or illiberal, can support international war crimes tribunals for any number of reasons, most of them more of political expediency than long-term policy.

Second, Western liberal states have supported war crimes trials precisely as an *alternative* to putting their soldiers at risk through military intervention. This is the "send in the lawyers" syndrome. It was the case in Bosnia and Rwanda, and, so far, in Sudan. Thus, as one scholar has noted, "some political interest remarkably short of liberal benevolence is an indispensable element in creating international criminal trials."[28]

Third, in citing the propensity of liberal states to be more interested in war crimes trials for offenses against their own soldiers rather than foreigners, Bass is in fact pointing to an international society tendency rather than true legalism.[29] Fourth, if liberal states are moved to push for war crimes trials by domestic legal opinion, then the (realist) arguments of the political philosophers Benedict de Spinoza and Jean-Jacques Rosseau, who assert that the interest of the domestic political community is paramount, are actually brought into play, and so the motivation, again, is not that liberal–internationalist at all. The same could be said of pressure from NGOs as a motivating factor. It is clear, then, that "in terms of sheer causality, liberalism hardly works wonders"[30] in this sphere of international relations. It has further been observed, critiquing Bass, that "if liberalism is just a predisposition . . . and it is crucially in the conjunction of that predisposition and a realist interest that makes the creation of international criminal justice likely, then Bass seems to have heaped up so many qualifications on his hypothesis that it no longer stands."[31]

Bass agrees that liberal states also commit atrocities, not at home but abroad, and that this hypocrisy does pose a considerable moral dilemma.[32] Although he treats this matter as a footnote, the exclusion of the crimes of powerful states from the sphere of international justice is one of its *central* features. It is not just an unfortunate sideshow to liberalism's claim to export its values abroad. Thus it is not the exception; it is the rule. If this is the case, it follows that the liberal paradigm is not the best one into which to fit war crimes tribunals. The better perspective from which to examine war crimes justice is that of a pluralist international society in which the self-interest of states, the frequent use of war crimes tribunals to construct particular kinds of order in international relations, and some liberal ethics combine. If liberal legalism was the dominant factor in the establishment of war crimes tribunals, there would have been many more such Security –Council-mandated tribunals before the permanent International Criminal Court (which is a treaty-based court that only willing states sign on to), established consistently as a matter of course, to address the numerous conflicts for which the option of war crimes trials has been foregone by the great powers.

DOES INTERNATIONAL LAW MATTER?

Many things, including war crimes trials, have been said and done in world politics in the name of international law. What is it, and does it really matter? Again, the answer to this question has important implications for war crimes justice. Since war crimes trials are held to enforce international humanitarian law, it follows that to understand war crimes trials and the context in which they happen, we must understand international law and its relevance. In a contemporary assessment of the English School, Peter Wilson has identified its three essential elements as (a) the absence of a common government that regulates the international society; (b) the importance of normative rules, with international law as its core, in shaping international societal behavior; and (c) the absence of solidarity among members of the international society.[33] The English School sees the absence of solidarity as a cause of the unavoidable existence of a significant degree of anarchy in international society, and posits that this lack of solidarity has important consequences for the *nature* of international law, important as the latter is in the architecture of the international society. As Wilson notes, "sense can only be made of international law by making sense of international society."[34] It is by making sense of the international society that we can see why and how the absence of complete solidarity within it—despite the advanced stage of that society—makes the prospect of a world justice that transcends the states' system a distant one indeed.

Theorists have spent much ink on whether international law, lacking as it does the centralized, coercive power or structure of law in the municipal sphere—a government with power to legislate, police and prisons to enforce, is indeed law. It is, but for different reasons. As one scholar has posited, "those who would draw a clear distinction between law and politics are to be found more in ivory towers than in the corridors of power."[35]

The nature of public international law, like most law in fact, is that "[P]olitics decides who the lawmaker and what the formulation of the law shall be; law formalizes these decisions and makes them binding."[36] From the positivist point of view, law must meet three tests in order to be valid: clear legislation in accordance with recognized procedure, uniform possibility of adjudication, and enforcement or sanction. By this light, then, if we apply these three tests to international humanitarian law, we find that only the first, legislation, is uniformly present. Adjudication and enforcement exist only partially, as I have discussed above, and this suggests that international law, especially in the political domain of the use of force and international humanitarian law, is, as Oppenheim opined, "weak law" but "nevertheless still law."[37] This is why international law is obeyed more in some spheres of international relations than in others.[38]

In order to understand international law a slightly different paradigm is needed, especially in light of the absence of a single sovereign and the presence of a multiplicity of sovereigns. What this suggests is that international law is law, but not always on a basis positivists are wont to look out for. States obey and respect international law, first, because members of the international society of states can enforce it on their own in certain circumstances; second, because of national interest; and third, because of the influence of international or domestic public opinion—the interstate equivalent of peer pressure. From this standpoint, "law is enforced because it is obligatory, not obligatory because it is enforced," and so it is not necessarily the case that international law is not binding because it cannot always be enforced.[39]

Any way we look at it, however, it is impossible to get away from the reality that international law is a weaker kind of law than national law, or law that is nationally enforced. While international law as a "social reality" is an important factor in international society, it is not necessarily a dominant one in world politics. Seen from this sociological perspective, international law is a reflection of hierarchies of power in the international society, despite the formal sovereign equality of states in the United Nations. Gerry Simpson has persuasively explained this fundamental aspect of the nature of international law in his book *Great Powers and Outlaw States*.[40] Voting rights in the International Monetary Fund and the World Bank are not equal, and "states of chief industrial importance" have special privileges in the International Labor Organization.[41] It is for this reason that international law often binds the weak more effectively than the strong—which is why the enforcement of legal justice for war crimes is so uneven. For these reasons, the nature of international law allows it to be constantly "updated," adapting even to violations of it in certain circumstances.

The problem of power relations—and its relationship to the international rule of law—will not go away in the foreseeable future. This problem is especially acute in the numerous periods in history where there have been "hyperpowers." The nature of power and dominance is that those who have it seek to maintain it, and history is very short indeed on examples of the possessors of such power giving it up voluntarily. Michael Glennon, in a realist essay on the nature of international law regarding the use of force, captures the inherent tension between hegemony and equality: "Hegemons have ever resisted subjecting their power to legal restraint. When Britannia ruled the waves, Whitehall opposed the limits on the use of force to execute its naval blockades—limits that were vigorously supported by the new United States and other weaker states. Any system dominated by a 'hyperpower' will have great difficulty maintaining or establishing an authentic rule of law."[42]

WAR CRIMES JUSTICE AS HEGEMONY

Other scholars have ascribed the motivations of states in war crimes trials to realism.[43] Realism is probably too extreme a political perspective from which to define the creation of war crimes tribunals, although some elements of it undoubtedly play a role. Realism—at least in its classical sense—encompasses the use of violence where necessary. Moreover, hardcore realists do not believe that international war crimes tribunals established by international institutions are a relevant, necessary, or desirable element of conflict resolution. The international society approach, which mediates the extreme self-interest of states through cooperation in consciously designed institutions, producing an ever-present tension, is more apposite.

As a result of its nature, whether interpreted from the realist, liberal or international society perspective, international justice is also hegemonic. Adam Watson, one of the founding members of the English School, has defined hegemony as "the material condition that enables one great power, or a group of powers, or the great powers in a system acting collectively, to bring such great pressures and inducements to bear that most other states lose some of their freedom of action de facto, though not de jure."[44]

Watson notes the two senses in which hegemony tends to be used in international relations. In the first, it refers to power relations and distribution—military, technological, financial. In the second it is "the dominance of a particular idea or set of assumptions, such as economic liberalism and globalization." While Watson aligns his definition of hegemony to the first sense of the word, I would apply it to international war crimes justice in both its senses, with the second even more directly applicable to war crimes tribunals—seen as the latter are as "liberalism." In fact, the first serves as the path-breaker for the second, for it is as a result of the military, technological, and financial prowess of the great powers that their ideas and assumptions—including ideas about justice—have become global.

Importantly, Watson also notes that the concept of a hegemonic system is not restricted to governments, but finds expression as well in the activities of transnational civil society. This insight is of special relevance to the International Criminal Court, where Western NGOs, some acting as straightforward activists, others as "technical advisers," influenced the decisions of several governments to sign the Rome Treaty that established the court. All of this is not to say that international justice for war crimes is good or bad, only that for a more complete understanding it is necessary to go beyond epiphenomena to examine its underlying currents. It is only when we understand its nature and the context in which it operates that we can make a more informed judgment about its benefits and drawbacks.

The politics around international war crimes tribunals are often expressed in the form of ideas. This process has resulted in such institutions being at the forefront of what has been described as "norm entrepreneurship." In this sense international or domestic tribunals articulate and enforce certain norms of state conduct and pressure states into adopting those norms in order to be seen as law-abiding members of international society.[45] This is one role that international war crimes tribunals play in the construction of international and domestic order.

There are, however, others who see this phenomenon as "facade legitimation,"[46] with norms providing "the kinder, gentler face of naked power considerations in the pursuit of state interests."[47] This hegemony is cloaked as a globalization of norms, and the increasing resistance to it is precisely why the trajectory of international trials for war crimes is now in decline, with an increased preference for trials in national or mixed national–international courts. Thus it is that one man's norm entrepreneur may be another's hegemon, for where the norms in question are not applied equally across the board, but rather selectively, it is a selective norm and is clearly a form of ideological hegemony. In this sense, legalism as a response to mass atrocity is a Western ideal that those countries have sought to impose on countries of other political or historical cultures. It advances the power and influence of the states that project the norms and are keen to universalize them while retaining the freedom to deviate from the same norms for self-serving reasons.

In what is certainly a paradox, such norms may be objectively defensible or even desirable, but that perspective coexists with others that are not necessarily any less valid. Japanese reaction to the Tokyo war crimes trials characterized them at the time as Western racism and imperialism, notwithstanding the fact—conveniently forgotten—that Japan was a militarily expansionist state that attacked the United States and dragged it into World War II. Allied troops did not face trials for war crimes, which were undoubtedly committed in the Allied bombings of cities with numerous civilian casualties. What right, then, an appraisal of norm entrepreneurship might ask, do powerful states have to impose their concept of war crimes trials on, say, African or Asian societies that may have other historically preferred notions of justice, or none at all in the case of war crimes?

The United Nations diplomat Shashi Tharoor has given an apt example of the hegemony of thought that is found in international war crimes trials: "When the United Nations helped reconstruct East Timor from the devastation that accompanied the Indonesian withdrawal, we had to rebuild an entire society, and that meant, in some cases, creating institutions that had never existed before. One of them was a judicial system of international standards, which in practice meant Western standards, complete with the adversarial system of justice in which a prosecutor and defense attorney attempt to demolish each other's arguments in the pursuit of truth. The UN experts had to train the Timorese in this system. But they discovered that there was one flaw. In Timorese culture, the expected practice for the accused was to confess his crimes and justice to be meted out compassionately. In order to promote the culture of the not guilty plea required by the Western court systems, the UN experts had to train the Timorese to lie. Their mental processes—their imagination—had now been truly globalized."[48]

2

Prosecute or Pardon?

Nothing is to be preferred before justice
—Socrates

Humanity and good policy dictate that the benign prerogative of pardoning
should as little as possible be fettered or embarrassed ... In seasons of insur-
rection, a well-timed offer of pardon to the insurgents and rebels may restore
the tranquility of the commonwealth
—Alexander Hamilton

This chapter will examine how the international society responded to the
newly emergent movement for international prosecutions of war crimes in
the first half of the twentieth century. It will analyze how political considerations conditioned the choices states made when confronted with two
possibilities: prosecuting or supporting prosecutions, on the one hand, and
pardons (political responses that do not invoke criminal trials) on the other.
The aim is to demonstrate the tensions between cosmopolitan notions of legalism and order, and how political considerations (sometimes mixed with,
or cloaked, in the guise of liberalism) determined or influenced the responses
to the war crimes of the German Kaiser Wilhelm II after World War I, and the
Nazis and the Japanese Emperor Hirohito after World War II. These historical developments, of course, have had ripples and parallels in contemporary
international society, to be elaborated upon in subsequent chapters.

THE DILEMMA

There are no straightforward answers to the question of whether violators of international humanitarian law should be prosecuted or pardoned—especially when they are the political leaders the prosecution of whom might lead to a greater breakdown of order. It all depends on the context of the case in question. Political exemptions from prosecutions are not new. They are, in fact, a not infrequent approach to the goal of order in some circumstances. The conundrum goes to the heart of the contest for primacy between order and justice in certain circumstances. The question is: do political exemptions or pardons promote order or do they encourage a culture of impunity?[1] Should justice be done in every deserving case, though the heavens fall?

The proposition is made here that, while there is no "best way" to tackle the question of justice, there is a "better way" in which, while the option of pardons in some circumstances cannot be ruled out, political exemptions from prosecution for violations of international humanitarian law should be the exception and not the rule. In other words, on balance, legal accountability has a better track record than most of its alternatives (the real issue is: what kind of legal justice?). This proposition is not based on the liberal theory of a Kantian peace, but, as I will seek to establish later, on the international society perspective that combines the recognition of the sovereignty of states, the need to place increased value of the individual human life that is violated by genocide, crimes against humanity, and war crimes, and the wishes of a political community, ascertained either through a democratic process or by consensus.

Meeting the challenge calls neither for excessive cynicism nor for cosmopolitan and overly legalistic formulas. To say that perpetrators of genocide, crimes against humanity, and war crimes should routinely be put beyond the reach of legal justice, in the name of order, is a perspective that denies the evolution of the international society. To say, on the other hand, that they must be prosecuted in all cases is to fail to take account of other factors that tend to complicate the picture in cases where the dilemma is present. Such a position would be a false assumption that the world has entered a Kantian age of universal justice. It has not.

The realist perspective is that the problem of what to do with conquered leaders or those in transition from the Olympian heights of power, with blood on their hands, is best left to political settlements and not to law courts. The argument is that, in some cases, insisting on prosecutions can do more harm than good. A peaceful settlement of a conflict can be precluded, triggering a breakdown of order. Or an escalation of a breakdown where one has already begun can occur. This can be the case where defeated parties renew conflict, or undefeated parties, seeing only prosecutions at the end of the tunnel, lose any incentive to put swords into plowshares and seek the "total victory"—and the sovereign state power that comes with it—that can serve as protection from accountability. In other words, better to make a sacrifice for the future by sweeping violations of international humanitarian law under the carpet for the sake of peaceful societal transitions or interstate relations.

Ramesh Thakur has argued: "Criminal law, however effective, cannot replace public or foreign policy. Determining the fate of defeated leaders is primarily a political question, not a judicial one. The legal clarity of judicial verdicts sits uncomfortably with the nuanced morality of confronting and overcoming, through a principled mix of justice and high politics, a troubled past."[2] And as Henry Kissinger, commenting with admiration on the Congress of Vienna's magnanimous dispensation toward France after the Napoleonic wars, asserts: "It is the temptation of war to punish; it is the task of policy to construct. Power can sit in judgment, but statesmen must look to the future."[3]

The realist argument against legalism, especially as dispensed by the international war crimes tribunals, can be summarized as follows: legalism may claim jurisdiction over the actions of great powers, complicate global diplomacy, and attack the historical concept that only sovereign states may impose criminal justice.[4] The realist perspective is that attempting to isolate legal justice completely from political context is shortsighted. Legal justice is what a political community is prepared to enforce.[5] I define a "political community" as a duly constituted society—sovereign, part of a sovereign entity, or a conglomeration of sovereign entities—with a cohesive political consensus on its internal social organization, including what constitutes legal justice.

In the policy sense in which pardons are mainly examined here, compromise approaches have been adopted that are mute on the question of whether to prosecute or pardon, and instead seek to reconcile the requirements of peace and justice. A pragmatic approach is to negotiate peace agreements with warlords without sanctioning impunity. A classic example of a pragmatic approach with strong ethical component is that of the former Yugoslavia, where the United States negotiated the Dayton Peace Agreement between the warring parties in 1995, with Slobodan Milosevic, President of the rump Federal Republic of Yugoslavia playing a key role in the negotiations. That agreement explicitly called for the prosecution of war criminals. Milosevic was not indicted at the time, but there was no deal to guarantee him immunity from indictment or prosecution, although the fact of his being NATO's negotiating partner may have led him to believe he would not meet that fate. Yet, Milosevic was subsequently indicted by the International Criminal Tribunal for the former Yugoslavia (ICTY) for genocide and crimes against humanity and put on trial.[6]

Inherent in this approach is a deferral to a later stage of the determination of whether to prosecute or pardon, putting peace well before justice.

Here, the timing of the indictment is critical. The cart of justice cannot—and, indeed, should not—be put before the proverbial horse of peace, for a warlord may opt to continue a war in the hope of victory rather than come to the negotiating table were an indictment for violations of humanitarian law will be dangled over his head.

Another factor in prosecute-or-pardon situations is the position of the United Nations, which is involved in most negotiations and settlements of armed conflicts. While the UN must frequently navigate between the idealism of the goals of its Charter and the realism of world politics, it has taken a decidedly principled and ethical position on the prosecute-or-pardon question. It does not, and cannot, derogate from a sovereign political authority's right to pardon crimes under domestic law. But it has staked out a moral high ground regarding violations of international humanitarian law for which the international institution refuses to recognize that any amnesties can be valid.[7] This is a solidarist position, consistent with the UN's interpretation of sovereignty since the end of the cold war. It supports the view that certain crimes are of international concern and cannot be the subject of purported amnesties by sovereign states, even if committed within their territories.

Having set out the dilemma, I now turn to an examination of some cases where the dilemma of whether to apply legal norms and prosecute individuals for war and other heinous crimes or to seek a political solution in the interests of order has been acute.

KAISER WILHELM II AND THE TREATY OF VERSAILLES

Efforts by Allied countries to prosecute the German kaiser following World War I represented the second major attempt in the twentieth century, after the Constantinople war crimes trials for the massacres of Armenians, at international justice for crimes committed during World War I. Like Constantinople, it failed woefully. Gary Jonathan Bass has provided an excellent and much more detailed account of these unsuccessful efforts.[8]

Following Germany's defeat in the Great War in 1918, the Allied Powers (especially Britain and France), motivated by the public and political outrage at atrocities by German soldiers, called for the trial of the German emperor, Kaiser Wilhelm II, for the crime of aggression and other crimes such as violating Belgium's neutrality. At the time, aggression was not codified as a crime in international law and a trial on that basis would have amounted to retrospective jurisdiction. The Treaty of Versailles, by which Germany formally surrendered on June 28, 1919, included severe punitive measures such as sharp reductions in the strength of the German armed forces and disarmament, the payment of reparations to the Allies, the especially resented "war guilt clause" (Article 231) in which Germany accepted responsibility for World War I as a result of its aggression, the return of territory to

Belgium, Luxembourg, Austria, France, Poland, and Czechoslovakia, and the trial of the kaiser and other German war criminals. Articles 227 of the treaty provided:

> The Allied and Associated Powers publicly arraign William II of Hohen-zollern, formerly German Emperor, for a supreme offence against international morality and the sanctity of treaties.
>
> A special tribunal will be constituted to try the accused, thereby assuring him the guarantees essential to the right of defense. It will be composed of five judges, one appointed by each of the following Powers: namely, the United States of America, Great Britain, France, Italy, and Japan.
>
> In its decision the tribunal will be guided by the highest motives of international policy, with a view to vindicating the solemn obligations of international undertakings and the validity of international morality. It will be its duty to fix the punishment which it considers should be imposed.
>
> The Allied and Associated Powers will address a request to the Government of the Netherlands for the surrender to them of the ex-Emperor in order that he may be put on trial.

In Article 228 of the Versailles Treaty, Germany recognized the right of the Allies to prosecute in the latter's military tribunals Germans accused of violations of the laws and customs of war. It agreed to hand over all persons requested by the Allies for this purpose, and acceded to a jurisdictional primacy clause in which the provisions of Article 228 would supersede any prosecutions or proceedings in German tribunals or those of her allies.

Since the Allies did not occupy Germany, however, they were unable to compel the handover of suspected war criminals. Other key provisions of the Versailles Treaty were also not enforced, mainly as a result of disagreements and reluctance among the Allied Powers over their approach to a defeated Germany.[9] Thus, the Allies "were strong enough to win the war, but not strong enough to secure the peace."[10] In a sequence of events with contemporary resonance in former Liberian President Charles Taylor's departure from Liberia and his exile in Nigeria (which for over 2 years steadfastly refused to hand him over to the Special Court for Sierra Leone for a trial despite the Court's formal indictment and warrant for Taylor's arrest), the kaiser had abdicated his throne in November 1918 and gone into exile in the Netherlands.

Bringing the kaiser to trial became a major issue in the internal politics of several Allied States. In Britain, Lloyd George's government had called a general election in December 1918 and, as Gary Bass notes, "British members of Parliament were eager to translate Wilhelm II's massive unpopularity into votes."[11] George and several members of his government went on the campaign trail with ringing demands for the prosecution of the German emperor, with cries of "Hang the Kaiser" frequently uttered and heard. Their victory at the elections reflected the overwhelming popular mood in Britain on the trial of the kaiser.[12] Similarly, French President Georges Clemenceau and Italian President Vittorio Orlando were staunch supporters of the Allied effort to bring the kaiser to trial. Despite repeated Allied demands that the kaiser be surrendered to stand trial, including assertions of Dutch obligations based on the legal postulations of the seventeenth-century Dutch international lawyer Hugo Grotius and threats to severe diplomatic relations, the Dutch government stood firm in its refusal to surrender the former monarch, and the kaiser eventually died in his country of exile.[13]

The Versailles Treaty and the failure to bring Wilhelm II to trial foreshadowed many of the same conceptual and practical issues embedded in the prosecute-or-pardon conundrum, as well as others that affect international justice for war crimes to this day. The abortive effort to try the kaiser demonstrates how issues of justice for violations of international humanitarian law remain a lighting rod in international diplomacy and domestic affairs. These issues include those of whether legalism advances or opposes order (the heart of the matter); command responsibility and sovereign immunity, which presaged the Nuremberg Trials, the UN ad hoc war crimes tribunals, the Special Court for Sierra Leone, and the International Criminal Court; who defines aggression in international law; victor's justice; and the impact of domestic political or foreign policy calculations on judicial intervention.

The Boomerang Effect

The humiliation inflicted by the provisions of the Versailles Treaty triggered deep resentment in Germany and radicalized domestic politics, galvanizing the extreme right wing of the political spectrum. Of special significance for Germans in this respect were the war guilt clause and the terms of reparations, both of which the Germans protested. In a telegraph from the German National Assembly to the Allies in Versailles, the Germans asserted: "The Government of the German Republic in no wise abandons its conviction that these conditions of peace represent injustice without example."[14] The government of the day refused initially to accept Articles 227 and 228 and experienced a period of severe instability induced by the internal domestic backlash from the Versailles Treaty.

Examples of Germany's parlous state at this time include the Kapp Putsch of March 1920, an uprising in Berlin by a right wing group led by Wolfgang Kapp (a right wing journalist who blamed the German government for the Versailles Treaty) and supported by several members of the German paramilitary forces and some army officers.[15] The uprising failed as a result of a general strike staged by German citizens against it. In 1923, right wing politicians in Bavaria attempted to overthrow the government, with support from Adolf Hitler and the Nazi party, in the midst of the prevailing economic malaise and turmoil. When the Bavarian politicians hesitated in executing the plan, Hitler and his Storm Troopers staged an uprising in November 1923.[16] Sixteen Nazi storm troopers were killed in a gun battle with police during the Munich Putsch. Hitler was put on trial and imprisoned for 9 months, during which he wrote his famous book *Mein Kampf.* That trial transformed him from an obscure extremist into the leader of the right wing political forces in Germany. Meanwhile, the Rhineland had declared its secession from Germany, and a state of emergency had by now been declared in the country.

Under threat of a military occupation issued by British Prime Minister Lloyd George and French President Georges Clemenceau, the German government had finally signed the Versailles Treaty.[17] Adolf Hitler reportedly met his would-be top lieutenant, Herman Goring, at a right wing political rally protesting French demands for the trial of German war criminals.[18]

There is a parallel in contemporary Serbia, where a nationalist backlash to the indictment and arraignment of extremist Serb leaders such as Slobodan Milosevic and Vojislav Seselj before the International Criminal Tribunal for the former Yugoslavia at The Hague combined with the general economic stagnation to stimulate a marked increase in the popularity of the Radical Party, headed by Seselj, and of Milosevic. Ultimately, however, this trend was not strong enough to translate into an electoral victory. In the wry comment of a Serbian politician: "My genuine belief is that Mrs. Del Ponte [Chief Prosecutor of the Hague Tribunal] was the best head of an electoral campaign that the Radical Party ever had."[19]

This is what might be termed "the martyrdom effect" of international criminal justice, whereby villains become heroes in the eyes of populations that feel humiliated either by the power of military conquerors, or by the failure of irredentist military adventures. Is this a valid argument against prosecutions? Clearly, German bitterness over the Treaty of Versailles and the Allies' failure to occupy Germany after World War I combined with several other factors to bring about World War II, resulting in the kind of changes imposed on that country in the wake of that war. In that context, despite the criticisms that attended it, the international prosecutions of German war criminals in Nuremberg did more good than the harm wrought by the half-hearted domestic prosecutions of war criminals at Leipzig. This was a compromise suggested by Germany after it refused to hand over German war criminals to the Allies as required by Article 228 of the Versailles Treaty. Rather, Germany proposed, it would try the accused persons before the German Supreme Court at Leipzig. In February 1920, the Allies agreed to this compromise. The increasingly likely and unpalatable alternative would have been for the Allies to march into and occupy Germany and arrest the accused war criminals themselves. Allied threats to occupy Germany had been issued simply to obtain the defeated nation's signature to the Versailles Treaty, but the Allies were reluctant to mount a physical occupation in order to enforce justice for war crimes. From initial Allied lists of suspects that ran into a thousand names, agreement was eventually reached to par these down to 45 names, broken down according the extent of the impact of German war crimes on each Allied country—sixteen from the Belgian list, eleven from the French, seven from the British, five from the Italian, and four from other countries.[20]

These trials, which began in May 1921 after much wrangling between the Allies and Germany over the latter's apparent intention to use the trial process to protect the real culprits from prosecution and instead try obscure minions, were an abject failure.[21] Virtually all the defendants convicted were given ridiculously light sentences, and several escaped from custody. Whereas Nuremberg-style trials after World War I, even if victors' justice, might have established the criminality of German atrocities such as unrestricted naval warfare against civilian targets, all the sham trials at Leipzig achieved was to reinforce the sullen defiance of the German leadership and its determination to emerge as the victor in World War II. Ultimately, concern for the preservation of the stability of the Weimar Republic was to lead Britain to back off from demands for the surrender of German war criminals.[22]

Command Responsibility

Following the armistice that ended the war on November 11, 1918, and preceded the more formal Treaty of Versailles, there was much agonizing and heated internal debate in the British government over the fate of the German emperor. Winston Churchill, the future Prime Minister, was cautious about the principle of command responsibility, which was Lloyd George's main ground for arguing for a trial of the ex-kaiser. He argued that while it was well "within our rights to kill him as an act of vengeance, but ... if you are going to deal with him on the basis of what is called law and justice, it is difficult to say that the ex-kaiser's guilt is greater than the guilt of a great many very important persons in Germany who supported him."[23] He wondered if a case against Wilhelm II would be sustainable in a court of law. Several other members of the cabinet opposed a trial of the kaiser because it had no precedent and were convinced it would be bad law.[24]

Ultimately, Britain's position on whether to try the kaiser boiled down to a case for command responsibility—essentially the basis of the international justice trend driven by the ad hoc and permanent international war crimes tribunals in the second half of the twentieth century. The case was eloquently made by Smith, the then attorney general of the UK, to the Imperial War Cabinet. The chief law officer of the Crown predicated his case on the argument that a trial of German soldiers for war crimes without one of the kaiser as their leader would be, in effect, a travesty:

> The ex-Kaiser's personal responsibility and supreme authority in Germany have been constantly asserted by himself, and his assertions are fully warranted by the constitution of Germany. Accepting, as we must, this view, we are bound to take notice of the conclusion which follows: namely, that the ex-Kaiser is primarily and personally responsible for the death of millions of young men; for the destruction in four years of 200 times as much material wealth as Napoleon destroyed in twenty years; and he is responsible—and this is not the least grave part of the indictment—for the most daring and dangerous challenge to the fundamental principles of public law which that indispensable charter of international right has sustained since its foundations were laid centuries ago by Grotius. These things are very easy to understand, and ordinary people all over the world understand them very well. How then, I ask, are we to justify impunity? Under what pretext, and with what degree of consistence, are we to try smaller criminals? Is it still proposed—it has been repeatedly threatened by the responsible representatives of every Allied country—to try, in appropriate cases, submarine commanders and to bring to justice the governors of prisons? . . . In my view you must answer all these questions in the affirmative. I am at least sure that the democracies of the world will take that view, and among them I have no doubt that the American people will be numbered. How can you do this if, to use the title claimed by himself, and in itself illustrative of my argument, "the All Highest" is given impunity? . . .

> Prime Minister, in my judgment, if this man escapes, common people will say everywhere that he has escaped because he is an Emperor. In my judgment they will be right. They will say that august influence has been exerted to save him. . . . It is necessary for all time to teach the lesson that failure is not the only risk which a man possessing at the moment in any country despotic powers, and taking the awful decision between war and peace, has to fear. If ever again that decision should be suspended in balanced equipoise, at the disposition of an individual, let the ruler who decides upon war know that he is gambling, amongst other hazards, with his own personal safety.[25]

France, which had the greatest numbers of victims from World War I, was an even stauncher—and consistent—advocate of prosecutions of the kaiser and other German war criminals at the end of the war. Unlike the British, France at no time considered extra-judicial, summary execution for the kaiser, and President Clemenceau anchored his support for a trial on the principle of command responsibility. He was, as were the British, motivated by the pressure of domestic public opinion.

Victors' Justice and Ex Post Facto Law

The question of the legal basis for trying the kaiser for aggression, as was clearly implied in the Versailles Treaty, and that of might as right, arose early in the internal debate in Britain's Imperial War Cabinet, mixed with the discussions about command responsibility. Initial exchanges in the war cabinet between Jans Smuts, the South African Defence Minister, Lloyd George, Robert Borden, Prime Minister of Canada, and W.M. Hughes, Prime Minister of Australia, turned on whether the kaiser could lawfully be tried for waging war. The British and Canadian leaders held the strong view that the kaiser had a criminal case to answer for "plunging the world into war," which, in Borden's opinion constituted a crime against humanity. But Australian Prime Minister Hughes had a penetrating response: "You cannot indict a man for making war. War has been the prerogative of the right of all nations from the beginning ... he had a perfect right to plunge the world into war, and now we have conquered, we have a perfect right to kill him, not because he plunged the world into war, but because we have won. You cannot indict him, Mr. Prime Minister, for breaking the law."[26]

The preceding dialogue puts into bold relief debates about the legality of war in international law that continue to this day—from the ultimately unsuccessful General Treaty on the Renunciation of War (Kellogg-Briand Pact, 1928), and the inclusion of aggression as a crime in the 1998 Rome Statute of the International Criminal Court.[27] The Kellogg-Briand Pact failed because it was not a positive law with any penalties for its breach or an enforcement mechanism, but rather a moral and policy declaration which several of the signatory states, including Germany (which had commenced a rearmament program) had no strategic interest in implementing. As such, it did not constitute clear international law, as I argue later in this chapter. Even before World War II, the pact had been violated on several occasions, including the Japanese and Italian aggressions in Manchuria and Ethiopia respectively.

The legality of, and limits to, the use of force, is at stake in this debate. We shall return to this topic when we consider the International Criminal Court. This debate captures as well the twentieth century roots of the assault on the concept of sovereign immunity—even if, in this case, for selfish reasons of national interest rather than an altruistic concern for humanity that proponents of pardons believe constitutes a threat to order in an international society of sovereign states.

Sovereign Immunity Shields the Kaiser

The Kingdom of the Netherlands' adamant refusal to surrender Kaiser Wilhelm over to the Allies for a trial was based on several factors: its neutrality, an absence of enthusiasm for what it considered the Allies' self-serving campaign for victors' justice, and on the view that the kaiser enjoyed sovereign immunity. Of even greater importance for the kaiser's ultimate escape from the then short arm of international justice was the extreme reluctance of U.S. President Woodrow Wilson to support the campaign for Wilhelm's extradition from Holland.

The American position was based on three major grounds. First, Wilson viewed the British and French campaign as dubious, self-interested legalism, and opted instead to use the end of the Great War as a means to a wider, more universalist framework for international law through the establishment of the League of Nations. He believed that a narrow pursuit of Kaiser Wilhelm would complicate the chances for the creation of the League, a project he pursued with messianic zeal. He toured Europe before the negotiations in Paris that ended World War I, selling his vision of a new international order to great acclaim. The League was, in Wilson's vision, no less than a grand compact to reorder international relations along the best aspirations of liberal internationalism. Pursuing the kaiser was a distraction from the larger strategic picture. "What we are striving for is a new international order based upon broad and universal principles of right and justice—no mere peace of shreds and patches," he proclaimed.[28]

Second, through his delegates to the Paris Peace Conference, Wilson argued that the kaiser was protected by the principle of sovereign immunity— a remarkably nuanced view for so liberal and purist an internationalist. Third—and in a reflection of the national self-interest that is never far from the surface in the calculations of statesmen—American casualties in World War I were few relative to those of France and Britain. Indeed, the United States joined the war only in 1917, following a German naval attack on a ship carrying American citizens that claimed 128 American casualties—an event that outraged and engaged American public opinion.

To the consternation of other Allies, the United States staked out its disagreement with war crimes trials of the Germans at the Commission on the Responsibility of the Authors of War and the Enforcement of Penalties, established by the Paris Peace Conference and chaired by no other than Robert Lansing, the American Secretary of State. The American delegation filed a memorandum in which it stated the United States' opposition to the proposed war crimes tribunal and distanced itself from the proposal.[29] In the memorandum, the Americans contended that the distinction between offenses "of a legal nature" and those of "a moral nature" had become blurred by "a determination to punish certain persons, high in authority, particularly the heads of enemy States, even though heads of States were not hitherto legally responsible for atrocious acts committed by subordinate authorities."[30] Lansing and James Brown Scott, the other American delegate, cited a decision of the U.S. Supreme Court in 1812 that affirmed the immunity of sovereigns from judicial process.[31] They emphasized that a head of State could only be tried by his country and not by others, and ridiculed the retrospective criminalization of aggression: "The laws and customs of war are of a certain standard, to be found in books of authority and in the practice of nations. The laws and principles of humanity vary with the individual, which, if for no other reason, should exclude them from consideration in a court of justice, especially one charged with the administration of criminal law."[32]

Lansing and Scott, echoing President Wilson, recommended not war crimes trials, but a formal condemnation of German war atrocities. In a telling phrase with echoes in the contemporary impulses to prosecute or pardon, the American diplomats wrote: " These are matters for statesmen, not for judges."[33] A quarter-century later, in a demonstration of how the policies of many states toward international prosecutions for violations of humanitarian law are subordinate to strategic interests, this position was to be repudiated at the Nuremberg Trials.

NUREMBERG

You'll get a fair trial ... and then I'm gonna hang you
Sheriff Dad Longworth to Marlon Brando
in the movie *One-Eyed Jacks* (1961)

The history of the twentieth century has been one of an active effort to make individual justice an active element in international politics. The rights and duties of individuals in armed conflict, negotiated and then codified at the Hague Peace Conference in 1899, out of which emerged, among three conventions, the Hague Convention with Respect to the Laws and Customs of War on Land, was the main catalyst for this development.[34] The motivation for the meeting was not as lofty as its title: it was, as one commentator has put it, "a disarmament conference initiated by the Tsar of Russia who found himself in a financially unbearable arms race" and had delegates from twenty-six self-styled "civilized states."[35] Neither did the conference presage to a casual observer that it would spawn an effective body of law in the absence of an enforcement mechanism. The Conference and the Convention were essentially aspiratory, and the delegates, who were predominantly representatives of sovereign states, expected that it would be incorporated into national laws. A follow-up Second Hague Conference was held in 1907 and updated the texts of the original conference, even if not with significant differences. There was no intention among participants to make radical changes to the international legal order, and indeed the German Kaiser Wilhelm II is reported to have privately made clear his reluctance in participating in the Second Hague Conference, noting that he would in practice not abide by its resolutions and would continue to find confidence in his "God and sharp sword."[36]

Nonetheless, two important principles emerged from the Ha
Conference: First, that individuals have rights that deserve prote
in times of war, a principle necessary to protect prisoners and civ
ulations in wartime and limit the scope of action of occupying powers.
Second, certain international laws and customs were inviolable and could
not be changed even by treaty.[37] Moreover, the Hague Convention was significantly relied upon for the prosecution of German war criminals at the
Nuremberg Trials.

Not even the Nuremberg and Tokyo trials, however, were the first attempts at international justice for war crimes. Several attempts had been
made, without success, even in the twentieth century.[38] Indeed, the trial of
Peter Hagenbach, governor of the Austrian town of Breisach in 1474 (pre-
dating even the system of sovereign states that was symbolized by the Treaty
of Westphalia in 1648) is indicative of the long history of this idea. Hagenbach was put on trial, following a popular revolt, for what today would
qualify as war crimes and crimes against humanity. More than five centuries
ago, in what is considered the first war crimes trial in recorded western history, the prosecutor indicted the accused as having "trampled under foot the
laws of God and man."[39] Von Hagenbach, who acted on the instructions
of his master, Charles of Burgundy, in seeking to subjugate Breisach, was
accused of engaging with his henchmen in acts of extreme brutality: murder,
rape, and pillage among others. "No conceivable evil," wrote a contemporary historian, "was beyond him."[40] The defense of superior orders argued
by the defendant did not avail him, and a court of twenty-eight judges found
von Hagenbach guilty and sentenced him to death.

But it was certainly the precedent of the Nuremberg Trials that captured
the world's imagination and established international war crimes justice
as policy and strategy. Adolf Hitler's rise to power in Germany in 1933
provided the vehicle for his pursuit of expansionist dreams, inspired by
theories of racial superiority, which culminated in World War II. Beginning
inside Germany and continuing outward through aggression and conquest
in Europe, it is estimated that 30 million people were killed during the
12 years of Hitler's dictatorship—on the battlefields of his wars, in forced
labor camps, and in gas chambers.[41]

Violations of the human rights of minorities and crimes against humanity were transparently part of the official policies of Hitler's Nazi government. Widespread outrage at the atrocities of the Nazi regime among Allied
nations that united to repel the aggression by Hitler and other Axis Powers
led to a determination to punish the Nazi leaders at the end of the war. Thus
was the International Military Tribunal (IMT) at Nuremberg established in
1945 to try the political leadership and officer corps of the German government and military high command.[42] The four Allied Powers appointed
the tribunal's judges, one from each country (with each backed up by an
alternate). The United States appointed Francis Biddle, a former attorney

general of the country whom President Harry Truman had dismissed in an act of political vengeance but now wanted to placate.[43] France appointed Henri Donnediue de Vabres, a scholar of international law and a former law professor at the University of Paris who was one of the early visionaries of a permanent international criminal court. The Soviet Union's Nuremberg judge was Ion Nikitchenko, vice chairman of the Soviet Supreme Court and one-time lecturer in criminal law at the Academy of Military Jurisprudence in Moscow. And the British judge was Sir Geoffrey Lawrence, a law lord on the appeals bench in the House of Lords, who was later elected president of the IMT thanks to American-led internal intrigues (the American chief prosecutor had not wanted Biddle, who nursed ambitions for the presidency of the tribunal, in the position, arguing that it would make the United States too dominant in the proceedings).[44]

Nuremberg was a prosecutor's court, in the sense that the prosecution was far more dominant than the judges in the proceedings. The prosecution was composed of four national teams from the four victorious Allied Powers. United States Supreme Court Justice Robert Jackson, a respected lawyer who had become a lawyer without going to law school, was appointed chief American prosecutor by President Truman. Sir Hartley Shawcross, the British attorney general, headed the British prosecution team, although he did not effectively vacate his duties in London and so his deputy, Sir David Maxwell-Fyfe, was the de facto leader of the British prosecution. Roman Rudenko, the Procurator of Ukraine, was the Soviet prosecutor, and Francois de Menthon was the French prosecutor.

The road from Nazi crimes to their punishment was by no means a straightforward one. In between, a gamut of first instincts, approaches, and positions were evident. There was sheer laziness, bureaucratic incompetence, a fear of venturing into unknown territory, conflicting legal approaches among the Allies, and, most prominently, Winston Churchill's (and, by extension, his government's) advocacy for summary executions of Nazi leaders as retribution.[45] Josef Stalin, while in favor of summary executions in off-the-cuff remarks to fellow Allied leaders, officially supported a trial of the Nazi leaders. In the words of the historians Ann Tusa and John Tusa, "Stalin wanted Nazi leaders put to death, but only after a trial."[46] The strong instinct for rough justice was predicated on a belief that the guilt of the Nazi leaders and the scope of their crimes were so obvious as to be undeserving of an effort to discharge the burden of proof. For the proponents of summary executions, the St. James Declaration of 1942 that announced the intention of the Allies to bring to justice the direct perpetrators and political authors of Nazi atrocities were all but forgotten.[47]

In the United States, a similar policy battle raged between Henry Morgenthau, the influential secretary of the treasury who favored summary executions and the destruction of Germany's industrial economy, and Henry

Stimson, the secretary of war who argued for a war crimes trial, reflecting America's internal value of due process. The resolution of that in-fighting by President Roosevelt in Stimson's favor, after Morgenthau's draconian proposals became public and generated a furious public reaction, was the deciding factor that provided the impetus and blueprint for a trial designed to provide basic safeguards of due process to the Nazi leadership.[48] The IMT tried twenty-two members of the Nazi leadership in a 315-day trial that opened on November 20, 1945.[49]

The defendants included Karl Dönitz, Supreme Commander of the German Navy from 1943 to 1945, who was named Hitler's successor in the latter's will, and, following Hitler's death, led the rump Nazi government in the last days of the war; Herman Goering, commander-in-chief of the German Air Force, originally designated by Hitler as his successor, but dismissed by the führer for treachery when he attempted to take over the leadership in April 1945; Rudolf Hess, Hitler's former private secretary, who was arrested in Britain when he made an unauthorized flight to Scotland with the hope of meeting the Duke of Hamilton and convincing the British government of Hitler's bona fides. Others included: Alfred Jodl, major-general and chief of the German Armed Forces Operations Staff, who signed Germany's unconditional surrender to the Allied Powers on May 7, 1945; Ernst Kaltenbrunner, Austrian lawyer and head of the feared Gestapo, who administered the gas chambers and the extermination program; Joachim von Ribbentrop, foreign minister of Nazi Germany from 1938 to 1945, who negotiated the Molotov-Ribbentrop Pact with the Soviet Union that facilitated Hitler's invasion of Poland; and Julius Streicher, Nazi propagandist and wealthy newspaper proprietor.[50]

The defendants were charged with crimes against peace (conspiracy to wage aggressive war and waging aggressive war), crimes against humanity (which included the persecution and mass extermination of Jews and other ethnic minorities and civilians in other countries), and war crimes (violations of the laws and customs of war). Eighteen of them were convicted on various counts on their indictments and given sentences ranging from 10 years imprisonment to death by hanging.[51] Eleven defendants including Goering, Jodl, Kaltenbrunner, Streicher, and von Ribbentrop were sentenced to hang. Three, including Hess, were sentenced to life in prison, while Doenitz was sentenced to 10 years in prison. Others received prison sentences of varying numbers of years, while three defendants were acquitted. In a major blow to the whole effort to bring the Nazi leadership to justice (especially as Hitler, Heinrich Himmler, and Bormann were already dead), Goering committed suicide with a cyanide pill before his execution by hanging. Based on a modified version of the Nuremberg Charter (Control Council Law No. 10) twelve other war crimes trials were subsequently held under the prosecutorial direction of the American lawyer Telford Taylor.

Nuremberg's Legacy

Just as remarkable as the precedent it set in being the first modern international war crimes trial is the fact that Nuremberg was purely the justice of the victor (Hermann Goering, upon receiving a copy of his indictment by the Nuremberg Tribunal, wrote on it: "The victor will always be the judge and the vanquished the accused").[52] "For all its devotion to legalistic forms" Barry Gewen has written, "Nuremberg was in the end a political trial with a foregone conclusion. . . ."[53] But this does not necessarily diminish the gravity of the crimes committed by Nazi Germany. It is noteworthy in this context that the United Nations General Assembly unanimously affirmed the Nuremberg Principles and Judgment in 1946.

As the Nuremberg judgment argued:

The making of the [Nuremberg] Charter was the exercise of the sovereign legislative power by the countries to which the German Reich unconditionally surrendered, and the undoubted right of these countries to legislate for the occupied territories has been recognized by the civilized world. The Charter is not an arbitrary exercise of power on the part of the victorious nations, but in the view of the Tribunal, ... it is the expression of international law existing at the time of its creation; and to that extent is itself a contribution to international law ... for it is not to be doubted that any nation has the right to set up special courts to administer law. With regard to the constitution of the court, all that the defendants are entitled to ask is to receive a fair trial on the facts and the law.[54]

It was of course perfectly legitimate, in the historical context of the time, where a state has waged aggressive war and lost, for the prerogatives of victory to go to the victor. This is all the more so where international order is undermined in such a fundamental manner as it was by Hitler's Third Reich. It was justified, and indeed remarkable in the context of the time, that the victorious powers embraced justice as a strategy. That strategy, in this case, was to ensure, through accountability and the stigmatization that accompanied the historical documentation of Nazi crimes, the permanent defenestration of Nazi ideology and leadership—that Germany would never again threaten international order after provoking two world wars within a quarter-century. The path to future cooperation between Germany and the Allied Powers was to be paved by severing the delinquent state's troubled past from its postwar future.

The American chief prosecutor Robert Jackson foresaw that the tribunal's credibility would be attacked with the tag of "victor's justice." His famous response during his opening address at the trial showed a keen appreciation of the judgment of history: "That four great nations flushed with victory and stung by injury, stay the hand of vengeance and voluntarily submit their captive enemies to the judgment of the law is one of the most significant tributes that Power ever paid to Reason."[55] The influence of liberal views in some states that were part of the Allied Powers ultimately ensured a form of justice that the Nazi government, had its military aggressions been successful, would hardly have afforded its enemies.

Notwithstanding the victor's justice it was, the Nuremberg Charter and the trials based on it have left an important legacy in international law and world politics. That legacy is decidedly mixed. Nevertheless, by demonstrating the moral and legal limits that there must be in the conduct of states, it was part of an important shift away from an international system to an international society that occurred in the first part of the twentieth century and laid the foundation for advocacy for a further movement toward a cosmopolitan world society.

Genocide

A major legacy of Nuremberg was the codification of the crime of genocide that followed in its wake. While the extermination of the Jews and other minorities in the course of Hitler's wars of aggression (tried at Nuremberg as crimes against humanity) was undoubtedly genocidal, and the word genocide was used in the course of the trials, Nuremberg did not have a mandate to try the Nazi leaders for genocide because the term, coined by the Polish international lawyer Raphael Lemkin, was not technically a legal crime at the time. That offense was only legally codified as a crime in international law by the Convention on the Prevention and Punishment of Genocide adopted by the United Nations General Assembly in 1948 (Genocide Convention). This is an important distinction, for the Genocide Convention opened up a markedly wider front in the quest for international justice. This legacy was extended through the attempts to develop international law by the International Law Commission of the United Nations. Although these efforts have tended to outpace positive international law and the actual practice of states in some instances, and called into question some interpretations of the guidance provided by that august body, they have led inexorably to the establishment of a permanent International Criminal Court.

Crimes against Humanity

Similarly, the establishment of a rubric called "crimes against humanity" in international law ranks as one Nuremberg's greatest achievements. Although that genre was defined in the context of the war for which the Nazi leaders were on trial, it has survived as a distinct category of crimes, whether committed in war or "peace." When this is combined with the manner in which the nature of conflicts have changed in the past 50 years—becoming far more "internal" than international, although with undoubtedly international ramifications—the implication of this innovation becomes clear. It has become the legal Achilles heel of dictators, at least in theory if not always in practice. What "maximum rulers" and "Big Men" despots do within their borders has become fair game for external interest and even inquiry. But meddlesomeness has rarely led to intervention or other sanctions, owing to political considerations that are characteristic of the international society.

Individual Responsibility

Perhaps the most important legacy of Nuremberg was the expansion in judicial practice of the principle of individual criminal responsibility for violations of international humanitarian law. The Nuremberg Tribunal rejected the argument that international law at the time governed the actions of sovereign states only, and provided no punishment for individuals. It rejected as well an extension of this argument, namely that where an act is done by a state, those who did it are not personally responsible, but are protected by the state's sovereignty. The defense of superior orders, so frequently invoked as moral and legal justification of conduct that violates the laws of war and mass atrocities in times of war and peace, was also expressly curtailed. Predictably, many defendants at Nuremberg relied on that defense, but it did not avail them. Today, the statutes of the ad hoc international criminal tribunals and the ICC (International Criminal Court) make clear that superior orders provide no exemption from the culpability that flows from individual responsibility, but may only be an extenuating factor in punishment.

Command Responsibility

It is only a short step away from the principle of individual criminal responsibility to that of command responsibility, or the responsibility of military or political superiors for the acts of their subordinates when the superior knew, or should have known, that such persons were committing genocide, crimes against humanity, or war crimes. Again, the Nuremberg Trials paved the way to the firm establishment of this principle in positive law.

But the principle of command responsibility automatically calls into question that of sovereign immunity. If a sovereign has command responsibility for the acts of his subordinates is he or she then immune from the legal consequences of those acts? It is here that the normative impact of the Nuremberg Trials confronts the nature of international order in terms so stark that it remains extremely controversial. Nuremberg's legacy is that heads of state and government can be tried for genocide, crimes against humanity, and war crimes in certain circumstances for acts performed while in office. The Nuremberg Charter proclaims: "The official position of defendants, whether as Heads of State or responsible officials in Government Departments, shall not be considered as freeing them from responsibility or mitigating punishment." The statutes of the war crimes tribunals for the former Yugoslavia and Rwanda, and the ICC, have similarly done away with substantive immunity for these crimes. But this should not be confused as being the general position in international law. The denial of that immunity is limited to cases where the victor or victors in a war become an occupying power, assume sovereignty over the vanquished, and try the leaders of the defeated party under special laws such as the Nuremberg Charter and Tokyo Charter. Sovereign immunity is also clearly suspended where an international tribunal with competent jurisdiction is established by the United Nations Security Council (e.g., The Hague and the Arusha Tribunals), or where an international criminal tribunal with competent jurisdiction is established by treaty, such as the ICC. Outside these circumstances, the substantive immunity of heads of state and government and other high officials of state (such as ministers of foreign affairs) remain solid in customary international law. Efforts to prosecute sovereigns outside these confines have been fraught with controversy and, so far, generally unsuccessful.

The Rise and Decline of International Law and Tribunals

In another important legacy, the Nuremberg Trials established the contemporary superiority of international law over domestic laws in legal responses to mass atrocities. This legacy was to be established in the "primacy" of the jurisdictions of the two international tribunals for Rwanda and the former Yugoslavia, in the former even more so.[56] Why was this so? First, in the era in which the Nuremberg Trials took place, wars were almost always waged across national frontiers. Jurists and politicians therefore believed that judging violations of international humanitarian law would best be undertaken through a "law of nations" rather than domestic criminal law.

Second, the Nuremberg Trials were framed by prosecutors such as Jackson as a contest between good and pure evil, with the law of the Nuremberg Charter having risen to the gallant defense of "civilization" or "civilized nations." This (in the case of Nuremberg, self-interested) defense of the greater whole, which today is captured by the more politically correct phrase "humanity" or "international community" was also more naturally handled through international law as a vehicle for the establishment of a post-World War II order.

International law's supremacy in this arena, however, has come under threat. This new reality arises because the nature of conflict, as noted a moment ago, has changed dramatically in the past half-century, with civil wars *within* states replacing wars *between* states as the main source of carnage. With this has come a slow but sure rethinking, on the basis of assertions of national sovereignty, of the balance of jurisdictions between international and municipal laws. Thus, some states have incorporated international law into nationally legislated laws or expanded their criminal law to accommodate such concepts. To illustrate: even in the context of the permanent International Criminal Court, that Court's jurisdiction was made *complementary* to national jurisdiction, reversing the Nuremberg trend adopted in the creation of the Hague and Arusha courts where national jurisdictions were seen in practice as poor cousins to international justice. Moreover, constrained by their nature as ad hoc tribunals and faced with the imperative of completing their work by the end of this decade, the international tribunals at Arusha and The Hague have turned to national courts for help with easing the burden of heavy case loads.

International tribunals as a favored institutional means for rendering justice for international crimes have also suffered a certain decline, with the trend now more in favor of hybrid courts that combine national and international jurisdiction and judges, such as the Special Court for Sierra Leone and the Extraordinary Chambers of Cambodia.

Ex post facto Law

The issue of retroactive or ex post facto law is an important characteristic of Nuremberg that goes to the heart of the nature of the IMT and has cast a pall over its legitimacy ever since. The legal principle *nulla poena sine lege* (no punishment of a crime without preexisting law on which punishment is based) has been a cardinal rule of criminal law in many countries for several centuries. It is now explicitly acknowledged in the statutes of the international war crimes tribunals. But the Nuremberg Trials violated this fundamental legal norm when they included "crimes against peace" (planning and waging aggressive war) as one of the crimes for which the Nazis were put on trial. Not prepared to allow the Allied Powers a monopoly to claims of defending civilization, the Nazi defendants challenged the very legitimacy of the IMT by arguing that retroactive punishment was anathema to the law of all civilized nations. Aggressive war was not a crime in positive international law at the time Hitler embarked on his irredentist military campaigns, at least not as defined in any statute. Nowhere had a penalty for waging such a war been stipulated, and there was no court created to try and punish offenders.

Even as they planned the Nuremberg Trials, its architects, including Robert Jackson, had foreseen this conundrum. Yes, the Nazis committed despicable acts that infringed morality at its most basic, but had they broken any *laws* in invading their European neighbors?[57] Germany was one of sixty-three signatory nations to the General Treaty for the Renunciation of War, referred to as the Kellogg-Briand Pact or the Pact of Paris, of 1928, which renounced war as an instrument of national policy. It was a signatory to the Hague Rules of Land Warfare of 1907 and the Geneva Conventions of 1929. Jackson constructed his response to these predictable arguments on the premise that the establishment of a court with punishment procedures (the IMT) filled in the previously blank space of enforcement of these treaties: "Let's not be derailed by legal hairsplitters," he argued. "Aren't murder, torture, and enslavement crimes recognized by all civilized people? What we propose is to punish acts which have been regarded as criminal since the time of Cain and have been so written in every civilized code."[58]

The judgment of the Nuremberg Tribunal dismissed the ex post facto defense with an elegant, stretched disquisition that was based more on international morality than interpretations of positive international law. The tribunal first sought to establish that the maxim *nullum crimen sine lege*, while a principle of justice, was not a limitation on the sovereignty of the Allied Powers.[59] It could not therefore become a valid excuse for violating treaties. "To assert that it is unjust to punish those who in defiance of treaties and assurances have attacked neighboring states without warning is obviously untrue, for in such circumstances the attacker must know that what he is doing is wrong, and so far from it being unjust to punish him, it would be unjust if his wrong were allowed to go unpunished."[60]

The IMT then analyzed the legal effect of the Kellogg-Briand Pact. In rejecting the Nazi defense that the pact lacked the force of positive law, the tribunal recalled the preamble to the pact and its first two provisions, in which the signatories, including the Axis Powers Germany, Italy, and Japan had pronounced themselves

> "Deeply sensible of their solemn duty to promote the welfare Of mankind; persuaded that the time has come when a frank Renunciation of war as an instrument of national policy should be made to the end that the peaceful and friendly relations existing between their peoples should be perpetuated ... all changes in their relations should be sought only by pacific means ... thus uniting civilized nations of the world in a common renunciation of war as an instrument of national policy ...
>
> Article I: The High Contracting Parties solemnly declare in the names of their respective peoples that they condemn recourse to war for the solution of international controversies and renounce it as an instrument of national policy in their relations to one another.
>
> Article II: The High Contracting Parties agree that the settlement or solution of all disputes or conflicts of whatever nature or of whatever origin they may be, which may arise among them, shall never be sought except by pacific means."

The tribunal was of the opinion that "the solemn renunciation of war as an instrument of national policy necessarily involves the proposition that such a war is illegal in international law; and that those who plan and wage such a war, with its inevitable and terrible consequences, are committing a crime by doing so." It likened the Kellogg-Briand Pact to the Hague Convention of 1907 that prohibited certain methods of warfare (inhumane treatment of prisoners, the use of poisoned weapons, and so on) without designating them criminal or stipulating sanctions, or establishing a court to try the offenders.

This comparison to the Hague Convention was convenient, but is inapposite. As the IMT itself noted, the acts condemned in the Hague Convention had been prohibited under customary international law long before the Convention. The same cannot be said of planning and waging war, which was, and still is, one of the common currencies of international relations. Therein lies the essential difference between the Hague Convention and the Pact of Paris. In any event, there was a clear understanding during the negotiation of the Hague Convention that national courts would enforce its principles, or at least bear them in mind when trying war criminals. There was nothing of the sort as a background to the Kellogg-Briand Pact. From the standpoint of objective legal analysis, the Nuremberg judges' attempts to establish a historical linkage between the Pact of Paris and a number of draft international treaties which preceded it and explicitly declared aggressive war an international crime[61] is unpersuasive. None of those hortatory declarations saw the juridical light of day in the sense of ratification because states were, in the end, not prepared to criminalize war in itself.

It is quite arguable that the atrocities perpetuated by the Nazis could have been effectively tried and punished under the rubric of war crimes (violations of the laws and customs of war) and crimes against humanity. Fifty years after Nuremberg, Drexel Strecher, one of its surviving American prosecutors, presented an important insight into Jackson's frame of mind on the question of aggressive war: it was, to Jackson, the linchpin of the case against the Germans, for it was the conspiracy to wage the war (another controversial charge) and the waging of it that propelled all the other crimes.[62]

The Nuremberg Tribunal either believed it was interpreting the Kellogg-Briand Pact to establish the missing link of its signatories' intentions, as it asserted, or else—and this is more likely—imposed a stretched interpretation in order to achieve the political objectives of the Nuremberg Charter. "In interpreting the words of the Pact, it must be remembered that international law is not the product of an international legislature, and that such international agreements as the Pact have to deal with general principles of law, and not with administrative matters of procedure," the tribunal ruled. "This law is not static, but by continual adaptation follows the needs of a changing world."

Meanwhile, evidence that the world had not changed very much at all lay in the more realistic provisions of the Charter of the United Nations adopted in 1945. That document remained true to the aspiration to a world free of war in its preamble: "We, the peoples of the United Nations, determined to save succeeding generations from the scourge of war, which twice in our lifetime has brought untold sorrow..." But it avoided the mistakes of the League of Nations—and that of the Kellogg-Briand Pact—when it recognized that the use of force is a hardy constant in international relatioı but sought to stipulate the circumstances in which it is lawful or unlawfuı.

The Nuremberg judgment, insofar as it relates to aggressive war, can now be seen as an attempt to turn a policy or aspiratory declaration into the force of law, because the Allied Powers *could*. The question, then, is—if the Nuremberg Charter was retroactive law, was it by that reason unjust, or was it a bad law that made real justice possible? This is an important query, for it goes to the heart of the debate about the nature of war crimes justice. The Nazi defense of the ex post facto nature of the Nuremberg Charter was in itself an exercise in hypocrisy, for Nazi rule and its persecution of minorities was based squarely on a subversion of that very principle. An international meeting of criminologists hosted in Germany in 1935 provided stark indications of the Nazi agenda.

Addressing delegates in a speech titled "The Idea of Justice in German Penal Reform," Franz Gurtner, the Reich minister of justice informed his learned audience that Germany would no longer rely on the principle of *nulla poena sine lege*. Rather, it would now adopt the exactly opposite one of *nullum crimen sine poena* (no crime without punishment). "Everyone who commits an act deserving of punishment shall receive due punishment regardless of the incompleteness of the law. . . . National Socialism imposes a new and high task on criminal law, namely the realization of true justice."[63] Gurtner explained, in his logic, that the advantage of this new approach was to free judges from the constraints of gaps in the law, whereby they could adjudicate only that which the legislature had defined as law.[64] The whole point, he stated, was to bridge the divide between morality and legality and so achieve "true justice." From this synthesis, criminal law would now benefit from "the valuable forces of ethics."[65] This discussion was taking place in the same period that the obnoxious Nuremberg laws were being formulated in the German ministry of the interior.

Thus it was that at Nuremberg the Nazi leaders got a taste of their own medicine—retroactive, instant-brew justice. This fact has been overlooked in many assessments of the trials. It is trite wisdom that two wrongs do not make a right, and it is helpful to bear in mind this whole aspect of the Nuremberg Trials as we review its legacy and competing claims to the defense of civilization as a tool in the service of agendas that are essentially political. But the scope of Nazi crimes called for an equally decisive response, as Jackson made clear in his moving opening statement at the trial.

Coupled with the issue of victor's justice noted earlier, the whole framework of the Nuremberg Trials, including ex post facto law, was established to exclude the crimes of the Allied Powers. Allied lawyers, including Jackson and Maxwell-Fyfe, anticipated the so-called "tu quoque," the "so-did-you" defense.[66] Both sides had committed war crimes during the war—in the case of the Allies most famously the bombing of Dresden and other cities that claimed hundreds of thousands of civilian lives. Jackson's position was that it simply had to be an invalid defense—and so, indeed, it was in the Nuremberg Charter. He argued that the scale of Nazi crimes, committed in the course of wars started by Hitler, utterly dwarfed the crimes committed by Allied forces. Here the legacy of Nuremberg has been one of subsequent attempts to create a more equitable framework in the establishment of contemporary international criminal tribunals. As we shall see in later chapters, the problem has not gone away.

Anglo-Saxon Common Law

The Nuremberg Trials also established a legacy in which the adversarial, Anglo-Saxon common law trial system became the dominant procedure in trials proceedings in the UN-sponsored ad hoc war crimes tribunals, over the continental European system that is sometimes referred to as "inquisitorial."[67] There were political motives at play in this process, but let us first examine the "technical" ones. Both systems have their merits and demerits. The adversarial system tends to drag out trials because of direct examinations and cross-examinations of accused persons and witnesses and would include an initial plea of "guilty" or "not guilty" by the defendant, but is seen as affording the accused a trial with full respect for his or her rights. The Nuremberg trial, however, was remarkable for its relative brevity— 8 months for the trial of twenty-two defendants for crimes committed in more than ten countries over several years, with a four-nation prosecution team.

The civil law system, on the other hand, is a heavily investigative process in which the judges are dominant, and lawyers—certainly defense lawyers, at any rate—and the accused have less scope for action. A criminal case that advances to the point of a docket has, in all probability, a high level of the burden of proof already discharged through the investigative process. It has already been noted that the Nuremberg trial was a "prosecutor's court," and it is clear that Jackson and his fellow Anglo-Saxon lawyers wanted to shape the nature of the proceedings at Nuremberg to a far greater extent than the civil law system would have allowed. Logically, then, the judges at Nuremberg were not the dominant force at the trial. Historical accounts of the IMT bear out this proposition, for they are unquestionably dominated by accounts of the courtroom heroics and oratorical flair of the Anglo-Saxon prosecutors Jackson, Shawcross, Maxwell-Fyfe, and their colleagues. Moreover, the balance of military roles among the four Allies in ending the war fell heavily in favor of the United States, with the roles of the French and Russian forces considered relatively less decisive. And American forces had captured most of the high-profile Nazi defendants. The cards were stacked in Jackson's favor.

As Joseph Persico recounts of the negotiations among the four Powers at a meeting to set the framework of the trial held in London in late June 1945, with the common law lawyers led by Jackson and Maxwell-Fyfe, and the

continental lawyers led by the Soviet Union's Nikitchenko and the Fr
delegation:

> "To the continental Europeans it seemed that the Anglo-Saxons were trying to ram an alien court system down their throats. Nikitchenko listened as Jackson and Maxwell-Fyfe explained adversarial law, with its opposing attorneys, direct examination, and cross-examination, before a judge who acted as an umpire. That was not how it was done in his country, he said. The French agreed. Their judges did not demean themselves by prying battling lawyers apart like a referee in a prize fight. Judges took evidence from witnesses, from the accused, from the police, from the victims, sifted it, weighed it, and arrived at their decisions. Lawyers were merely to help the accused prepare a defence. They had little role in the court itself. Lawyers are not so important, Nikitchenko concluded in a lecturing tone; judges are important. And this matter of pleading guilty or not guilty: Were they really going to allow a man like Ernst Kaltenbrunner, responsible for the Gestapo and the concentration Camps, to stand up in a court of law and declare himself Not Guilty?"[68]

Moreover, there were almost certainly other political reasons, inspired by a mixture of national pride and strategic goals that contributed to the ultimately successful American and British effort to ensure the dominance of their national legal cultures at the Nuremberg Trials. It would best facilitate the historical defeat of the Nazi ideology in Germany, backed up as the prosecution case was by damningly incriminating documents. Jackson fully appreciated the historical significance of the Nuremberg Trials. And it should not be surprising that he sought to put a distinctly American stamp on the proceedings in light of the disturbing tensions that were already developing between the West and the Soviet Union despite their "shotgun marriage" at Nuremberg.[69]

Nuremberg's Legacy in Historical Context

Nuremberg's legacy is interwoven into a number of important historical developments. First, the Nuremberg Trials were perhaps the most important postwar factor that shaped a democratic and prosperous Germany (West Germany) that became a key member of the Western alliance during the cold war that divided Germany between East and West. By demonstrating so vividly the crimes committed by the Nazi Party, the trials effectively banished Nazi ideology from the domestic political sphere. The deep introspection it generated in subsequent years—not very apparent during the trials themselves or even shortly afterward—helped make room for real democracy. Hitler and the Nazi era became a badge of shame to be lived down. Across the Atlantic, Stimson was proved right and Morgenthau wrong. Prophecies by Nazi defendants at the trial that they would go down in history as martyrs for the German nation—Goering in his typical vainglory predicted that statues would be erected in his image years after the trials—have remained a chimera. While this advantage from Nuremberg's legacy has accrued far more to Germany—and Japan, courtesy of the Tokyo Tribunal—than in any other theater of conflict in contemporary times, even in its limited impact it has had important implications for world politics and economics.

Second, the establishment of the permanent International Criminal Court, the hope of which Nuremberg so ardently inspired in human rights campaigners, is one of the most important legacies of the Nuremberg Trials. To be sure, the ICC as it exists today is not quite what was sketched out in the visions of its prophets—the Court came along half a century late as a result of the cold war; even some liberal democracies were opposed to its creation; its jurisdiction is secondary to national prosecutions; and its future prospects and impact are decidedly debatable.

Third, at a more philosophical level, Nuremberg, romanticized as it has been in the mainstream liberal tradition, did not achieve its ultimate and unrealistic goal of deterring aggression with the specter of accountability. Between 1945 and 1992, just before the United Nations established its first ad hoc international tribunal the following year, there were twenty-four wars between nations, at a cost of over 6 million lives.[70] Another ninety-three civil wars took an additional 15 million lives.[71] Millions more have died in the past decade, from Liberia to Sri Lanka, from Rwanda and the former Yugoslavia to Colombia and Sudan. No one can wish wars or evil away. Perspectives of international relations that draw on adaptations of the realist paradigm propose only how wars can be made fewer and farther between.

The Nuremberg prosecution of "crimes against peace" thus seems likely to remain frozen in mists of history. As we shall see when we examine the politics of the ICC, and as is apparent from even the most cursory look at contemporary events in a world now fundamentally altered by the war against terrorism and what Samuel Huntington famously called the "clash of civilizations," the meaning of "aggression" depends on who is defining it. It does not look very much different from the dilemma that beset the members of the League of Nations when they were faced with drafts of the Treaty of Mutual Assistance in 1923 and the Geneva Protocol a year later.

Nevertheless, aspects of Nuremberg's legacy became firmly established by the judgments handed down by the international tribunals established as a response to two contemporary tragedies—the genocides in Rwanda and Bosnia–Herzegovina in the early 1990s. The *Dusko Tadic* trial at the ICTY in 1994 became the first time an individual was judged and convicted for war crimes and crimes against humanity on the basis of individual criminal responsibility by an international tribunal since Nuremberg. But, if Nuremberg's standards of political consequence were to be strictly applied,

Tadic, being a lowly camp guard, would not have merited the judicial tention of a major international war crimes tribunal. The avowed goal these institutions is to make examples of the powerful by bringing them to accountability. The *Tadic* trial nevertheless served to reawaken the legacy of Nuremberg and led the Hague Tribunal to more significant quests that resulted in the historic indictment in 1999 of Slobodan Milosevic, the first sitting head of state, to be indicted by an international criminal tribunal.

As it relates to the ultimate crime of genocide, however, the nature of events in Rwanda in 1994, the uncontested fact and gravity of the worst genocide since the Holocaust, lent the International Criminal Tribunal for Rwanda at Arusha, Tanzania, the opportunity to become the first international criminal tribunal to apply Nuremberg's legacy at a consistent level of political consequence—trying the ringleaders of a genocide. I have discussed the pursuit of justice at the Arusha Tribunal—along with the politics intertwined in that effort—at length in another book, *Rwanda's Genocide: The Politics of Global Justice*.[72]

The Nuremberg trial left a mixed legacy. Barry Gewen has characterized this legacy as "ambiguous," noting: "It has taken a long time for the muddled legacy of the Nuremberg trials to make itself felt, but we all now live in its shadow."[73] But, warts and all, it remains the defining war crimes trial of the twentieth century. This is as much for what it teaches us about justice as policy as for the lessons it provides—for those willing to see beyond its halo—about the political and strategic context of war crimes justice. The legacy mentioned above is one that combines in itself the romantic view of international justice and more cynical motivations. What I have done is to show how that legacy has constituted an advance from where we were in the years before international justice for war crimes became a major dimension of international law and politics.

BEYOND LEGALISM: HIROHITO AND THE TOKYO TRIBUNAL

While the concept of command responsibility was having its heyday at the International Military Tribunal at Nuremberg, the subsequently established International Military Tribunal for the Far East (IMTFE, or the "Tokyo War Crimes Trials"), which sat from May 1946 to November 1948, proceeded along somewhat different lines. The IMTFE, which comprised eleven judges of various nationalities, tried twenty-five high-ranking political and military leaders accused of unprecedented war crimes and classified as Class A war criminals.[74] These included four former prime ministers, three foreign ministers, four war ministers, two navy ministers, two ambassadors, three economic and financial advisers, an influential imperial advisor (Koichi Kido), one admiral, and one colonel (Kingoro Hashimoto).[75] All had served in successive Japanese governments and the military during the war. By a majority decision, seven defendants were sentenced to death by hanging, sixteen were sentenced to life imprisonment, one to 20 years, and another to 7 years.[76]

To be sure, the Tokyo Tribunal also had aspirations as avowedly lofty as those of the Nuremberg Tribunal. The element that has chiefly triggered the ambivalence of historians toward the Tokyo war crimes trials is the extent to which the commitment to justice was compromised by the double standards of the political and strategic considerations of the Allied Powers. It was General Douglas MacArthur, Supreme Commander of the Allied Powers in the Pacific (the "American Caesar" who accepted the unconditional surrender of Japan at the end of World War II), rather than the Chief Prosecutor of the IMTFE, Joseph Keenan, that made the most important decision of the Tokyo trial process. That decision—a deliberate and political, rather than judicial one—was to exempt Hirohito, the emperor of Japan, from prosecution for war crimes even as the country's military, the political leadership, and even Hirohito's royal household faced trial. Britain supported the U.S. position, but the Soviet Union insisted on a trial of the emperor.[77] In Tokyo, even far more than at Nuremberg, America was the dominant ally and its position naturally prevailed.

History has taken a mixed view of this double standard. Some commentators have been critical of the political exemption of Hirohito from prosecution, and the Tokyo war crimes trials have historically been viewed as inferior to Nuremberg in terms of its relative success and international public awareness of the proceedings. Not least among the reasons for this divergent assessment is that, at Nuremberg, legalism (victor's justice though it was, with a significant dose of political considerations thrown in) was utilized to the full—a fact that was seen as a progressive deployment of power. Regarding Japan, however, many analysts saw MacArthur's exemption of the emperor as a retrograde step, a missed opportunity. William Webb, the Australian judge who presided at the IMTFE, believed that the trials were fundamentally flawed by reason of Hirohito's absence from the dock.[78] So did Justice Henri Bernard, the French judge on the tribunal.[79]

But there is nothing to suggest that, with the exception of the exemption of Hirohito and a number of differences of a technical nature, the Tokyo Trials were fundamentally different from Nuremberg in its nature as victor's justice. In the words of John Dower: "Like Nuremberg, the Tokyo trial was law, politics and theater all in one."[80] Moreover, as Dower also recounts, several senior military and civilian officials of the Allied Powers privately viewed the Tokyo Trials as a sham. A top American military intelligence officer in the Allied Pacific Command Headquarters confided to a judge of the Tokyo Tribunal his view that "this trial was the worst hypocrisy in recorded history." In March 1948 George Kennan, the head of policy planning at the U.S. Department of State, visited Japan and issued a stinging commentary on the Tokyo Trials as "ill-conceived, political trials ... not law." The trials surrounded the punishment of enemy leaders "with the hocus-pocus of judicial procedure which belies its real nature," despite having been "hailed as the ultimate in international justice."[81]

If the Tokyo Trials were not regarded as being at par with Nuremberg, is this solely because of the failure to try Hirohito, or does this judgment arise from Western ethnocentrism, in which the West attaches the greatest importance, even in the context of justice, to European theatres, victims, and defendants?[82] After all, critics have asserted that there were a number of cover-ups in the Nuremberg trial. There, Russia tried to avoid references to the Molotov-Ribbentrop Pact that parceled out "spheres of interest" between the Axis Germany and the Allied Soviet Union in August 1939, the existence of which was only indirectly affirmed through examinations of Ribbentrop at the trial, and it emerged as well that that Germany attacked Norway only to forestall a planned attack by Britain.[83] No less an authoritative figure than Nuremberg prosecutor Telford Taylor observed, "On these matters, the tribunal was engaging in half-truths, if indeed there are such things."[84]

Moreover, if MacArthur's decision to exempt Hirohito is the rallying point of critical assessments of the Tokyo war crimes trials, it is important to address on the merits the question: was that decision justified? In order to better appraise MacArthur's use of pardon power, it is essential to understand the unique cultural context of Japan at the time, and differing views of the link between that context and the politico–military one. Prior to World War II, the Japanese considered their emperor divine—the Son of Heaven. In Japanese culture, the emperor's subjects could not look him in the face and were obliged to bow and avoid eye contact for as long as they were in his presence. In short, the emperor was deeply embedded both in the Japanese psyche and history as a central factor, and at a far deeper level than the monarchies of Europe. In this context, then, he was seen as the embodiment of Japanese society and central to societal order.

Yet, in the first part of Hirohito's reign (between 1926 and 1945), the influence of the military in government steadily increased apace with Japan's rise in the early twentieth century as a military and irredentist power in the Far East. The Japanese Imperial Army and the Imperial Navy exercised veto power over the formation of the country's civilian governments since 1900. From 1932, following the assassination of the moderate Prime Minister Tsuyoshi Inukai, the military held virtually all political power in Japan and executed policies that fed into its military expansionism in Asia and set the country on an irreversible path to World War II.

It is against this background that there has been heated historical argument about Hirohito's role in Japanese involvement and atrocities in World War II, and the extent of his personal guilt. There is widespread belief that he bore a great degree of command responsibility and was not the figurehead he was claimed to be as a justification for his non-prosecution. Especially in Asia, he was seen by many as the region's Hitler. In this view, he was considered the head of state. Under Japanese law, only the emperor had authority to declare or launch a war. In any case, the war was fought by the Japanese military in his name, and he did not deny knowledge of military plans by Japanese generals to wage aggressive war against China, the Philippines, and the United States. From a strict perspective of the equal application of justice and the rule of law (which, as noted earlier, though embraced by human rights advocates and the moral philosophy of liberalism, is tenuous at the international plane) it is easy to be scandalized at Hirohito's exemption from the Tokyo war crimes trials. Yet there is a view of him as a figurehead who was unable to influence events in the face of the voracious military irredentism of Japan's generals. He was no more than a mild-mannered fellow, who wore a moustache, had a fondness for bacon and eggs, wore a Mickey Mouse watch, and was obsessed with marine biology. The Japanese government at the time certainly advanced the "figurehead" argument in supporting the Allied decision that made Hirohito immune from the legal process of the Tokyo Tribunal.

But the weight of evidence suggests a strong case of the emperor's command responsibility. In the saber-rattling lead-up to Japan's attack on the United States, Hirohito was initially distant from military decision-making, and was concerned about the bellicose nature of Japanese demands that the United States and Britain give it carte blanche to invade China. Faced with the Imperial Cabinet's unanimous support for war, however, Hirohito shook off his doubts and became a cheerleader of the war effort that was executed in his name. It fell to him, the "voice of the marble," to make the radio broadcast that announced Japan's unconditional surrender after the atomic bombing of Hiroshima and Nagasaki by the United States in 1945.

Although MacArthur did not favor the emperor's abdication and allowed Hirohito to remain as emperor, the god-king was forced to renounce his divinity—a significant humiliation in the Japanese cultural context. Perhaps this was a concession to senior members of the American government in Washington that had sought an investigation of the emperor's war role. MacArthur resisted with an authoritative interpretation, in a secret cable to Washington, of the reality on the ground in Japan after the war.[85] Hirohito was, in MacArthur's eyes, vital for the future of Japan under the Occupation Government (1945–1952) and beyond. The American general wanted to guarantee the continuity of Japan's body politic and, in what was the ultimate strategic goal, facilitate the democratization process that would culminate in a transformation of the divine emperor into a constitutional monarch.[86] This was the fundamental reason why MacArthur decided to shield Hirohito from the inconvenient searchlight of the judicial process of the IMTFE. The "American Caesar" believed he needed Hirohito as a symbol of continuity and cohesion of the Japanese people following their defeat. With the societal trauma among the Japanese population in the wake of their defeat, especially the humiliation of the atomic bomb, MacArthur saw Hirohito's survival as a necessary counterweight to a fragile situation. "Seeing their God-monarch in the dock of a Western-run trial" could hardly have helped the situation.[87]

MacArthur's cable warned Washington that indicting Hirohito would plunge Japan into chaos from which the country would not recover, trigger guerilla warfare and a communist upsurge, and dash all hopes of introducing a liberal democracy—the ultimate goal of the Occupation Government.[88] In sum, indicting the emperor would lead to a total breakdown of order, requiring at least a million troops and thousands of additional civil servants to reverse.[89] As an intelligence specialist who advised MacArthur on the issue recalled, he favored retaining Emperor Hirohito on the throne "because otherwise we would have had nothing but chaos. The religion was gone, and he was the only symbol of control. Now, I know he had his hand in the cookie jar, and he wasn't any innocent child. But he was of great use to us, and that was the basis on which I recommended to the Old Man [MacArthur] that we keep him."[90]

MacArthur did not stop at exempting Hirohito from trial. Occupation policy shielded the emperor from criticism, and ensured a conspiracy of silence about Hirohito's war role at the Tokyo war crimes trials—directly tampering with witness testimony, or what can only be accurately described, in common parlance in the American domestic legal system, as "obstruction of justice." Hideki Tojo testified in the course of his trial that "there is no Japanese subject who would go against the will of His Majesty; more particularly, among high officials of the Japanese government. . . ." He later recanted (under subsequent pressure from American officials), stressing Hirohito's "love and desire for peace."[91] In a conversation that took place between General Fellers, a senior aide to MacArthur, and the former admiral and Prime Minister Yonai Mitsumasa before the Tokyo trial began, the American is reported to have said: "It would be most convenient if the Japanese side could prove to us that that the emperor is completely blameless. I think the forthcoming trials offer the best opportunity to do that. Tojo, in particular, should be made to bear all the responsibility at his trial. In other words, I want you to have Tojo say as follows: 'At the Imperial Conference prior to the start of the war, I had already decided to push for war even if His Majesty was against going to war with the United States.' "[92] Moreover, in pursuit of this policy, physical evidence in the form of documents and materials that might incriminate the emperor were deliberately ignored and suppressed. Thus the prosecution at the Tokyo Tribunal under Keenan functioned, in the words of Dower, "as a defense team for the emperor."[93]

Sordid as this direct tampering with evidence is, and as unflatteringly as it undoubtedly portrays the Tokyo war crimes trials, it is clear that a majority of Japanese, then and now, view the decision not to put Hirohito on trial as justified. It would be unhelpful to question whether the decision is "right" or "wrong," as that inquiry would not produce a satisfactory answer in the world of politics and strategy that shapes decisions to prosecute or pardon in international criminal justice: realists who see little value in prosecuting political leaders, only the potential complications legalism can bring to political settlements, would call it the "right" decision and argue that it is justified, while universalists would surely view it as an outrage. An international society perspective on international justice that is conditional would recognize the uniqueness of this case given its cultural context. It might, depending on what part of the international society spectrum (rationalist or solidarist) the observer were to be, criticize the process by which Hirohito was saved from justice, but consider the outcome "typical" of the nature of that society. For, as already noted, the Japanese belief in the divinity of their emperor was a serious one indeed, and to have stripped Hirohito of that aura was already a serious strategic blow. To have stretched the policy to the point of putting him on trial may have generated a backlash that might have undermined the goal of order itself. Random samplings of the opinions of Japanese citizens on this question indicate that many in Japan would have committed suicide in response to the embarrassment or loss of face that is taboo in Japanese culture.[94] At the very least, then, MacArthur's decision was understandable.

Not everyone agrees that by saving the Japanese throne MacArthur paved a solid path to democracy in Japan. Sterling Seagrave and Peggy Seagrave are of the firm view that the prospect of real democratic reforms was actually undermined by putting Hirohito beyond accountability for war crimes.[95] In a contrarian interpretation of MacArthur's decision, they argue that the real story was as follows: Japan owed U.S. lenders huge sums of money by 1945. Former U.S. President Herbert Hoover, a Quaker, conspired with fellow Quakers in the Japanese elite to preserve the royal family in order to prevent Japan from lurching toward communism and to ensure that the country's financial barons stayed in place and that debts to wall street financiers were repaid. In this account, MacArthur ensured Hirohito's pardon in the hope that it would facilitate his well-known presidential ambitions by obtaining support from Hoover and other powerful Republicans.

For whatever reason, the prospect of Hirohito's accountability was sacrificed to the imperative of order. Thus, a negative exercise of prosecutorial prerogative may have been justified by a successful outcome in an important societal transition that has benefited not only Japan, but international society and the world economy as well. Moreover, the Tokyo war crimes trials exposed to the Japanese people the excesses of the militarist policies of their governments and laid an important foundation for a constitutionally guaranteed pacifist foreign policy.[96] In this sense, the numerous "big fish" that were tried at the Tokyo Tribunal appears to have effectively counterbalanced the exemption of Hirohito. Despite academic criticisms, there is nothing in this especially unique situation to suggest that, 50 years afterward, the Japanese society essentially regrets MacArthur's decision to spare the emperor. And if that is so, the argument for that decision appears to have essentially been vindicated.

But the pros and cons of the political decision to exculpate Hirohito is one thing. Whether Japan has handled the legacy of its irredentist history astutely is quite another. The benefits of sparing Hirohito remain mingled with the deep wounds Japanese war crimes have left in some countries in Asia to this day and a certain moral ambivalence within Japanese society on the question of a formal apology by Japan for those crimes.[97] Asian countries that had suffered conquest and occupation at the hands of Japanese forces have long argued for a formal apology by Japan, and it was not until June 6, 1995, that the Japanese government issued a declaration expressing "deep remorse" for its aggression.[98]

The conspicuous pardon granted the Japanese emperor is hardly the only decision *not* to prosecute at the Tokyo Tribunal. In his review of the Tokyo trial Yves Beigbeder has highlighted some fundamental examples of the endogenous qualities of international humanitarian law in deciding not just *who*, but *what*, gets prosecuted or pardoned.[99] The first is the atomic bombing of Hiroshima on August 6, 1945, and of Nagasaki 3 days later. The second is the exclusion from prosecution at the Tokyo trial, for political/strategic reasons, of the development of biological weapons by the Japanese army's notorious Unit 731 and the use of these devastating agents on prisoners of war.

The atomic bombing of Hiroshima and Nagasaki was the decisive factor in Japan's surrender and ended the country's military expansionism. The bombings caused massive physical destruction and loss of human lives. But its most enduring legacy, other than the political controversy that has trailed President Harry Truman's decision to authorize its use and questions about its legality (to which we will return momentarily), was its crushing psychological impact. The first (Hiroshima) bomb, with fission produced by 0.85 kilograms of uranium, released an explosive power equivalent to 13,000 of TNT, reached a temperature of 7,000 degrees centigrade that killed persons within one kilometer range through intense burns and rupture of internal organs.[100] It released radiation that injured people within a 2.3-kilometer radius, generated atomic ash and "black rain" that resulted in the deaths of 140,000 persons by year-end in 1945. The Nagasaki bomb claimed 60,000 to 70,000 victims in the same period.[101]

Hirohito's imperial address announcing Japan's surrender bears witness to the psychological humiliation inflicted by America's nuclear weapons:

To our good and loyal subjects:

After pondering deeply the general conditions of the world and the actual conditions obtaining in our empire today, we have decided to effect a

settlement of the present situation by resorting to an extraordinary mea-
sure.... Moreover the enemy has begun to employ a new and most cruel
bomb, the power of which to do damage is incalculable, taking the toll
of many innocent lives.... We have resolved to pave the way for a grand
peace for all the generations to come by enduring the endurable and suffering what is insufferable....[102]

In their destructive, indiscriminate impact, the atomic bombings were
clearly beyond anything the world had seen, and certainly far beyond the
prohibitions of the Hague Conventions and the poison warfare that was
employed by the Japanese and was condemned by the United States during the war. Attempts by the defendants at the Tokyo trial to introduce
the atomic bombings in evidence at their trial were ruled inadmissible by
the Tokyo Tribunal and omitted from the majority judgment.[103] But two
of the tribunal's judges held starkly opposing views on the matter, expressed
in their concurring and dissenting opinions. Justice Jaranilla opined that the
means justified ends, and thus the atomic bombing was justified because
it brought Japan to its knees and ended the war. Justice Pal, on the other
hand, believed that "As a matter of fact, I do not perceive much difference
between what the German emperor is alleged to have announced during the
First World War in justification of the atrocious methods directed by him
in the conduct of that war and what is being proclaimed after the Second
World War in justification of these inhuman blasts."[104] In 1993, nearly
40 years after Hiroshima and the Tokyo trial, Justice Röling, reviewing
both the massive Allied aerial bombardments of Japanese cities that caused
thousands of civilian deaths and the atomic bombs, wrote: "I am strongly
convinced that these bombings were war crimes.... It was terror warfare,
"coercive warfare" ... forbidden by the laws of war."[105]

In an Advisory Opinion[106] in response to a majority resolution of the
UN General Assembly (narrowly adopted after contentious debate, and in
the face of vigorous opposition from France, Russia, Britain, and the United
States), the International Court of Justice (ICJ) addressed the question: "Is
the threat or use of nuclear weapons in any circumstance permitted under international law?" The fifteen-member Court's ruling was an equivocal one.
It unanimously ruled that neither customary nor conventional international
law specifically permits the threat or use of nuclear weapons, but, by eleven
votes to three, that neither did both sources of international law "compre-
hensively and universally" prohibit it. By seven votes to seven, with a casting
vote by its president, the ICJ ruled "the threat or use of nuclear weapons
would generally be contrary to the rules of international law applicable in
armed conflict, and in particular the principles and rules of international
humanitarian law, but that in view of the current state of international law
and the facts before the Court, it could not conclude definitively whether
the threat or use of nuclear weapons would be lawful or unlawful in an

extreme circumstance of self-defence, in which the very survival of the state would be at stake." The Court then ruled, unanimously, that there was an obligation to pursue in good faith and conclude negotiations that result in nuclear disarmament under international control.

Effectively, beyond the Nuclear Non-Proliferation Treaty (NPT), there is no positive international law that governs the possession of nuclear weapons by the pre-NPT nuclear powers, that is to say, all five members of the UN Security Council. Thus, the use of such weapons is really beyond law, resting more in the domain of diplomacy and high politics. By that logic, whether or not using nuclear weapons is a crime is indeterminate, and so it can be said to have been defined out of any possible prosecutorial framework. The fact that such weapons have not been used in a war since 1945 owes itself not to the constraining power of law or the possibility of criminal accountability, but to the doctrines of deterrence and mutually assured destruction that such use would portend.

The decision not to prosecute the members and activities of Unit 731 exposes even more poignantly the arbitrariness inherent in the definitions of who or what are prosecuted or pardoned by international war crimes justice. As Beigbeder reports, the Unit, euphemistically tagged a "Water Purification Unit," was the Japanese army's main bacteriological warfare research institution, and was led by Army Medical Lieutenant General Ishii Shiro. Employing 5,000 Japanese personnel and motivated by doctrines of racial superiority similar to those that drove the medical experiments of the Nazi doctor Josef Mengele, Unit 731 performed sinister medical and biological experiments on between 3,000 to 12,000 prisoners of war—mainly Chinese and Russian but including some British and Dutch nationals—between 1932 and 1945.[107] These experiments involved exposure to bubonic plague, anthrax, typhoid, mustard gas, and other deadly bacteriological conditions. The human "subjects" of these experiments were incinerated afterward.

In 1947 the U.S. authorities granted Shiro and other participants in Unit 731's experiments immunity from war crimes prosecution in a secret deal. In return, the United States obtained the Unit's surviving scientific "research" secrets. Japanese authorities officially denied the existence of Unit 731 for nearly 50 years after World War II, even as the Unit's activities were revealed in various public reports.[108]

3

The Balkans: The Trial
of Slobodan Milosevic

He was not brought to judgment, but he was brought to justice
—Edgar Chen

The creation of an international war crimes tribunal in 1993 to prosecute violations of international humanitarian law in the former Yugoslavia was the first such institution since Nuremberg nearly 50 years earlier. Paradoxically, although some advocates for the creation of the tribunal saw it as the modern day genesis of a sweeping movement to take war crimes justice global and make legalism a constant factor in dealing with the aftermath of wars and mass atrocity, for the diplomats who ultimately created the International Criminal Tribunal for the former Yugoslavia (ICTY) based in The Hague, it was nothing of the sort. Creating the tribunal was, for many of them, a fig leaf to pacify critics calling for action, including military intervention, to stop the war in Bosnia and Herzegovina. It was not at all clear that the tribunal would ever actually indict any of the senior level protagonists in the Balkan wars, and several diplomats were wary of its potential to complicate diplomacy, the favored approach to end the wars in the region.

Thus the Hague Tribunal was a bundle of contradictions, a showcase of the tensions between liberal legalism, realism, and the international society perspective. From humble and inauspicious beginnings the trials at the Hague Court were to lead a revolution in international law and politics—the indictment of a sitting head of state and his trial after he left office.

MILOSEVIC AND THE DISINTEGRATION OF YUGOSLAVIA

To understand the political context of the trials at the Hague Tribunal, it is necessary to have a brief recollection of the historical trends that led to the break-up of the Socialist Federal Republic of Yugoslavia in 1991–1992, and the political role of Slobodan Milosevic as the most influential actor in this historical drama.

Ethnic conflict in the Balkans is nearly a millennium old, going back 700 years. The people that made up the former Yugoslavia—Croatia, Serbia, Montenegro, Bosnia and Herzegovina—are all Slavs who speak one language (Serbo-Croatian), but their different historical experiences, which led in turn to their having different religions, created disparate ethnic identities that ultimately proved stronger than any common bonds.[1]

As far back as the ninth century, most inhabitants of the Balkan region were Christians. The western part of the region (now Croatia and Slovenia) was largely Roman Catholic, while the eastern part (Bosnia and Herzegovina, Serbia, Montenegro, and Macedonia) adhered to Eastern Orthodoxy. In 1389, Ottoman Turks, in pursuit of empire, defeated Serbian forces in the battle of Kosovo Polje (Field of the Blackbirds), beginning a lengthy occupation of the eastern portion of the Balkans that would only end in the early twentieth century. This battle, which occurred on June 28, 1389, assumed mythic proportions in Serb history and nationalism. Serbs celebrate the day as a testament to their bravery, although they were defeated, thus leaving something of a chip on their collective shoulder. This battle established Kosovo as a fulcrum of the Serb historical experience, with severe implications for modern history and the Balkan wars of the 1990s.

The Turkish expansion was to be checked by the competing ambitions of the Austro-Hungarian empire, which wrested the area of Bosnia–Herzegovina from Ottoman rule in 1878 and occupied and administered it. While under Ottoman rule, some Balkan peoples preserved their cultural identity by accepting second-class citizenship of the empire. But others, mostly in the area that is now Bosnia and Herzegovina, converted to Islam, the religion of the Turks, in order to avoid persecution. This is partly the genesis of the Serb antipathy toward Bosnian Muslims today—the Serbs see the Muslims as people whose ancestors betrayed the faith and entered an alliance with their Ottoman conquerors.[2]

The Serbs eventually freed themselves from Ottoman rule through rebellions, the first of which occurred from 1804–1830 and brought Russian and Greek support based on the religious solidarity of the Eastern Orthodox Church,[3] and the second in the Balkan wars fought in 1912 and 1913 that resulted in the expulsion of the Turks from most of the Balkan region. With the Turks now expelled, Serb nationalists next focused on ending the Hapsburg Empire's occupation of Bosnia and Herzegovina. The assassination of the Austrian Archduke Franz Ferdinand on June 28, 1914, (anniversary of the battle of Kosovo) helped set off the World War I. With the war over 4 years later, the yoke of foreign domination was lifted when the great powers allowed the establishment of the kingdom of the Serbs, Croats, and Slovenes under King Alexander of Serbia. The Kingdom's name was later changed to Yugoslavia ("land of the South Slavs").

But the Croats, who had originated this concept, existed in an uncomfortable relationship with the Serbs, who nursed the ambition of a Greater Serbia. The tensions came to a head during World War II. The Axis Powers occupied Yugoslavia and created an independent Croatian state led by Croatian fascists (Ustashas) allied with the Nazis. This state included the territory of Bosnia and Herzegovina. Under the leadership of Ante Pavelic, the Ustasha state of Croatia committed horrendous atrocities against Serbs and Jews. Josip Broz Tito, a Croatian-born Serb, emerged as the leader of the predominantly Serb communist forces, the Partisans, which resisted the Axis occupation with the support of the Allied forces. Another group of Serbs, the monarchist Chetniks, also fought the occupation, but Tito's group ultimately gained the military upper hand. Bosnian Muslims fought on both sides—Ustasha and Serbs. But "the memories of the Ustasha locked Serbs and Croats in mutual suspicion."[4] This led to the massacre of more than 100,000 Croatian prisoners by the Partisans in revenge killings after the Ustasha surrendered in 1946.[5]

It was against this background that Tito established a communist regime after World War II that sought to bind Yugoslavia's disparate groups into one state made up of six republics—Serbia, Croatia, Bosnia and Herzegovina, Macedonia, and Montenegro. Kosovo and Vojvodina were autonomous provinces located inside Serbia. The effort was successful for the nearly four decades that Tito was at the helm. But it began to unravel after his death in 1980 and the collapse of communism later that decade, as long-suppressed nationalism among Yugoslavia's constituent republics came to the fore and progressively gained ascendance. Economic inequalities between the constituent republics of Yugoslavia tugged at an already strained fabric, with Slovenia and Croatia complaining that they had to subsidize poorer regions, such as Macedonia and Bosnia, and resenting Serb dominance of the bureaucracy, the police, and the army.[6]

Into this combustible mix came the rise of Slobodan Milosevic, a Serbian Communist Party apparatchik who was a trained lawyer and former banker. Milosevic's rise to the leadership of the Serbian Communist Party in 1986 marked the beginning of a virulent strain of Serbian nationalism that was to lead to the disintegration of Yugoslavia and the wars that followed in its wake. Kosovo, where he made a famous nationalist speech in 1986 in the face of an ethnic crisis between Kosovars and the minority Serb population, was to be his launch pad. Milosevic sought to create a more centralized Yugoslavia under Serbian dominance, but this led to a backlash of anti-Serb nationalism in Croatia and Slovenia, and resistance from the presidents of the two republics, Franjo Tudjman and Milan Kucan.

WAR, AND A WAR CRIMES TRIBUNAL

In 1991 Milosevic used his political clout to prevent Stipe Mesic, a Croat, from becoming the president of the Socialist Federal Republic of Yugoslavia, despite the provision in the federal constitution for a rotation of the presidency among the republics. This act of bad faith was the last straw that triggered the breakup of Yugoslavia. On June 25, 1991, Croatia and Slovenia unilaterally declared their independence. Their failure to provide concrete guarantees for the security of Serbs living in their territories provided Milosevic an excuse to invade the two former republics with the Serb-dominated Yugoslav National Army (JNA). The Yugoslav forces were successfully repulsed by the Slovenes. Under the face-saving cover of a ceasefire brokered by the European Community, Milosevic withdrew his forces from Slovenia.

Croatia was not so fortunate. The JNA, aided by local Serb militias, inflicted heavy casualties on the Croatian army, seized a third of Croatia's territory (later to be recaptured by the Croats during "Operation Storm" in 1995) and committed atrocities that included a destructive siege of the Croatian town of Vukovar and the massacre of 200 patients at the Vukovar hospital. The victims were buried in mass graves.

In late 1991 the United Nations Security Council imposed an arms embargo on the territory of the former Yugoslavia, and in January 1992 negotiated a ceasefire between the warring armies that led to the deployment of UN peacekeepers in Serb-held territories. In April 1992 Bosnia and Herzegovina declared its own independence from Yugoslavia. As with Croatia, the Yugoslav army invaded Bosnia. Serb forces committed numerous atrocities, including the slaughter of 7,000 Muslim men in Srebrenica, during the 3-year conflict in Bosnia.

A Yugoslav journalist, Mirko Klarin, first proposed an international tribunal to prosecute crimes committed in the Balkan wars in an article he published in Belgrade on May 16, 1991, in the newspaper *Borba*. Titled "Nuremberg Now," Klarin's article called for a tribunal made up of "impartial foreign experts in the international laws of war" to be immediately set up to try "big and small leaders" for crimes against humanity in Yugoslavia.[7] A year later, a creeping, hesitant process toward the creation of such a tribunal by the great powers began.

An influential turning point came at the London Conference on the former Yugoslavia, held on August 26, 1992. There the German foreign minister, Klaus Kinkel, called for accountability for war crimes.[8] His French counterpart, Roland Dumas, took up the idea in his own statement at the same meeting, and the London Conference specifically decided that governments and international organizations would "take all possible legal action to bring to account those responsible for committing or ordering grave breaches of the Geneva Conventions."[9]

The response of the international society to the wars and atrocities in the former Yugoslavia was at this time full of rhetoric but little concrete action. None among the great powers wanted to intervene with force to stop the ethnic cleansing and other crimes initiated by Serbs but also committed by other sides in the conflict. When, on October 6, 1992, the United Nations Security Council voted unanimously to adopt resolution 780, under which it created a Commission of Experts to investigate and collect evidence of violations of international humanitarian law in the region, several commentators and even some members of the commission believed it lacked the political and financial support it required to do a speedy, effective, and credible job.[10] France and Britain were believed not to have been, in practice, much in support of creating a war crimes tribunal because it would interfere with peacekeeping efforts.[11] And a member of the commission charged that even some senior UN officials played an obstructionist role.[12]

Despite the early frustrations the Commission faced, its creation nevertheless represented a significant advance in the response of the international society. An additional boost to the prospect of accountability for Balkan war crimes came when Lawrence Eagleburger, the U.S. secretary of state, delivered his famous "naming names" statement at the International Conference on the former Yugoslavia in Geneva on December 16, 1992, presided by the peace negotiators Cyrus Vance of the United States (on behalf of the UN) and Lord Owen of Britain (on behalf of the European Community).

Noting the predominant, but not exclusive, responsibility of Serb leaders and military commanders for the ethnic cleansing and other war crimes being committed in the conflicts in Bosnia and Croatia, Eagleburger declared: "My government also believes it is time for the international community to begin identifying individuals who may have to answer for having committed crimes against humanity. The fact of the matter is that we know that crimes against humanity have occurred, and we know when and where they occurred. We know, moreover, which forces committed those crimes, and under whose command they operated. And we know, finally, who the political leaders are to whom those military commanders were—and still are—responsible."[13]

Eagleburger then named leaders who the United States believed directly supervised persons accused of war crimes and who may have ordered those crimes. These individuals included Zeljko "Arkan" Raznjatovic, the baby-faced head of the feared paramilitary forces known as the "Tigers," and Vojislav Seselj, head of the "White Eagles" force. Arkan and Seselj were later indicted by the Hague Tribunal. Seselj was surrendered to the tribunal for trial, but Arkan was assassinated before he could be captured.

The U.S. diplomat then went further and named leaders, such as Slobodan Milosevic, the then president of Serbia, Radovan Karadzic, the then president of Serbian Bosnian Republic, and General Ratko Mladic, the commander of the Bosnian Serb military forces, as leaders with political and command responsibility and a case to answer. This was a dramatic intervention that, in the political context of the time, could only have been made by a great power like the United States. Analysts have underrated its significance,[14] seeing as military intervention by U.S. forces was nearly 3 years away. But in hindsight, it was a major policy statement that foreshadowed the latter-day evolution of the effort to establish meaningful accountability for war crimes in the Balkans, and Eagleburger surely deserves credit for it. Eagleburger, in turn, credits a conversation he had with the Holocaust survivor Elie Wiesel as having inspired him to call for a war crimes tribunal in such bold terms.[15]

On February 22, 1993, having received an interim report of the Commission of Experts, which suggested that the establishment of an ad hoc international war crimes tribunal would be "consistent with the direction of its work,"[16] the Security Council adopted resolution 808.[17] The resolution decided "that an international criminal tribunal shall be established for the prosecution of persons responsible for serious violations of international humanitarian law committed in the territory of the former Yugoslavia since 1991."[18]

Since the creation of the Hague Tribunal, law and politics have constantly intersected in its work, with the prosecutorial and judicial activities of the tribunal frequently shaped, directly or indirectly, by political context, and the tribunal's judicial work advancing the ends of political justice.[19] Examples of this politico–legal synergy include the political battles between states in the Security Council over the appointment of the tribunal's first chief prosecutor, Serb claims that the tribunal was singling Serb leaders out for victor's justice, the tribunal prosecutor's investigation of possible war crimes charges over the NATO bombing campaign in Kosovo, and the ultimate political justice—the indictment, trial, and eventual death of Slobodan Milosevic. Each of these aspects of the work of the Hague Tribunal deserves a concise review and analysis.

THE PROSECUTOR

The politics that pervaded the selection of the Hague Tribunal's first prosecutor actually went back to the appointment of the Commission of Experts. It appeared to be a search not for who might be the best man or woman to do the job of prosecuting war crimes in the Balkans, but for the lowest common denominator—a person who would be acceptable to all the great powers. When the commission was being set up, the Secretary-General of the

UN, Boutros Boutros-Ghali, wanted the international criminal law professor Cherif Bassiouni to head it.[20] Bassiouni is an Egyptian-born lawyer of U.S. nationality. But when the commission's line-up was actually announced, Fritz Kalshoven, a retired Dutch law professor with a retiring personality, was named the commission's chairman. Bassiouni, who had consistently exhibited a zeal for accountability for the Balkan atrocities, was named a member of the commission, but believes he was passed over for the chairmanship of the expert group because the Balkan negotiator Lord Owen sabotaged his appointment with the argument that Bassiouni, a Muslim, would bring a pro-Bosnian Muslim bias to the job.[21] Bassiouni later became the commission's chair when Kalshoven resigned in late 1993.

This perception problem, or more accurately, an initial reluctance on the part of diplomats to take an activist approach to war crimes investigations and prosecutions, followed Bassiouni when he subsequently wanted to become the first prosecutor of the Hague Tribunal. Madeleine Albright, then the U.S. ambassador to the UN, wanted a strong prosecutor for the court, and supported Bassiouni's candidature in the summer of 1994. The decision lay with the Security Council, which, under the Hague Tribunal's statute, appoints the prosecutor on the recommendation of the Secretary-General.

But other countries on the Council, led by Britain and Russia, were more cautious. Meanwhile Warren Christopher, the American Secretary of State, had developed second thoughts about whether an American should be the prosecutor. His reticence thus overruled Albright's instincts and sent Bassiouni's candidature into a nosedive—with the willing help of other reluctant states. As the candidate himself put it, "There are certainly some members of the Security Council that are not too enthusiastic about having an aggressive prosecutor who is likely to disrupt political processes."[22]

Britain then nominated an alternative candidate, a Scottish prosecutor named John Duncan Lowe. Boutros-Ghali decided to force a decision by formally nominating Bassiouni. Britain vetoed his candidature, arguing that the Egyptian-born scholar had no courtroom prosecutorial experience, while America blocked that of the Briton Lowe. Boutros-Ghali then proposed the attorney general of India, but Pakistan opposed the nomination, effectively blocking it.[23] Next, the Secretary-General nominated Ramon Escovar Salom, attorney general of Venezuela. With no country objecting, the Security Council appointed Salom as prosecutor. But the Venezuelan had little interest in the job, and resigned even before he could formally assume the post, taking a new position as interior minister of his country.

After America nominated a former U.S. attorney whose nomination was opposed by Russia, "tempers were running short."[24] It was Nelson Mandela's agreement to the nomination of Richard Goldstone, a South African Constitutional Court judge, that brought to an end this diplomatic war over the selection of a war crimes prosecutor at The Hague. The tribunal finally got a prosecutor, more than a full year after it was formerly established.

THE DAYTON ACCORD—AND ITS PARADOXES

With the very limited political and financial support the Hague Tribunal received in its early years, arresting the key planners and commanders accused of the war crimes in Bosnia and Croatia proved difficult. Its first trial, the first international war crimes trial since World War II, was of a "small fry" defendant, Dusko Tadic. Tadic was a low level camp guard at Omarska camp in Bosnia, one of the concentration camps where Bosnian Muslims were held and tortured during the war. His arrest at a nightclub in Munich was an accident of fate that occurred because one of his victims at Omarska, now a refugee in Germany, recognized him on the street and alerted the German police.[25] German authorities initially wanted to prosecute him in their own courts for violations of the Geneva Conventions, but Goldstone requested that he be handed over to the Hague Court, which had primacy of jurisdiction under its statute. The Tadic trial was, in the larger scheme of things, a minor event. But the tribunal and its supporters in the human rights groups and the western media, seeking to lift the Hague Court out of its initial despondency, saw to it that it was promoted as the "trial of the century."[26]

In July 1995, well before the Tadic trial began in May 1996, the Hague Tribunal had taken the first step toward affecting the political evolution of the former Yugoslavia when it indicted the Bosnian Serb leaders Karadzic and Mladic for war crimes, crimes against humanity, and genocide. Soon afterward, peace talks began between the parties to the Yugoslav wars and the "Contact Group" (the United States, Russia, France, Britain, and Germany) in Dayton, Ohio. These talks, chaired and driven by the American diplomat Richard Holbrooke, led to the Dayton Accord that sought to end the war in Bosnia by partitioning its territory between Bosnian Muslims, on one hand, and Bosnian Serbs on the other.[27] The two entities would have a large amount of autonomy, but were to be governed by a three-person presidency consisting of a Muslim, a Croat, and a Serb.

The Dayton Accord, though chiefly aimed at ending the war in Bosnia, was nevertheless intricately linked to the pursuit of international justice in the former Yugoslavia in three ways. First, Holbrooke's chief interlocutor on the Serb side was Slobodan Milosevic, who had now positioned himself as a "peacemaker" with whom the great powers had to contend if they hoped to end the Balkan wars. Karadzic and Mladic, having been indicted by the Hague Tribunal, were politically marginalized in the international society but nevertheless still participated in the negotiations. In this sense it can be said that the Hague Tribunal was an indirect political actor in the Dayton process, and its indictments of Karadzic and Mladic helped pave the way for the successful negotiation of the peace accord. This situation also created important contradictions that demonstrate the manner in which order and justice clash at a fundamental level, with the option of justice giving way to an immediate need to establish peace in the sense of the absence of conflict. In this sense, order, in fact, becomes an agent of justice—"peace first, justice later." The synthesis of that contradiction was the outcome of Dayton, with help from the tribunal, as I have indicated earlier.

One contradiction was that the presence of Karadzic, a person indicted for violations of international law, on American territory, was a violation of international legal obligation created by the Hague Tribunal's arrest warrant that any state that finds the accused should arrest and hand him over to the international tribunal. Another contradiction involved Milosevic. He was widely known as the author of the Greater Serbia project, and yet here he was, negotiating as a legitimate interlocutor. But that particular contradiction was easy to resolve as of Dayton. Milosevic had not been indicted by the Hague Tribunal.

Second, the Dayton Accord provided that each party must cooperate with the Hague Tribunal where it sought the arrest and transfer for trial of any indicted person in its territory. Furthermore, in a provision that began the process of eroding the platform of Serb extreme nationalist politicians, it provided that no one indicted by the Hague Tribunal could stand for elections in Bosnia and Herzegovina. Thirdly, the Dayton Accord led to the deployment of a NATO force known as the International Force (IFOR) to implement the accord. Implementing the accord meant also arresting accused war criminals.

THE IDES OF KOSOVO

Kosovo, with which Milosevic had long been fixated, was to be his undoing. Tensions between the majority ethnic Albanians and Serb in the province eventually led to the emergence of an Albanian guerrilla movement, the Kosovo Liberation Army (KLA) in 1997. When Serbian police tried to arrest Adem Jashari, a KLA leader, in January 1998 and met with resistance, Serb police killed Jashari and fifty members of his family including twelve women in a gun battle.[28]

The KLA became radicalized and mobilized by this event, with dramatically increased public support among Kosovo Albanians. Their increasingly successful attacks on Serb forces led Milosevic to order Serb troops into Kosovo in mid-1998. These Serb troops committed numerous atrocities in response to what became a military and political struggle for independence for Kosovo by the KLA. Branding the KLA a terrorist organization, Serb forces began the "ethnic cleansing" of Kosovo villages, leading to massive flows of nearly 300,000 Kosovar refugees to Macedonia and Albania.[29]

The Hague Tribunal's prosecutor, Louise Arbour, ordered investigations of war crimes in Kosovo in late 1998. Holbrooke, who had led the Dayton negotiations, met with Milosevic in October 1998 and threatened the Serb leader with military strikes by North Atlantic Treaty Organization (NATO) forces if he did not end the fighting in Kosovo. That same month, NATO authorized air strikes on Serb forces if Milosevic did not comply with a UN Security Council resolution that ordered him to establish a ceasefire, withdraw Serb forces, allow the return of refugees, and begin negotiations for self-rule by Kosovo.[30]

But in January 1999 Milosevic launched a full-scale attack on Kosovo. The discovery of the massacre of forty-five Albanian civilians in the village of Racak galvanized the Western powers, leading to a peace conference between Serb and Albanian leaders at Rambouillet, France, in February 1999. That attempt to end the war and atrocities in Kosovo failed, largely because Milosevic, obstinately refusing to relinquish Serb control of Kosovo, instructed the Serb delegation not to sign an agreement by which NATO troops would be stationed in Kosovo. Faced with the choice between a NATO force to ensure a ceasefire in the province and a NATO bombing campaign, Milosevic insisted that Kosovo was sacred land for Serbs and could not come under the occupation of a foreign power. On March 24, NATO began its bombing campaign against Serbia. Paradoxically, Serb forces in Kosovo accelerated their ethnic cleansing campaign as the NATO bombing progressed.

On May 27, 1999, war crimes prosecutor Louise Arbour unveiled an indictment of Milosevic by the Hague Tribunal for war crimes against humanity in Kosovo. With the indictment of a serving head of state, international justice had made history. In June, Milosevic finally caved to the NATO bombing campaign and agreed to a peace accord that placed Kosovo under international administration by the United Nations.

But even as Louise Arbour prepared to indict Milosevic—undoubtedly the high point for the Hague Tribunal and for her own professional career—she kept looking over her shoulder, afraid that the UN might make a peace deal that would spare Milosevic from prosecution for war crimes.[31] "I felt when we have a strong a case we must move rapidly so that there's no risk that some deal will be made providing him with a de facto amnesty. *If the Security Council didn't want us to[indict Milosevic] they could stop us any time.* Until the phone rang I felt I have been asked to do something and I'm going to do it," she told a journalist.[32]

That the prosecutor of an international war crimes tribunal could make such a remarkable admission is a testament to the political nature of war crimes justice. This political influence and control over prosecution policy is a reality check on the avowals of liberal legalism as the impartial pursuit of justice in the fight against impunity. But Arbour's worries were unnecessary for three reasons. First, in the advanced international society in which international war crimes trials take place, amnesties for violations of international humanitarian law are no longer acceptable public policy or acceptable diplomacy. This is an important advance for liberal legalism, demonstrating the increased impact of ethnical values in world politics. The world may not be perfect, and may never be in the sense the cosmopolitan world peace movement would want it. But some things simply don't fly anymore. This is why the Western powers did not consider granting Milosevic an amnesty from prosecution at the Dayton Peace talks.

Second, and following from the new reality above, United Nations policy is that it does not recognize formal amnesties from prosecutions for violations of international humanitarian law in armed conflicts. Thus the UN instructed its representative to the 1999 Lome Peace Accords on the Sierra Leone civil war—which provided for amnesties for some of the protagonists—to append a reservation that the UN would not recognize such an amnesty.

Third, the practical and political situation was that Milosevic had outlived his usefulness to the Western powers as an interlocutor in the Balkans. If proof was needed, his intransigence over Kosovo and the ethnic cleansing there provided it. Thus, while the great powers could, conceivably, have sent signals against any preparations to indict Milosevic, the stakes were no longer high enough to do so. The situation might have been different had the Hague Tribunal tried to indict Milosevic before or during the Dayton Peace Talks. This analysis does not preclude what happened later in Sierra Leone, where the prosecutor of a UN-backed war crimes tribunal was to unveil an indictment against another serving head of state precisely as he was involved in peace negotiations (see Chapter 5). But then, such a dissonance can easily be explained from the standpoint of strategy: the stakes, from a geostrategic perspective, were certainly higher in the Balkans than in West Africa.

UNEQUAL JUSTICE

When the Canadian law professor Michael Mandel and others including Russian legislators filed a complaint with the Hague Tribunal regarding war crimes allegedly committed by NATO forces during their 78-day bombing campaign, there was much buzz, but no indictment.[33] The allegations set out cases where scores of civilians were killed by NATO bombs, including the bombing of a bridge as a passenger train was crossing it, a strike against a refugee convoy near Djakovica, and one against a Serbian television building in Belgrade.[34] Arbour ordered an investigation, but her successor, Carla Del Ponte, ultimately declined to file an indictment because she was unable "to pinpoint individual responsibilities."

But even the mere fact of an assertion of jurisdiction implicit in an internal review by the chief prosecutor at The Hague met with resentment in the circles of power and influence in NATO capitals.[35] To begin with, the Hague

Court's investigation was initially internal and confidential, though it was later made public. The tribunal has a mandate to investigate and prosecute violations of international humanitarian law committed in the territories of the former Yugoslavia from 1991. At a theoretical level at least, NATO did not question that remit. The real demonstration of the limits of international justice lay in the actions and statements by the United States government, the normally "fearless" Del Ponte, and other officials of the Yugoslavia Tribunal. At a press conference in December 1999, Del Ponte asserted the will to hold NATO accountable should evidence of crimes be confirmed, consistent with her responsibilities as an independent international prosecutor: "If I am not willing to do that, then I am not in the right place," she said. "I must give up my mission."[36] But Del Ponte soon issued a statement in which she backpedaled, emphasizing that "NATO is not under investigation" and that "no formal inquiry" was underway."[37]

While NATO shrugged off the tribunal's investigation and its spokesman asserted the military alliance's respect for the laws of war in its Kosovo campaign, the U.S. government reacted differently: A White House spokesman asserted NATO's exemption and characterized the tribunal's investigation of the legality of the NATO bombings as "completely unjustified."[38] Spokesmen for the tribunal later made it clear that an indictment or a prosecution of NATO leaders and officials accused by Mandel was out of the question.

The reasons for this turn of events are not farfetched. The United States, a great power, is a major financial and diplomatic backer of the Hague Tribunal. The turnaround in the tribunal's fortunes following its frustrating early years in which it was able only to apprehend and try low-level Serb military personnel, to the arrests of higher-profile political figures indicted by it, including Slobodan Milosevic, has depended almost exclusively on NATO's military and American political muscle. Del Ponte was initially under pressure to demonstrate the tribunal's independence, but ultimately, the international court could not bite the finger that has fed it. This is not mere conjecture, for NATO spokesman Jamie Shea is quoted as saying, in 1999, that: "NATO countries are those that have provided the finance to set up the Tribunal . . . we want to see war criminals brought to justice, and I am certain that when Justice Arbour goes to Kosovo and looks at the facts, she will be indicting people of Yugoslav nationality. I don't anticipate others at this stage."[39] More generally, the United States has consistently opposed any possibility that its military personnel or political leaders will be brought under the purview of international criminal tribunals, in particular the International Criminal Court.[40] Critics like Mandel have asserted that America supported the establishment of the UN tribunal simply in order to further its strategic interest in the Balkans.[41]

States rarely punish their own war criminals. This holds true even more for a great power. Great powers often see themselves as guardians of international order, and one of the unspoken prerogatives of their muscular military exertions, frequently in the service of a national interest but also sometimes on behalf of international society, is a lower threshold of accountability. When U.S. soldiers killed over 300 Vietnamese civilians during the war in Vietnam including infants and elderly persons, "no captains, majors, or generals were ever convicted" despite the precedent of command responsibility for the acts of subordinates set by the International Military Tribunal for the Far East in the famous *Yamashita* case.[42] The U.S. military chain of command tried to suppress the story until it was broken by journalists, leading to a trial of the lowly Lt. William Calley who was convicted of war crimes but paroled after a brief imprisonment.[43]

IN THE DOCK: THE ARREST AND TRIAL OF MILOSEVIC

The NATO bombing campaign took more than a physical toll on Serbia. It brought home to Serbs the consequences for them of the Balkan wars Milosevic had instigated. His political standing thus took a heavy hit. Milosevic's approval rating in Serbia dropped to 20 percent, the lowest in his 13-year rule.[44] With the country's economy severely weakened by international sanctions as well, Milosevic was defeated in the September 2000 presidential elections by Vojislav Kostunica, the compromise candidate of several opposition groups.

That election defeat was preceded by two sets of events that were connected indirectly to the Hague Tribunal. The first was a series of gangland-style assassinations of a number of close associates of Milosevic that people believed were done to prevent their cooperation with the international tribunal against Milosevic. Most notable of these were the assassinations of Arkan in January 2000 and the subsequent killings of Yugoslavia's defense minister and Ivan Stambolic, Milosevic's former political mentor and friend whom Milosevic had ousted from his position as head of Yugoslavia's Communist Party in the late 1980s in order to acquire ultimate political power.[45] That Milosevic ordered the murder of Stambolic was confirmed, several years later, by the Serbian Supreme Court.[46] The second was the successful mass protests against Milosevic by Serbian students and opposition leaders when he tried to steal victory in the September 2000 elections he lost. The protests were successful because Zoran Djindjic, the opposition mayor of Belgrade, made a secret deal with Milorad Lukovic, the commander of Milosevic's elite Interior Ministry Commandos, that Lukovic would not be handed over to the Hague Tribunal if he supported the protests or at least did not obstruct them.[47]

While Milosevic was in power, the Hague Tribunal's indictment against him, while legally valid, could not be executed on the practical grounds of sovereignty. NATO would have had to invade Belgrade to snatch Milosevic. Despite the prior bombing campaign undertaken on humanitarian grounds—which was already controversial enough because it did not have the approval of the United Nations Security Council—the great powers were clearly unwilling to go to such lengths to support international justice. As U.S. President Clinton put it: "I do not believe that the NATO allies can invade Belgrade to try to deliver the indictment, if you will."[48]

Following Milosevic's resignation in October 2000, however, his handover to the Hague Tribunal—and that of his coindictees and other indicted Serb leaders—became the central issue in Yugoslav politics. This tension was intricately tied up with Serbia's—and indeed the whole region's—need for economic aid and admission to European institutions. It was, in a real sense, the political economy of war crimes justice.

For a motley combination of reasons, all tied up with Serb nationalism and sovereignty, Yugoslav President Vojislav Kostunica, a former law professor, stoutly resisted pressure from Carla Del Ponte, the Hague Tribunal's prosecutor, to surrender Milosevic to the Hague Tribunal for trial. Serb public opinion detested the tribunal just as much as it disliked Milosevic because the court was seen as anti-Serb (the vast majority of its indictees at the time were Serbs). Belgrade was crowded with Serb refugees from the wars in Bosnia, Croatia, and Kosovo, and Del Ponte had declined to prosecute NATO commanders for alleged war crimes in the Kosovo bombing campaign.[49] Kostunica insisted he would try Milosevic in Yugoslav national courts, and then for economic crimes, not war crimes.

But the train of legalism had now been unleashed by the indictment. It seemed illogical to stop it, especially with Milosevic no longer in power. From a legal–sovereignty standpoint, Kostunica's position was untenable: the Hague Tribunal was established under the peace enforcement powers of the UN Security Council under Chapter VII of the UN Charter, and under the Charter, UN member states are obliged to accept and carry out decisions taken by the Security Council in accordance with the Charter. This is a clear limitation on sovereignty, which exists by virtue of membership of international institutions such as the United Nations, and is emblematic of the distinction between an international society such as exists in contemporary world politics from the international system that existed in the twentieth century.[50]

Carla Del Ponte embarked on a diplomatic campaign in Europe and the United States that sought to persuade these countries to make a proposed one-billion-dollar aid program to Yugoslavia conditional on the surrender of Milosevic to The Hague. She found support from some American congressmen. Mitch McConnell, Chairman of the U.S. Senate Finance Committee, inserted into the appropriations act a provision that made handing Milosevic to The Hague a condition precedent to aid to Serbia.[51] Despite continued resistance from Yugoslav president Kostunica, supported by a ruling of a Yugoslav federal court against surrendering Milosevic, Serbian Prime Minister Zoran Djindjic arranged the surrender of Milosevic to the

Hague Tribunal through the U.S. military base in Tuzla, Bosnia.[52] Milosevic was transferred from that base to The Hague on June 28, 2001. Djindjic was to pay for this act of bravery, which was inspired not necessarily by a commitment to legalism but by Serbia's need for economic aid, with his life. He was subsequently assassinated in what was clearly a vengeance killing by Serb extremist nationalists.

The trial of Milosevic began on February 12, 2002. Carla Del Ponte and the British barrister Geoffrey Nice, Queens Counsel (QC) led the prosecution. Milosevic refused to recognize the legitimacy of the Hague Tribunal and so refused to formally appoint a defense counsel. He was charged with the crimes committed by Serb forces in all the major wars that followed the disintegration of Yugoslavia—in Croatia, in Bosnia, and in Kosovo. In the beginning, Milosevic was charged with crimes against humanity and war crimes, specifically grave breaches of the Geneva Conventions and violations of the laws and customs of war. There was no charge of genocide. This was not surprising, for while what happened in Rwanda in 1994 was clearly genocide, it was a matter of debate whether ethnic cleansing in the Balkans constituted the ultimate crime. Genocide is primarily a crime of intent. It thus requires the intent to completely or partially destroy members of an ethnic, racial, or religious group by reason of who they are. It was clear that the massacres committed by all sides in the Yugoslav wars—Serbs, Croats, Bosnian Muslims, and Kosovo Albanians—were politically motivated. This made the massacres of civilians, in addition to war crimes, crimes against humanity. Ethnic cleansing in the former Yugoslavia was largely a struggle for territory, independence, and the ethnic purity of the inhabitants of these territories.

Because Milosevic was a wily operator, to whom little or no direct evidence of physical involvement in these crimes could be traced, the prosecution's case for his individual criminal responsibility rested mainly on his alleged participation in a "joint criminal enterprise" as a "co-perpetrator."[53] In the indictment against Milosevic for war crimes in Croatia, the other persons identified as part of that "joint criminal enterprise" including leading Serb politicians, army, and paramilitary commanders such as Borislav Jovic, president of the SFRY presidency from May 1989 until April 1992, Branko Kostic, General Veljko Kadijevic, former federal secretary for national defense, General Aleksandar Vasiljevic of the Yugoslav National Army (JNA), Tomislav Simovic, defense minister of Serbia in 1991, Milan Babic, "president of the republic" of the breakaway republic of Serbian Krajina from 1991 to early 1992, and Goran Hadzic, who succeeded Babic in the same position until 1994.[54] Others included the paramilitary commander Arkan, Vojislav Seselj, the leader of the Serbian Radical Party (SRS) who openly advocated the creation of a "Greater Serbia" by violent and other unlawful means, and Momir Bulatovic, former president of the Republic of Montenegro.[55]

Regarding the war crimes in Bosnia, many of these individuals were also named as part of Milosevic's "joint criminal enterprise." Notable additional figures in this particular indictment were Radovan Karadzic, president of the self-proclaimed Serbian Republic of Bosnia and Herzegovina ("Republika Sopska"), Momcilo Krajisnik, a copresident of "Republika Srpska," Biljana Plavsic, a former president and vice president of Srpska and the only woman to be indicted and convicted by the Hague Tribunal, and the notorious Serb military commander General Ratko Mladic, who commanded JNA forces in Knin, Croatia, and later assumed similar command in Sarajevo.[56]

Unlike the Bosnia and Croatia indictments, in the Kosovo indictment Milosevic was charged jointly with four of his political and military associates. These men were Milan Milutinovic, foreign minister of the Federal Republic of Yugoslavia (FRY, consisting of Serbia and Montenegro), Nikola Sainovic, deputy prime minister of the FRY, Colonel General Dragoljub Ojdanic, chief of the general staff of the armed forces of the FRY (VJ) that succeeded the JNA, and Vlajko Stojiljkovic, Minister of Internal Affairs of Serbia.[57] This was because in the cases of the wars in Bosnia and Croatia, Milosevic's control over the Serb paramilitary forces in those countries was seen as de facto but not de jure. The clearest indication of Milosevic's influence over Serb policies in Bosnia can be seen in the role he played at Dayton in negotiating and speaking for Karadzic and the so-called Republika Srpska. Kosovo, however, was legally part of the FRY, even if an autonomous province, and so Milosevic's responsibility for the crimes committed by Yugoslav forces was seen as more direct.

Another plank of prosecution strategy, in addition to the "joint criminal enterprise" approach was the command responsibility argument. Whatever may be the political controversies around the Milosevic case, and we will address these below, there was a clear case for command responsibility against Milosevic—provided, of course, that the crimes alleged could factually be proved to have been committed, and by individuals under his command. Under the legal principal of command responsibility, developed for the first time in the *Yamashita* case at the Tokyo Tribunal, a superior is responsible for the criminal acts of his subordinates if he knew or should have known that his subordinates were about to commit such acts or had done so, and he failed to take necessary and reasonable measures to prevent such acts or to punish the perpetrators.[58]

This principle is enshrined in Article 7(3) of the statute of the Hague Tribunal. Either out of ignorance or in the fog of war, many political and military commanders seldom take steps to prevent incrimination for war crimes under this broad remit. Of course, it is easier to instruct commanders not to kill civilians or attack civilian targets—assuming that that in itself is not the very purpose of a military action, as in the Balkan wars—than it is to punish military commanders who do so.

One instance of the implications of command responsibility in a courtroom trial came with a dramatic confrontation between Milosevic and the British parliamentarian Paddy Ashdown in the courtroom at the Hague Tribunal in 2002. Ashdown was a prosecution witness. With Milosevic in the dock, Ashdown testified to how, on a visit to Kosovo in late 1998, he encountered and filmed the bombardment of a Kosovar Albanian village by Serb forces in a manner that was clearly "indiscriminate, systematic and of a nature to terrorize and drive out the civilian population."[59] He later traveled to Belgrade, where he met Milosevic and confronted him with the cinematographic evidence: "I warned you that if you took those steps and went on doing this, you would end up in court, and here you are," he told Milosevic in the Hague courtroom.

There was always the question, especially among human rights activists that observed the Hague trial closely, whether Milosevic would be charged with genocide. In late 2002, international prosecutor Carla Del Ponte amended the Bosnia indictment against the former Serb leader to add charges of genocide—the ultimate crime. Milosevic now had sixty-six charges against him. Was this move law or politics? Was it because new evidence of Milosevic's genocidal intent had now been discovered, or was it a prosecutorial decision that sought to achieve maximum political impact in the demonization of Milosevic in his war crimes trial? The latter appears to be the case, demonstrating the blend of politics and law in the war crimes trial. Del Ponte insisted on bringing genocide charges against the doubts of some of her own senior lawyers, who thought a charge for genocide would be difficult to prove.[60]

Many legal scholars shared these doubts.[61] To be sure, the Hague Tribunal had, in August 2001, convicted the Bosnian Serb general Radislav Krstic of genocide for the Srebrenica massacre of several thousand Bosnian Muslims. This was the court's first genocide conviction. But the Krstic conviction did not set a persuasive precedent for the genocide charges against Milosevic. The Serb leader's name was nowhere mentioned in the 250-page judgment, and superior command responsibility was instead pinned on Ratko Mladic, who visited the scene of the massacres before they happened.

Milosevic, meanwhile, mounted a robust self-defense. He sought to turn his trial into a political spectacle and cast it as a show trial by his NATO conquerors, stoking Serb nationalism back home in Serbia in the process.[62] He tried to accomplish these goals in a number of tactical ways. First Milosevic refused from the beginning to recognize the legitimacy of the Hague Tribunal. He refused to enter a plea when the charges against him were read out, and the judges entered a not-guilty plea for him. His opening statement lasted for a total of eleven hours. "I can only be proud and I can accuse my accusers and their bosses. They are free men, but they are not truly free. I, arrested, imprisoned, am nevertheless free. My name is Slobodan with a capital 'S,' which means 'free' in my language," he told the court on the fifth day of his trial.[63]

Second, in what was probably the most effective blocking tactic he used in his trial, Milosevic refused to accept representation by a defense counsel, whether one appointed formally by him or one assigned by the tribunal under its legal aid scheme. This impasse allowed a constant struggle between Milosevic's political filibustering at his trial and the judges' valiant efforts to impose order on the hearing, and derailed the trial significantly. The lengthy and messy trial of Milosevic, which lasted 4 years without coming to a meaningful conclusion, raised serious questions and disillusionment with international war crimes tribunals.[64]

Under international law and the tribunal's rules of procedure, an accused person has the right to defend himself or through legal assistance of his own choosing, to be informed of his right to legal assistance, and to be assigned a lawyer where the interests of justice so require, and at no cost to the defendant if he is unable to pay the costs of such legal assistance.[65] But, in an indication of the political stakes in the case, the trial judges did not want to allow Milosevic to defend himself because they believed it would militate against the impression of a fair trial that was necessary to give the Milosevic trial political and historical legitimacy.[66] The Hague judges ordered a team of three court-appointed lawyers, "friends of the court," to assist the tribunal by handling Milosevic's interests in the trial, but not to work directly with the defendant. The former Serb leader would henceforth shut up and let his lawyers do the talking and questioning of witnesses, though he could play a minor role in questioning witnesses. When the judges informed Milosevic of the imposition of defense counsel, his petulant reaction was to raise his hand and declare, "Well, you go ahead and deal with it."[67] He subsequently boycotted his own trial, and witnesses scheduled to testify in his defense cancelled their appearances, leading to a postponement of the trial.

Milosevic asserted that "you cannot deny me the right to defend myself," and appealed the decision of the trial panel.[68] The appellate chamber of the Hague Tribunal affirmed the trial court's decision,[69] but Milosevic in practice continued to defend himself. In reality, he also had a group of outside Serb legal advisers who had no official status at the international tribunal.

The politicization of the defense of accused war criminals, especially when they are erstwhile political leaders, is not new. The contemporary precedent had already been set at the Arusha Tribunal that is prosecuting the accused architects of the 1994 Rwanda genocide. The Arusha court, however, dealt more firmly with attempts by former Rwanda prime minister, Jean Kambanda, former diplomat and media proprietor Jean-Bosco Barayagwiza, and other defendants to defend themselves or otherwise manipulate their trials for genocide.[70] To be sure, a defendant at the Arusha or Hague tribunals has the right to defend himself. But bearing in mind that a war crimes defendant such as Milosevic might have a variety of reasons in wanting to do so, not least of which is the desire to make a political mockery of the proceedings by casting them as a show trial, the court is faced with the choice of balancing the right to self-defense with other interests of justice in the trial. Those interests include, but are not confined to, those of the defendant.[71] They include the need for an expeditious trial and the need of the victims to see justice done.[72] How the court should rule depends on the situation in the particular case.

A second major contributing factor to the fiasco the Milosevic trial progressively became was a combination of the defendant's ill health and the death of Judge Richard May, the British judge at the Hague Tribunal who first presided over the trial. Milosevic suffered from chronic cardiac problems and high blood pressure. Doctors appointed by the tribunal judged him at risk of a heart attack.[73] That created major delays in the trial and was part of what exerted pressure on the judges to appoint defense counsel for him. Although the judges declared the defendant "fit enough" for his trial to proceed by July 2004, when he was due to start his defense case, 66 trial days had already been lost by then as a result of Milosevic's poor health, with the trial postponed more than a dozen times.[74]

Milosevic, in the meantime, had sought to call more than 1,400 witnesses. The prosecution had called nearly 300 witnesses.[75] Milosevic's witness list included world leaders such as Bill Clinton, former U.S. president, Tony Blair, the British prime minister, and Kofi Annan, the United Nations Secretary-General. It was unlikely that these personalities would have given character testimony in favor of the former Serb leader. His unsuccessful attempt to have them in court was calculated at further politicizing his trial by grilling them for exculpatory statements that would advance his positioning as a "victim" of a political conspiracy.

Further complications arose with the death of Judge May in late June 2004. Starting the trial anew was not seen as a viable option. He was replaced by Lord Bonomy, a Scottish judge, who had to be appointed by the UN Secretary-General. Patrick Robinson, the Jamaican judge on the trial panel, became the presiding judge in the trial. The replacement of May by a new judge who now had to catch up on 2 years of prosecution evidence led some critics, seeing the trial through the lens of national judicial practices, to consider it as further evidence of the political imperatives driving this war crimes trial. Arguing that, in America or Britain the death of a presiding judge would have resulted in a retrial, a British commentator wrote: "Perhaps Milosevic is so bad that he doesn't deserve a fair trial. The important thing is to get a conviction and make an example of him. Certainly there is a political case for that. But let us not pretend that we are treating Milosevic with the normal rules of impartial justice."[76]

Meanwhile, the trial of Milosevic, which by mid-2004 had been running for 2 years, was running in parallel with changes in the evolution of the domestic political order in Serbia. In his political diatribes at The Hague, Milosevic was speaking as much to his domestic audience in Serbia, where Serbs watched the proceedings with rapt attention, as to the international lawyers, judges, and spectators in the courtroom. Although his popularity at home had waned long before his surrender to the war crimes tribunal, his trial and strident calls by prosecutor Carla Del Ponte for the handover of other Serb indictees to The Hague had the impact of giving some strength to radical nationalist politicians.[77] This was especially so with regard to the Serbian Radical Party led by the notorious Vojislav Seselj, who was already awaiting trial at The Hague.[78]

However, reformist political forces were already in the ascendant in Serbia. In June 2004 Boris Tadic, a pro-reform politician running on the platform of the Democratic Party defeated the ultranationalists' candidate of the Radical Party, Tomislav Nikolic, in the Serbian presidential elections.[79] Tadic declared the country's economic revival and taking it into the European Union as his priorities.[80] Achieving both goals is explicitly linked to Serbia's cooperation with the Hague Tribunal, to which Tadic also committed his government.[81] But the political balance in Serbia remains a delicate one, and will probably be so for years to come. Tadic won the elections in a second-round runoff, by a slim margin. The Radical Party, which was allied with Milosevic during the 1990s, had made strong gains in previous parliamentary elections in December 2003.[82] Vojislav Kostunica, now Prime Minister of Serbia, remained consistent in his antipathy toward the Hague Tribunal, though in his rhetoric he adopted the posture of cooperation.[83] Radovan Karadzic and Ratko Mladic remain at large as of this writing, and potential economic aid from the West and entry into the European Union for Serbia thus remain blocked. All of this, however, did not equate to any significant personal popularity for Milosevic among the Serbs.[84]

THE DEATH OF MILOSEVIC

On March 11, 2006, Milosevic died in his cell at the detention facilities of the Hague Tribunal, aged 64. He had died of cardiac problems. Speculation was rife: Had he committed suicide? Was he poisoned? It did not help matters that, a week before Milosevic's death, Milan Babic, who had been scheduled to testify against him, committed suicide. Controversy was further stoked by the fact that, shortly before his death, Milosevic had asked the tribunal for leave to undergo medical treatment in Russia. The tribunal's judges denied the request and insisted Milosevic continue receiving medical attention in The Hague.[85] The former Serb leader's appeal was pending at the time of his death. The ruling was handed down because the tribunal was not persuaded that the defendant would return to The Hague to complete his trial if he was granted permission to leave the Netherlands, despite personal guarantees from him and from the Russian government.

In light of the fiasco that surrounded the defense of Milosevic, this situation posed a true policy dilemma. But, despite the outcome of Milosevic's eventual death, the tribunal's decision was the right one, for Milosevic had a right to medical attention, but not necessarily to treatment in Moscow. A series of autopsies and toxicology tests ruled out poisoning or suicide, but confirmed that Milosevic had secretly been taking rifampicin, a tuberculosis drug that prevented the prescribed medication for his heart condition from working effectively.[86] While we can only speculate, this can be interpreted as a death wish if Milosevic knew that the unauthorized medication he was taking would have the effect it did. This is not a farfetched scenario, for Milosevic had a family history of suicides, both his parents having killed themselves. In any case, while medical experts disagree as to whether further tests than those undertaken by court-appointed doctors would have made a difference to his eventual fate, and valid questions exist about the level of care he received while in detention at the Hague tribunal, Milosevic was known to be "a sometimes difficult patient who defied doctors' orders."[87]

The death of Milosevic has been interpreted in several ways. The question is—was it a denial of justice to the victims of the crimes for which he was on trial, or was it in fact a final kind of justice? Carla Del Ponte, the Hague Tribunal's prosecutor, admitted that Milosevic's death represented "a total defeat" for her.[88] Her prize catch had slipped through her fingers, outfoxing the Hague Tribunal yet again by taking the spotlight on his own terms. Subdued, she characterized the unfortunate event at a press conference at The Hague as "a great pity for justice" and spared a thought for Zoran Djindjic. Richard Holbrooke, Milosevic's old foe at Dayton, characterized the former Serb leader in television interviews after his death as a "monster," and opined that his death was in fact justice that brought closure to Milosevic's controversial career.

One thing was not in dispute—that the death of Milosevic had dealt a near-death blow to the Hague Tribunal.[89] The anticlimax it created has highlighted the difficulties of using war crimes trials to establish the accountability of erstwhile powerful leaders for violations of international humanitarian law.[90] It was no precedent, however. Foday Sankoh, the Sierra Leonean warlord who was to be a star defendant at the Special Court for Sierra Leone, the UN-backed war crimes tribunal created to adjudicate the atrocities committed in the Sierra Leonean civil war, died before he could stand trial.[91] And more than half a century earlier, the Nazi kingpin, Hermann Goering, escaped the hangman's noose by committing suicide after his conviction at the Nuremberg Trial. It is thus a matter of opinion—and perspective—whether the death of Milosevic has made his aborted trial "the most important unresolved case in the history of international law."[92]

Although it took the shine out of the trials at The Hague, Milosevic's death will not preclude the outcome of the process of political justice underway at the International Criminal Tribunal for the former Yugoslavia. To begin with, it increases the pressure on the tribunal to capture and prosecute Karadzic and Mladic, who are important symbols, and whose trial has been made even more important, according to conventional wisdom in Western international policy, by the death of Milosevic. This will be no easy task. The chance exists that, with the Hague Tribunal scheduled to close down in 2009, these men too could elude justice, including by committing suicide, rather than face the tribunal. That would be a cowardly but thoroughly political act. It is commonly assumed that the arrest of Mladic, in particular, is polit-ically essential to re-establish the political relevance of the Hague Tribunal, but in an insightful and contrarian opinion essay, Timothy William Waters, a former prosecuting attorney at the Tribunal has argued that "Europe is making … lazy assumptions about the role of international justice in trans-forming societies," and that it is better for the European Union to proceed with talks with Serbia for its integration into Europe because of the larger strategic benefits of Serbian integration, than for the process to be held up by the absence of one defendant.[93]

Second, Milosevic's demise robs the Serbs of an opportunity to see with-out blinkers, and repudiate, the crimes that were committed in their name by the former Serb leader's political and military subordinates. That process, though, is already underway, even if it will not enjoy the boost a legal con-viction of Milosevic would have given it. Clearly, a majority of Serbs have already repudiated Milosevic's legacy. This is not because they all share the world's indignation at the crimes committed in the failed "Greater Serbia" project that accompanied the demise of the former Yugoslavia. Rather, this distancing has occurred because many Serbs were angry and disappointed at the sanctions and isolation they faced for several years as a result of the wars Milosevic instigated. Thus Milan Panic, who was prime minister of Yugoslavia from 1992 to 1993 and an opposition politician, has posited that Milosevic's death "cleanses the stains" on the Serbs' national pride.[94]

It is technically now a matter of speculation what the Milosevic trial's verdict would have been had it been completed, but it seems clear on close examination that he would have been convicted. The real question is—for what crimes in his indictment? He would certainly have been convicted of crimes against humanity and war crimes (violations of the laws and customs of war) in Kosovo, where he had direct command of the Yugoslav armed forces, and probably for the same category of crimes in Bosnia and Croatia. Such convictions would have been based on the principle of command responsibility and on the charge of Milosevic's participation in a "joint criminal enterprise" in three Balkan wars.

The principle of command responsibility is a fall-back, catch-all rubric that makes it difficult for political and military commanders to escape con-viction where there is clear evidence of crimes committed by their subordi-nates, and their commanders knew or should have known and did nothing to stop or punish such crimes. Command responsibility is an essential tool to accomplish the political objectives of war crimes trials—the trial of high-level political or military leaders—where the political factors at play permit the targeting of such leaders. In some cases the evidence of such command responsibility is clear. Nearly a decade earlier, the principle formed the backbone of the 1998 conviction of Jean Kambanda, prime minister and head of government of Rwanda during 1994, at the Arusha Tribunal. This was the first conviction of a former head of government for genocide by an international war crimes tribunal and a precedent for the Milosevic trial.[95]

But to establish Milosevic's command responsibility in Bosnia or Croatia (which would have been no easy thing to achieve) or his participation in a "joint criminal enterprise" (which would have been easier), it would have been necessary to demonstrate clearly that he was actively in charge, even though he was not formally in command of Serb paramilitary forces in Bosnia and Croatia. In the Rwanda case, Kambanda confessed to presiding over cabinet meetings where the progress of the genocide was discussed. Participation and leadership of a criminal activity rarely gets more obvious than that. In the Milosevic case, his control appeared more subtle. Nonetheless the prosecutors at the Hague Tribunal led some former Serb intelligence officials in evidence that appeared to link Milosevic in a supervisory role to the actions of Serb nationalists in the breakaway republics of Bosnia and Croatia.[96] In one instance, the Hague Tribunal listened to a Bosnian intelligence intercept of a conversation between Milosevic and Karadzic in which Milosevic told Karadzic to get arms from a JNA garrison inside Bosnia.[97] On the tape Milosevic also told Karadzic "Take radical steps and speed things up, and we shall see if the European Community is going to fulfill their guarantees, if they are going to stop that violence."[98]

The real problem in a Milosevic verdict, as indicated earlier, would have been the charges of genocide in Bosnia. Although Carla Del Ponte insists she would have secured a conviction for the ultimate crime, from a legal standpoint it would have been difficult to achieve that without—in the circumstances of the Srebrenica massacre—stretching the principle of command responsibility to an extent that would have been highly questionable. If the Hague Tribunal had done so, it would have been stretching the law to achieve political impact—exactly what the Nuremberg Tribunal did when it convicted the Nazis of aggressive war, something that was not a crime in international law at the time Hitler's army rampaged across Europe.

But, although Milosevic adeptly turned his trial into a political spectacle and an obstacle course for the prosecutors and judges, his arrest and transfer to The Hague was itself already a victory for the political justice that war crimes tribunals exist to accomplish. In his having been removed from the political space in Serbia, his defenestration by the Hague Tribunal was nearly complete.

Did Milosevic receive a fair trial? This important question is best answered not in the abstract, as is the wont of many critics, but in the context of the objective reality of the political nature of war crimes trials. On the balance, then, despite its shortcomings (and there are few perfect trials for war crimes), the answer is yes, although his supporters in Serbia view the Hague

Tribunal as a political kangaroo court. Like all war crimes tribunals, they are not wrong in seeing The Hague Court as "political" in the sense of its context and the forces that drive it. Whether this makes the Hague Tribunal a "kangaroo" court is another matter. The lopsided nature of many war crimes trials, inspired as they generally are by great powers or victorious parties in wars, often beclouds the objective fact of mass atrocities committed at the instigation of the persons on trial. Justice, and especially war crimes justice, is rarely neutral, let alone evenhanded. But the essentially political nature and function of war crimes tribunals, including the Hague Tribunal that prosecuted Milosevic, raises valid questions about prosecutorial independence.[99]

At a strategic level, however, the Milosevic trial was a major failure by and for the Hague Tribunal and provides object lessons to other war crimes trials. The selection of Judge May, a British judge and a national of a country that was part of the NATO bombing campaign against Serbia, presented a perception of unfairness in the eyes of some observers. The matter of Milosevic's defense counsel could have been better handled. The tribunal could have taken the alternative position, given the particular situation before it. The Hague Court appeared overly concerned with its own image in seeking to force defense lawyers on the former Serb leader and, while the rights of the defendant must be balanced with other interests such as those of the victims in obtaining a fair and expeditious trial, Milosevic had the right to defend himself under international law.

The policy perspective, anxious to avoid war crimes trials being turned into political soapboxes, is of course different, and most tribunals try to avoid situations where the accused person defends himself. But in this case that policy approach actually worked against the Hague Tribunal and allowed Milosevic to manipulate the proceedings into an appearance of unfairness to him. To the extent that he did not mount a sustained boycotting his own trial—in which case the court could appoint a lawyer to protect his interests and continue with the trial, as the Arusha Tribunal did in the Barayagwiza case[100]—his right to self-defense ought to have been respected. To prevent its abuse by the wily Milosevic, such a decision would be accompanied by strict time limits for his presentations and examinations of witness. If he failed to abide by such restrictions that are necessary for an efficient trial, the courtroom public address system would be turned off on him, as indeed it was on a number of occasions: Not even Milosevic's ill health deprived him of the right to defend himself if he so wished, so long as the implications of following that path were made clear to him, on the record. Judge May held the view that Milosevic could defend himself, but this was a minority position in the three-judge bench.[101]

A second major misstep in the Milosevic trial, this time by the prosecutor Carla Del Ponte, was her insistence on combining in one trial the charges against Milosevic for crimes committed in Bosnia, Croatia, and Kosovo over a near-10-year span. This overly ambitious strategy was bound to generate—and did generate—complications that bogged down the trial in serious delays.[102] Attempts to respond to these complications demonstrated once again the political factors that influenced the actions of various actors in the trial.

One of those influences was the impatience of public opinion and the governments in the UN Security Council with the seemingly endless trial of Milosevic and, in the case of the United States, even more broadly on the lifespan of the Hague and Arusha tribunals.[103] The dilemma this situation poses for war crimes tribunals is whether, in trying important political figures, to "throw the book" at the defendant and seek to establish his guilt for what is always a long list of alleged crimes, or to be selective about what crimes to prosecute for the sake of judicial economy. The latter tactic addresses one or two important crimes in order to achieve the desired symbolic (political) outcome in such trials while, from a legal standpoint, "wasting" prosecutorial opportunities.

The judges sought to break up the Milosevic indictment into smaller, more manageable parts, but both the defense and the prosecution objected, each for its own reasons.[104] Breaking up the case would most likely have led to an earlier verdict in at least one portion of it.[105] The prosecution wanted to show the atrocities committed by Serb forces in the various parts of the former Yugoslavia as part of an overall land grab. Milosevic's unofficial defense team of Serb lawyers, no doubt relishing the opportunity for Milosevic to state his own version of the contemporary history of the former Yugoslavia, objected on the grounds that the move amounted to changing the rules of the game midstream.

So attached was prosecutor Del Ponte to a single trial of Milosevic for his alleged crimes in the Balkan wars that she successfully appealed an initial decision by the trial judges to begin the trial with the Kosovo indictment. Here again, as with Louise Arbour when she worked toward indicting Milosevic, the prosecutors had the UN Security Council—the tribunal's political master—on their minds: they worried that the Council might press for a discontinuation of the trial once the Kosovo portion was concluded. "This was such an acute danger that we didn't want to take the risk," Graham Blewitt, Del Ponte's deputy said.[106]

Let us return to the larger significance of the Milosevic trial, the defendant's death, and its impact on the Hague Tribunal. The reason why, despite the anticlimax of Milosevic's death, the political and economic reconstruction of the Balkans through war crimes trials will continue is this: the strong psychological desire of the Serbs and other ethnic nationalities in the Balkans to become part of the mainstream Europe. Seeing this as their ultimate interest, political economy will trump nationalism on this question and Serbia's democratically elected leaders, despite their recent reluctance, will move inexorably to achieve that outcome. While Milosevic's abrupt death has foreclosed the option of legal, more certain closure to the historical questions of guilt for the Balkan wars and their atrocities, and it is important to note that even politically, Milosevic does not bear sole responsibility for the break-up of the former Yugoslavia, it provides an opportunity to bring that closure in a different manner that is just as political and economic as it is legal.

The death of Milosevic increased the pressure on Serbia's leaders from the Hague Tribunal's political sponsors to surrender Karadzic and Mladic. It is an open question whether the two men will be brought to The Hague for trial, as nationalist sentiment remains strong in Serbia. That the tribunal has indicted leading Croat, Bosnian Muslim, and Kosovar suspects for war crimes in recent years has blunted Serb charges that the international tribunal was set up to target and demonize them. The most dramatic of the non-Serb indictments by the international tribunal were those of General Ante Gotovina of Croatia[107] and Ramush Haradinaj, who was elected Kosovo's prime minister in a national elections after a career as a leader of the Kosovo Liberation Army, which was known to have committed atrocities against Serbs.[108] But the political challenge that must be overcome to ensure the eventual success of the Hague Tribunal is to ensure that hard-line nationalist forces do not return to power in Serbia.

Milosevic's victims would argue that he was a victim of a Western conspiracy to punish him, and thus a martyr. But this is self-delusion, for it refuses to recognize the reality of the crimes against the hundreds of thousands of victims in the wars Milosevic waged and lost. To say that Milosevic would have been convicted—on the basis of objective legal evidence—of at least several crimes with which he was charged is not to deny another truth that supporters of the Hague Tribunal conveniently ignore: that court and others like it in Rwanda, Sierra Leone, and Cambodia are more instruments of political engineering than impartial justice for war crimes.

This is why charges of war crimes that were leveled at the NATO bombing campaign in Kosovo were ultimately dismissed by Del Ponte. The real mandate of the Hague Tribunal is political, not just an abstract legal one. In his death, Milosevic snatched himself from the jaws of justice. But it leaves many questions unanswered, questions that must still be resolved. And it demonstrates the limits of legalism.

4

The Rise and Fall of Universal Jurisdiction

To define the interests of mankind is to lay claim to a kind of authority that can only be conferred by a political process
—Hedley Bull, *The Anarchical Society*

One dimension of the cosmopolitan view of international justice is the push to obliterate geographical (and jurisdictional) boundaries in the pursuit of alleged war criminals. This is what has been termed "universal jurisdiction" or "borderless justice." It is a campaign for accountability beyond the jurisdictional borders established in the centuries over which international law has developed. This chapter will examine that phenomenon. It will inquire into the legal basis of the assertion of this controversial form of jurisdiction that touches the heart of world politics, demonstrate how the concept of universal jurisdiction illustrates the tension between universalist conceptions of justice and the nature of the international society, and establish that, although the concept is not without legal and historical basis, those foundations are of limited scope. Certain clearly defined circumstances permit trials on the basis of universal jurisdiction. But excessively broad assertions of a right to try presumed war criminals in the courts of countries other than their own rest more on declarations of a cosmopolitan world society than on concrete legality.

UNIVERSAL JURISDICTION

Universal jurisdiction is a doctrine that asserts that some crimes are so shocking in the affront they represent to all nations that the national courts of any country can and should bring the perpetrators to justice. Accused offenders can be prosecuted in a country that asserts universal jurisdiction, whether or not a link exists between that country and the place where the crime was committed, or the nationality of the offender or the victim. In other words, universal jurisdiction, in its purest form, is one in which mankind acts on behalf of itself everywhere to ensure that the perpetrators of particularly heinous crimes will not escape justice on the basis of the limitations of national judicial systems or those of international courts. The doctrine assumes the existence of—or at least proposes—a community or a *world* society, rather than an *international* society of sovereign states. It is the strongest expression so far of the struggle to give birth to a cosmopolitan regime of legal justice in international relations.

Not surprisingly, then, it is arguably the hottest flashpoint of the tension between that worldview on the one hand and that of a pluralist, or even less expansively defined solidarist international society, on the other. Henry Kissinger complained in 2001 that

> "In less than a decade, an unprecedented movement has emerged to submit international politics to judicial procedures. It has spread with extraordinary speed and has not been subjected to systematic debate, partly because of the intimidating passion of its advocates. To be sure, human rights violations, war crimes, genocide, and torture have so disgraced the modern age and in such a variety of places that the effort to interpose legal norms to prevent or punish such outrages does credit to its advocates. The danger is in pushing the effort to extremes that risk substituting the tyranny of judges for that of governments; historically, the dictatorship of the virtuous has often led to inquisitions and even witch-hunts."[1]

Elder statesman in the eyes of some, the reincarnation of Machiavelli for others, Kissinger, a geopolitical strategist with few equals in contemporary history, had reason to be irked: as National Security Adviser and, later, Secretary of State of the United States, he is credited with several controversial policies, some of which had serious implications for human rights. His extremist critics on the ideological left see him as a prime candidate for the exercise of just such "universal jurisdiction."[2] It emerged from a declassified telephone conversation between him and President Richard Nixon, for example, that Kissinger, in the service of a liberal democracy that is the United States, actively supported the overthrow of Salvador Allende, a democratically elected president of the Latin American nation of Chile, by General Augusto Pinochet in 1973.[3] The goal was to protect capitalism—a strategic interest of the United States—by preventing the entrenchment of leftist governments in Latin America during the cold war.

In the still anarchical international society, powerful officials of state like Kissinger exist in many countries. And, because the nature of statecraft often involves tradeoffs between morality and cold calculations in foreign and domestic policy that in extreme cases results in violations of international humanitarian law, the doctrine of universal jurisdiction generates apprehension on the part of those whose duty it is to advance the strategic interests of states. The prospect of an arrest warrant served in an airport VIP lounge during an airplane stopover or on arrival at its destination is enough to cause discomfiture to many a traveling statesman. But there are those who are not high priests of *realpolitik* that have as well questioned the manner in which this controversial legal doctrine has sometimes been asserted.

The concept of universal jurisdiction is closely related to the international law principle of *jus cogens*—a norm of international law from which no derogation is permitted, not even by a treaty.[4] A clear example is the prohibition of piracy. Pirates have historically been considered *hostis hominis generis*, or "enemies of the human race."[5] It is widely accepted in international law that, largely because piracy often occurs on the high seas where no nation can assert jurisdiction, any or all states may apprehend and punish pirates captured on the high seas or the territory of the arresting state. The United Nations Convention on the Law of the Sea stipulates:

> On the high seas, or in any other place outside the jurisdiction of any State, every State may seize a pirate ship, aircraft, or a ship or aircraft taken by piracy and under the control of pirates, and arrest the person and seize the property on board. The courts of the State which carried out the seizure may decide upon the penalties to be imposed, and may also determine the action to be taken with regard to the ships, aircraft or property, subject to the rights of third parties acting in good faith.[6]

Thus, universal jurisdiction is a theory that clearly exists in positive international law.

Advocates of universal jurisdiction in relation to genocide, crimes against humanity, and war crimes have offered the need to combat impunity as the rationale for borderless justice. They see the doctrine as one way to bring to justice tyrants and errant high officials of state that are beyond accountability either because their acts are not contrary to domestic law or, where they indeed violate such laws, the legal system is in practice subordinate to the political authority wielded by such individuals. Alternatively, these individuals avoid accountability by reason of immunities or national amnesties conferred by truth and reconciliation commissions.

This is the heart of the matter. Who is fit to judge? Should the courts of one state judge the alleged infractions of leaders or citizens of another?[7] Universal jurisdiction in this context is controversial because (a) it transcends—or threatens to transcend—the sacrosanct principle of sovereignty without the consent of states or the support of other accepted exceptions in international law such as enforcement action by or under the aegis of the United Nations Security Council; (b) for this reason, it can be a serious threat to international order. Before examining some contemporary cases of the exercise of universal jurisdiction, it is necessary to review its legal basis—and its limitations—as a response to violations of international humanitarian law.

There are several misconceptions about universal jurisdiction, although the doctrine has gripped the popular imagination since the "legal soap opera" that was the Pinochet case in Britain (that case was, technically speaking, more one of extradition and immunities than of universal jurisdiction, although the latter doctrine was discussed at various stages of the legal proceedings against the former Chilean leader in several countries).[8]

Territory has been the strongest basis for the exercise of jurisdiction in legal history. Jurisdiction is strongest where the state exercising it is the one where the crimes occurred. Human rights activists have confused the extraterritorial application of territorial jurisdiction with universal jurisdiction. Mutations of territorial jurisdiction include the nationality principle (where a state exercises jurisdiction over its national territory); the passive personality principle (where a state claims jurisdiction to prosecute an individual for offences committed outside its territory which has or will impact nationals of the state—this was the basis of the celebrated trial of Adolf Eichmann in Jerusalem in 1961 following his abduction from Argentina);and jurisdiction by a state over foreign nationals when they have committed an act abroad that compromises the security of that state.[9] These kinds of jurisdiction are to be distinguished from the pure universality principle, where each and every state has jurisdiction to try specific offences.[10]

Universal jurisdiction should also be distinguished from the jurisdiction of international criminal tribunals, such as the ad hoc United Nations war crimes tribunals for Rwanda and the former Yugoslavia, or the permanent International Criminal Court. As Cherif Bassiouni has noted, none of the ad hoc international tribunals established since the end of World War II (Nuremberg, Tokyo, Yugoslavia, and Rwanda) has been based on the theory of universal jurisdiction.[11] The ad hoc tribunals represent an extension of national territorial jurisdiction. An occupying power acquires and exercises jurisdiction over a defeated enemy state by virtue of conquest and physical occupation, as was the case in Iraq from the end of the U.S.-led invasion in 2003 until the return of sovereignty to Iraq on June 30, 2004. In the case of the UN tribunals, these courts assume *concurrent* territorial jurisdiction by virtue of the peace enforcement powers of the United Nations

Security Council. Bassiouni clarifies the more nuanced case of the ICC by noting that the Rome Statute does not automatically confer the character of universal jurisdiction on situations referred to the Court. Rather, it only has a "universal scope" in relation to crimes *within its jurisdiction* [emphasis added]. In the case of the ad hoc UN tribunals, this limitation extends not only to crimes under their jurisdiction, but to the geographical boundaries of their jurisdiction as well—Rwanda and neighboring states in the case of the Arusha Tribunal and the states of the former Yugoslavia in that of the Hague Tribunal. In other words, the Hague Court can only try individuals for crimes committed in the territory to which its jurisdiction is confined, and this cannot be accurately described as "universal" jurisdiction.

This distinction may appear at first sight to be mere sophistry. But it is an important one. Bassiouni explains that, because cases can only be "referred" to the ICC by a state party or a nonstate party, the Court's jurisdiction cannot be seen as flowing from the doctrine of universal jurisdiction. The point, then, is that an international, but nonetheless limited jurisdiction that merely reacts to states is not what would normally be considered "universal," because the exercise of universal jurisdiction does not require an external trigger. Universal jurisdiction is either inherent by virtue of customary international law or specifically by treaty, or both. However, Bassiouni makes the distinction that a "referral" to the ICC from the Security Council (presumably in its capacity as a guardian of international security, with an automatic global reach) would constitute universal jurisdiction.

Against the background of the distinctions noted above, there are very few examples of actual trials based on the exercise of universal jurisdiction, with the exception of piracy.[12] The notable contemporary exception was the trial of four Rwandans in Belgium, under Belgian law, for crimes related to the Rwandan genocide of 1994. That case and the law on which it was based will be discussed below.

Most importantly, Bassiouni has sought to help clear the confusion between assumptions of universal jurisdiction on the basis of international human rights standards (at least in the view of the liberal human rights movement) and the actual state of international law on the matter. He establishes convincingly that the doctrine of universal jurisdiction is far more persuasive in the writings of scholars and human rights activists with a vested interest in a advancing the concept, than it is in the actual practice of states, and that human rights groups have engaged in self-interested misinterpretations of how widespread the doctrine is in practice. Coming from an eminent academic expert in international criminal law, this critique is a weighty one. It highlights the problems of universal jurisdiction and why, despite its potential benefits in certain circumstances, it is necessary to approach the doctrine with caution.

LEGAL BASIS: DECLARATORY V POSITIVE LAW

To understand the validity or otherwise of claims of universal jurisdiction, it is necessary to distinguish two situations. The first is one where
jurisdiction is asserted on the basis of what *ought* to be universally punishable by the courts of all nations, usually because such acts are an affront to
the collective conscience of mankind. This is the declaratory ethical tradition in action. The second is one where an act is actually made punishable
on the basis of universal jurisdiction by a law authoritatively declared in
accordance with recognized procedure, with a mechanism for adjudication,
whether international or national, and an enforcement mechanism—again,
whether national or international. This is legal positivism.[13] Advocates in
the declaratory tradition tend to believe that because the moral repugnancy
of certain crimes is self-evident, coupled with the firm establishment of
individual justice in international law, it must follow that jurisdiction over
those crimes cannot be hemmed in by geographical borders. Legal positivists
would share the same degree of moral outrage at these crimes, but interpret the applicability of universal jurisdiction against the standards of what
law, national or international, really is. We can now test this approach on
the three major violations of international humanitarian law—war crimes,
crimes against humanity, and genocide.

War Crimes

The Geneva Conventions of 1949 and Protocol I clearly provide for
the exercise of universal jurisdiction. However, some scholars are of the
view that, absent the Geneva Conventions, state practice does not reflect
the application of the doctrine to customary international law.[14] But the
view that the Geneva Conventions are somewhat tentative in their support
for universal jurisdiction is unnecessarily conservative.[15] In the first of the
four Geneva Conventions of August 12, 1949, the states parties to the treaty
undertook to enact laws that would punish persons who commit or order
the commission of any of the grave breaches defined in the Convention. In
a clear provision of universal jurisdiction

Each High Contracting Party shall be under the obligation to search for persons alleged to have committed, or to have ordered to be committed, such
gave breaches, and shall bring such persons, regardless of their nationality,
before its own courts. It may also, if it prefers, and in accordance with the
provisions of its own legislation, hand such persons over for trial to another
High Contracting Party concerned, provided such High Contracting Party
has made out a *prima facie* case.[16]

Amnesty International has asserted that at least 120 states have enacted legislation permitting their courts to exercise universal jurisdiction over conduct that would amount to war crimes.[17] These claims may be exaggerated by interpretation, as noted above. Even Amnesty notes that "the absence of authoritative commentary or jurisprudence, as well as ambiguities in wording, in many countries makes it difficult to say with some certainty whether courts may exercise universal jurisdiction over conduct amounting to war crimes." A few countries, such as Belgium, Canada, and New Zealand, have national legislation that expressly confers universal jurisdiction over war crimes committed not only in international armed conflict, but in noninternational armed conflicts as well. Considering that most contemporary armed conflicts are civil wars, this reality of so few states having the required national legislation is the more accurate indicator of the real state of universal jurisdiction over war crimes. Moreover, having a law on the books is often quite different from the political will to apply it in terms of a practical assertion of universal jurisdiction.

What has more often been the case is that several states have enacted laws that give their courts universal jurisdiction over certain ordinary crimes under national law (such as murder and crimes of sexual violence) which would amount to war crimes if committed in an armed conflict.[18] This was the basis for the trial and the conviction in Switzerland of a former Rwandan soldier for crimes committed during the 1994 genocide.[19] And it was the first by a national court exercising universal jurisdiction under the 1949 Geneva Conventions.[20]

Historically, there is a judicial track record that suggests a consistent, if partial reliance on the doctrine of universal jurisdiction for war crimes by the courts of the Allied Powers in the aftermath of World War II, although universal jurisdiction was not a basis for the Nuremberg Trials.[21] (The Nuremberg Tribunal was based on the territorial principle of jurisdiction because the Allies, relying on their status as an occupying power, promulgated the Nuremberg Charter in the exercise of their right in that context to establish special courts.) Accused war criminals were prosecuted by United States military courts for crimes against nonnationals of allied countries.[22]

In the *Hadamar* trial, for example, a U.S. military commission tried Germans charged with killing nearly 500 Russian and Polish civilians at a sanitorium in Germany. Even in this case there is a territorial link to Germany, in which the United States was an occupying power. However, the commission invoked the doctrine of universal jurisdiction, with the commission's judgment explaining the basis of its jurisdiction as follows:

> the general doctrine recently expounded and called universality of jurisdiction over war crimes; which has the support of the United Nations War Crimes Commission and according to which every independent State has, under International Law, jurisdiction to punish not only pirates but also

war criminals in its custody, regardless of the nationality of the victim or of the place where, the offense was committed, particularly where, for some reason, the criminal would otherwise go unpunished.[23]

In the same vein, another U.S. military commission in Shanghai asserted jurisdiction over Germans in China who were charged with the war crime of continuing hostilities against the Allies after the German surrender in 1945. Rejecting a defense claim challenging its extraterritorial jurisdiction, the commission ruled:

> A war crime is not a crime against the law or criminal code of any individual nation, but a crime against the *ius gentium* [international law]. The laws and usages of war are of universal application, and do not depend for their existence on national laws and frontiers. Arguments to the effect that only a sovereign of the *locus criminis* [place of the crime] has jurisdiction and that only the *lex loci* [law of the place] can be applied, are therefore without any foundation."[24]

Here the commission invoked universal jurisdiction in a case where the United States had a significant security interest and the accused persons were nationals of an enemy state occupied by the Americans. British military courts after World War II also adopted a similar jurisdictional stance in some cases.[25] And what the historical cases demonstrate is not so much clear examples of universal jurisdiction but rather, an apparent confusion as to what the doctrine really meant. That universal jurisdiction was cited by these tribunals is perhaps evidence of the doctrine's appeal even in the 1940s. Reference to it in this context is also not surprising, considering that its invocation served the strategic interests of the Allies.

Crimes against Humanity

With the exceptions of the International Convention on the Suppression and Punishment of the Crime of Apartheid (Apartheid Convention) adopted in 1973 and the Convention against Torture and Other Cruel, Inhuman or Degrading Treatment of Punishment (Torture Convention) adopted in 1984, there is no positive international law that establishes universal jurisdiction for the prosecution of crimes against humanity. Whether such crimes *should*, on ethical grounds, be the subject of universal jurisdiction, is another matter.

One reason for this state of affairs is that, unlike the 1949 Geneva Conventions on war crimes, there is no specific convention covering crimes against humanity. Crimes against humanity have been defined only in the statutes of various international criminal tribunals ranging from the Nuremberg and Tokyo tribunals, through the Yugoslavia and Rwanda tribunals, to the Rome Statute of the International Criminal Court. Over the years the definitions of that particular category of violations of international humanitarian law have evolved, with the definition in the Rome Statute the most detailed, incorporating the crimes of apartheid, torture, and various other more recent developments in international humanitarian law.[26] Crimes against humanity were first defined in the Nuremberg Charter as "murder, extermination, enslavement, deportation, other inhumane acts committed against any civilian population, before or during the war; or persecutions on political, racial or religious grounds in execution of or in connection with any crime within the jurisdiction of the tribunal whether or not in violation of the domestic law of the country where perpetrated."

One of the most important aspects of crimes against humanity is that they can be committed whether in times of peace or war, and thus do not require an activating element of armed conflict. The Nuremberg Charter's definitional link to armed conflict is thus peculiar to that document and is not a general requirement in contemporary international law as defined in the statute of subsequent international criminal tribunals. But it is precisely the fact that crimes against humanity can be committed in a context in which it cannot be said that there is a war or even an armed conflict, that makes it politically sensitive, for this wider definition covers the kinds of crimes that tyrants would usually commit in order to crush domestic political opposition in the name of order and national security in a time of "peace."

The most valid progressive statement of whether universal jurisdiction can automatically be asserted against crimes against humanity is that made by Robert Jennings and Arthur Watts: "no general rule of positive international law can as yet be asserted which gives states the right to punish foreign nationals for crimes against humanity in the same way as they are, for instance, entitled to punish acts of piracy," but there were "clear indications pointing to the gradual evolution of a significant principle of international law to that effect."[27]

As was noted earlier, the ad hoc tribunals for Rwanda and the former Yugoslavia have contributed, through judicial activism, to a progressive development of universal jurisdiction. In 1999 the Arusha Tribunal, allowing a motion by the prosecutor to drop charges against a former Rwandan soldier accused of genocide on policy grounds, explicitly encouraged all countries to exercise universal jurisdiction over violations of international humanitarian law within its jurisdiction, which include war crimes in non-international armed conflict. The tribunal stated:

> the Tribunal wishes to emphasize, in line with the General Assembly and Security Council of the United Nations, that it encourages all States, in application of the principle of universal jurisdiction, to prosecute and judge those responsible for serious crimes such as genocide, crimes against humanity and other grave violations of international humanitarian law.[28]

Four years earlier, the appeals chamber of the Hague Tribunal had declared, in a discussion on jurisdiction, that "It would be a travesty of law and a betrayal of the universal need for justice, should the concept of State sovereignty be allowed to be raised successfully against human rights. Borders should not be considered as a shield against the reach of the law and as a protection for those who trample underfoot the most elementary rights of humanity."[29]

These statements clearly indicate a universalist bent in the jurisprudence of those tribunals. But it is relatively easy, in the context of crimes with a clear territorial ambit such as those on trial at Arusha and The Hague, and on which there is general international political agreement that the perpetrators should be brought to justice, to propound a universal justice. That is not the same thing as saying that there is a widespread agreement, let alone practice, among states on asserting universal jurisdiction over crimes against humanity. The controversy between the United States and the International Criminal Court notwithstanding, the exercise of universal jurisdiction by international criminal tribunals does not pose as significant a threat to sovereign states as would the widespread exercise of such powers by the national courts of other sovereign states. As will be seen later, it is at the domestic judicial level that the stakes are much higher: international tribunals have no independent law enforcement institutions, but states that adopt universal jurisdiction can actually enforce it within their territories should they choose to do so. According to Amnesty International, only a few states, such as Canada, Belgium, New Zealand, and Venezuela have national laws that expressly authorize universal jurisdiction over crimes against humanity.

Genocide

Genocide is the "crime of crimes." But, incongruous as it may appear, and strong though the case for it undoubtedly is, positive international law, at least as it exists in the 1948 Convention on the Prevention and Punishment of Genocide, does not provide for the exercise of universal jurisdiction over the crime of genocide. This is in stark contrast to the Geneva Conventions on war crimes.

This legal gap was no accident: it was the result of a political process that recognized the gravity of the crime of genocide, but was unwilling to empower states at large to punish it without a strong jurisdictional basis. In the wake of the 1994 genocide in Rwanda, there has been much talk in the international society of states to "never again" allow a recurrence of genocide. But, despite the moral sense of outrage that genocide evokes, and the strenuous, aspiratory arguments of human rights groups, no explicit step has been taken in positive international law to make genocide a universally punishable crime.[30]

The Genocide Convention states, in pertinent part:

Article 1: The Contracting Parties confirm that genocide, whether committed in time of peace or in time of war, is a crime under international law which they undertake to prevent and punish.

Article 4: Persons committing genocide or any of the other acts enumerated in Article 3 [genocide, conspiracy to commit genocide, direct and public incitement to commit genocide, attempt to commit genocide, complicity in genocide] shall be punished, whether they are constitutionally responsible leaders, public officials or private individuals.

Article 5: The Contracting Parties undertake to enact, in accordance with their respective Constitutions, the necessary legislation to give effect to the provisions of the present Convention and, in particular, to provide effective penalties for persons guilty of genocide or any of the other acts enumerated in Article 3.

Article 6: Persons charged with genocide or any of the other acts enumerated in Article 3 *shall be tried by a competent tribunal of the State in the territory of which the act was committed, or by such international penal tribunal as may have jurisdiction with respect to those Contracting Parties which shall have accepted its jurisdiction* [emphasis added].

Article 8: Any Contracting Party may call upon the competent organs of the United Nations to take such action under the Charter of the United Nations as they consider appropriate for the prevention and suppression of acts of genocide or any of the other acts enumerated in Article 3.

From the plain text of Article 6, it is clear that the jurisdiction envisaged is a territorial one. Only if (a) an "international penal tribunal" is established, and (b) state parties to the Convention also become state parties to such a tribunal, can the latter have universal jurisdiction.[31]

Advocates of universal jurisdiction for genocide have sought to establish that, while Article 6 clearly affirms a territorial jurisdiction in the absence of an international tribunal, it does not *prevent* the exercise of other forms of extraterritorial jurisdiction such as active or passive personality jurisdiction.[32] Reviewing the Convention's *travaux préparatoires*, Amnesty International seeks to establish that this permissive extraterritorial jurisdiction over conduct that amounts to genocide is the result of a compromise that was arrived at by states negotiating the Convention after an initial draft of that article prepared by Raphael Lemkin was rejected. Similar proposals by Saudi Arabia and Iran introducing an express universal jurisdiction to prosecute offenders or extradite them to other state parties were rejected.[33] Article 7 (the original version of Article 6) read: "The High Contracting Parties pledge themselves to punish any offender under their Convention within any territory under their jurisdiction, irrespective of the nationality of the offender and or the place where the offence has been committed."[34] The Ad Hoc Committee on Genocide rejected that language and replaced it with the one that survived in the final version of the Convention.[35]

Raphael Lemkin, the Polish lawyer who coined the word "genocide" and lobbied hard for the adoption of the Genocide Convention, tried to obtain accountability through pure universal jurisdiction and not a permanent international criminal tribunal. He believed the world was "not ready" for such a court, which would be too obvious a threat to state sovereignty.[36] Even that roundabout route to justice was too much for the strategic interests of states. If, a full 56 years later, this tension persists in international society, it surely was bound to have been even sharper in 1948. As William Schabas has commented, Article 6 of the Genocide Convention "was a pragmatic compromise reflecting the state of the law at the time the Convention was adopted," and "although universal jurisdiction, and the related concept of *aut dedere aut judicare* (prosecute, or extradite), had long been recognized for certain crimes committed by individual outlaws, few in 1948 wanted to extend it to crimes which would, as a general rule, involve State complicity."[37]

A duty to prosecute perpetrators of genocide has not been formerly established, but a permissive right to do so, or extradite, is gaining ground. International law and the form of the international society are not static. Even if we discount the crusading writings of some publicists of international law, we cannot fail to notice the judicial pronouncements of the International Court of Justice and resolutions of the United Nations Security Council and General Assembly. These all point in a certain direction, even if individual states will still act in a mostly strategic and self-seeking fashion.

From a policy perspective, it is desirable that, where a strong basis for the exercise of jurisdiction by a national court exists (most appropriately by virtue of the criminalization of genocide in domestic law), the crime can be prosecuted by a court outside of where the crime was committed, or outside of an international tribunal with competence to do so. A careful reading of the Genocide Convention, especially when Articles 1, 4, and 5 of the Convention are taken together, suggests a basis for this approach. The caveat is that there must be strong links between the prosecuting state and the defendant.

Although the Genocide Convention consciously did not include a duty to prosecute or extradite, the International Court of Justice noted in 1996 that there are no territorial limitations to the obligations of all states to prevent and punish genocide. The Court has pronounced that the rights and obligations enshrined by the Convention are rights and obligations *erga omnes*, [in relation to everyone] noting that the obligation each State has to prevent and to punish the crime of genocide is not territorially limited by the Convention."[38]

THE PINOCHET CASE

The multiple law suits in the late 1990s against Augusto Pinochet Urgarte on the basis of the exercise of universal jurisdiction by courts in Spain and Belgium, and his arrest and 18 month detention in the UK, marked a high point for the doctrine of universal jurisdiction and its advocates. For many leaders around the world, however, it was a most unsettling development, one that brought home a new sense of vulnerability. Pinochet's travails, widely televised to millions around the world in an age of instant communications, were a giddy period that observers and practitioners of international justice pronounced as a revolution in international law and human rights.[39]

As Richard Falk has observed in an excellent review of the Pinochet legal proceedings, they meant different things to different people.[40] For many, it was a major blow against impunity. For others, it was a welcome lifting of the veil of sovereign immunity. And for many victims of his oppressive rule in Chile, it was a chance for Pinochet to face justice beyond borders after the self-amnesty that accompanied his exit from power had sealed his domestic impunity.[41]

While Pinochet was undergoing medical examinations in Britain in late 1998, Balthazar Garzon, a crusading Spanish investigating magistrate, issued an international warrant against Pinochet dated October 16, 1998, for alleged crimes against humanity.[42] The next day, a London magistrate issued a provisional warrant for Pinochet's detention. Pinochet mounted an initially successful legal response that saw the Divisional Court of the Queen's Bench unanimously quash the first Spanish international arrest warrant and a subsequent one with additional charges that included crimes of torture.

The Crown Prosecution service appealed on behalf of Spain to the House of Lords. This appeal dealt mainly with issues of immunity and extradition, and so was not so much about universal jurisdiction, although the doctrine was the underlying basis of Judge Garzon's attempt to bring Pinochet to justice. Several human rights groups, including Amnesty International and Human Rights Watch were invited as "intervenors" to clarify some of the issues of international law in dispute at the trial. By a vote of three to two on November 25, the House of Lords ruled in favor of extradition on the important ground that Pinochet did not enjoy immunity for crimes under international law. At issue: Were the alleged crimes part of his normal functions as a head of state?

Issues of immunity lie at the heart of the controversy over universal jurisdiction. The targets of attempts at universal jurisdiction are frequently sovereigns and other high officials of state. And concepts of sovereign immunity, sacrosanct in the international system of centuries past, remain a major plank of order in today's international society.

In the first House of Lords decision, a majority of the judges ruled that "international law has made it plain that certain types of conduct, including

torture and hostage-taking, are not acceptable conduct on the part of anyone. This applies as much to heads of state, and even more so, as it does
to anyone else; the contrary conclusion would make a mockery of international law." Lord Steyn stated in a separate opinion that the criminal charges
against Pinochet being "international crimes deserving punishment," it was
"difficult to maintain that the commission of such high crimes may amount
to acts performed in the functions of a Head of State."[43]

The pro-Pinochet arguments were made by the minority-opinion judges.
Lord Slynn stated: "it does not seem to me that it has been shown that
there is any State practice or general consensus let alone a widely supported
convention that all crimes against international law should be justifiable in
national courts on the basis of the universality of jurisdiction. Nor is there
any *jus cogens* ["compelling law" or "higher law" from which no derogation
is permited] in respect of such breaches of international law which require
that a claim of State or Head of State immunity, itself a well established
principle of international law, should be overridden."[44]

The British Secretary of State for Home Affairs, Jack Straw, was vested
with authority to make final decisions on extradition, on the basis of other
strategic, nonlegal considerations, and, in theory, his decision could directly
contradict the judicial decision.[45] Were Pinochet's opponents trying to settle
in law courts matters best left to diplomats and statesmen?

In the event, Straw authorized Pinochet's extradition, minus the additional charge of genocide in the Spanish request, on the basis that it was
not an extradition crime under British law.[46] The House of Lords decision
was eventually set aside as a result of a conflict of interest involving one of
the judges—Lord Hoffman, who had strong personal links with Amnesty
International, an intervenor in the case. At a rehearing of the original appeal
to the House of Lords (with an enlarged, seven member panel that excluded
Lord Hoffman), Chile supported Pinochet's immunity claim and asserted its
sovereign jurisdiction to prosecute crimes committed on Chilean territory.[47]

On March 24, 1999, the House of Lords ruled six to one against
Pinochet's claim of immunity. But the law lords based their decision on
the narrow ground of positive British law (its obligations under the Torture
Convention, which had been incorporated into domestic British law and
made torture a crime in the UK irrespective of the place of the crime or the
nationality of the perpetrator).

Pinochet eventually returned to Chile on March 2, 2000, with the 1978
amnesty law and his immunity as "Senator for Life" intact. However, subsequent decisions by Chilean courts stripped him of his immunities following
a legal complaint filed by human rights lawyers, and the former leader was
placed under house arrest on December 2, 2000.[48] Pinochet was later indicted for his responsibility in the abduction and murders of seventy-five
victims in the October 1973 "Caravan of Death." However, subsequent
medical examinations of the over-eighty former dictator led to the Chilean
Supreme Court to find him unfit to stand trial.

That appeared to have ended the Pinochet saga, with justice winning the day in principle, if not in practice. But a Chilean court reopened the controversy by ruling that Pinochet could stand trial, following the broadcast of a television interview in which he appeared lucid enough to defend himself as "a good angel" and passed blame for the atrocities committed during his rule to his subordinates.[49] Chile's Supreme Court upheld this ruling in a decision of January 3, 2005, thus closing all legal obstacles of a trial of Pinochet.

BELGIUM'S LAW V AMERICAN POWER

In the decade between 1993 and 2003, the Kingdom of Belgium became the epicenter of the doctrine of universal jurisdiction. An apparent judicial revolution was underway, with attempts at the globalization of justice and a conscious effort to bring the primacy of order to its knees at the altar of justice. In the heyday of universal jurisdiction that led to Kissinger's predictable plaint, this small European country was virtually alone in its will to authorize prosecutions in its domestic courts for genocide, crimes against humanity, and war crimes. The attempt was short-lived.

In 1993, Belgium made the 1949 Geneva Conventions and their two additional protocols part of its domestic law. The statute criminalized twenty acts that are "grave breaches" under the conventions as "crimes under international law." On February 10, 1999, Belgium amended and expanded the 1993 law to include genocide and crimes against humanity, adopting the definition of crimes against humanity in the Rome Statute of the International Criminal Court.[50] The new legislation gave Belgian courts sweeping, unconditional, and universal jurisdiction of utopian scope: "The Belgian courts shall be competent to deal with breaches provided for in the present Act, irrespective of where such breaches have been committed."[51]

It has been observed that the universal jurisdiction conferred on domestic courts by the Belgian law went well beyond its treaty obligations, as no international law required Belgium to prosecute crimes against humanity or genocide.[52] The decision to expand the Belgian law was the result of a domestic political process that had its genesis in the 1994 genocide in Rwanda, a former Belgian colony.[53] A colloquium organized by a liberal political party in the Belgian Senate in 1996 recommended an expansion of the 1993 law in order to close gaps that might exist in international justice.[54] The report of a parliamentary commission in 1997 provided further support for a new law, concluding that "it is necessary to include in domestic criminal law provisions that punish crimes against humanity, in particular the crime of genocide."[55]

The executive arm of the Belgian government through the Minister of Justice, made clear its intention that official immunities would be no barrier to prosecution, and that the new law would apply to crimes committed before it entered into force. But the attempt to strip away immunities was not altogether successful, as will be seen when an important decision of the International Court of Justice is discussed below. It is noteworthy that, even before the adoption of the new law in 1999, Belgian courts were already attempting to exercise universal jurisdiction over crimes against humanity by claiming support in customary international law. It was on this basis that, on November 6, 1998, Daniel Vandermeersch, an investigating magistrate in Brussels, ruled during proceedings against Pinochet that the court could assert universal jurisdiction over acts committed in Chile that amounted to crimes against humanity.[56]

The 1999 law engendered a flood of investigations, indictments, and prosecutorial attempts against the political and military leaders of various countries. These efforts warmed the hearts of human rights enthusiasts and the victims of rights abuses, presaging—in their expectations—a universal community in which justice for human rights violations would be borderless. In short order, cases were filed against Prime Minister Ariel Sharon of Israel by the survivors of the 1992 massacres at the Sabra and Shatila refugee camps in Lebanon by pro-Israeli Lebanese militia under Israel control when Sharon was Israel's Minister of Defence. Similar suits were brought against Saddam Hussein, the then President of Iraq, for attacks against Iraqi Kurds in 1991 that were alleged to be crimes against humanity; against Yassir Arafat, the then leader of the Palestinian National Authority, and against President Paul Kagame of Rwanda. Suits were filed against several other political leaders of foreign countries. It was becoming clear even to the many supporters of the Belgian law that assuming the role of the world's moral/judicial policeman created diplomatic and even practical logistical problems that could not be overlooked.[57]

One landmark case that was conclusively and successfully prosecuted in Belgium under the 1993 law involved offenses committed during the Rwandan genocide. On June 7, 2001, a Belgian court with twelve jurors sentenced four Rwandans—two Roman Catholic nuns, a physics professor, and a former government minister—to prison terms of 12 to 20 years for crimes committed during the genocide.[58] Although they were charged with war crimes under the 1993 law and not genocide or crimes against humanity, the precedent-setting case attracted much publicity because of the exercise of universal jurisdiction and because it was a jury trial. The case was relatively uncontroversial—the convicts were living in Belgium at the time of their arrest. *The New York Times*, in an editorial on the case, expressed support for the doctrine of universal jurisdiction.[59] It noted that "Ideally, trials should be conducted in the country where the crimes occurred, but Rwanda lacks the resources and judicial expertise to provide adequate trials."[60] The case was also viewed in some quarters as one of partial atonement by Belgium for its historical and contemporary responsibility for creating a national sociopolitical situation that ultimately gave rise to the genocide in Rwanda.[61]

If the Belgian trial of the Rwandans won general acclaim, the indictment of Ariel Sharon, a sitting head of government, generated contentious debate on the merits of the Belgian law and the extent to which it could complicate the country's diplomatic relations. Sharon cancelled a scheduled visit to the European Union's Brussels headquarters and recalled Israel's newly appointed ambassador to Belgium. The country's then foreign minister, Louis Michel, called the law "embarrassing" and hinted that it would be reviewed to protect the immunity of serving senior officials of state.[62] In a repudiation of the Belgian law's refusal to side step sacred cows, the Belgian Supreme Court would later rule that Sharon was immune from prosecution while serving as a prime minister, although the court upheld the principle of universal jurisdiction and left open the possibility of a suit once the Israel leader left office.[63] With nearly thirty suits against various world leaders filed under the Belgian law, and a British citizen reportedly arriving at a Belgian embassy abroad and requesting a Belgian investigation of his claim that the British Broadcasting Corporation was attempting to assassinate him, universal jurisdiction suits in Belgium had turned into what one Belgian newspaper editor headlined "The News from Absurdistan."[64]

The dam broke when indictments were filed against several U.S. political and military leaders in connection with the bombing of a civilian shelter in Baghdad that killed over 400 people in the Persian Gulf War of 1991.[65] The prosecutorial targets included former president George Herbert Walker Bush, Vice President Dick Cheney (who had served as a secretary of defense under Bush I), Secretary of State Colin Powell (former Chairman of the Joint Chiefs of Staff), and Gen. Norman Schwarzkopf, the American military commander in the Gulf War. Subsequent suits relating to the American and British preemptive war against Iraq in 2003 were filed against President George W. Bush, Powell, and U.S. military commander Tommy Franks.

These lawsuits were the most important factor that led to the ultimate death of the Belgian law in its potent form—and the inevitable decline of universal jurisdiction. The United States issued several warnings to Belgium, which also hosts the headquarters of NATO. American officials like Powell and Donald Rumsfeld, the secretary of defense, made it clear that the United States would withhold its financial contributions to the construction of a new NATO headquarters in Brussels, and would boycott meetings in Belgium until the Belgian law of 1999 was rescinded and the suits against U.S. leaders dismissed.[66] "Belgium needs to recognize," Rumsfeld said, "that there are consequences for its actions."[67]

Faced with this confrontation between the universal jurisdiction law and the world's most powerful nation, the cosmopolitan notions of justice represented by the law gave way to political reality. Belgian Prime Minister Guy Verhofstadt, previously a staunch defender of the law, pledged quick action to repeal it. Belgian Senator and human rights campaigner Alain Destexhe, one of the law's main sponsors, told a journalist that Rumsfeld's threat left Belgians with "a kind of vertigo." "Suddenly, the law became very unpopular. People like me were saying, 'We've got to get out of this.'"[68]

On August 1, 2003, the Belgian Parliament passed a new law amending the 1999 law, repealed the 1993 law, and established a mechanism for quashing pending complaints that were outside the new, strict confines within which the exercise of universal jurisdiction could now take place in Belgium. Under the new law's provisions, Belgian courts could assert universal jurisdiction over international crimes only where the accused is of Belgian nationality or lives in Belgium; where the victim is Belgian or has lived in Belgium for at least 3 years prior to the commission of the crimes, or where Belgium has a treaty obligation to prosecute.[69] Unless the accused is Belgian or lives in Belgium, it is entirely up to the state prosecutor to decide whether or not to proceed with a complaint. The prosecutor could reject a complaint without investigation if he considered it "manifestly without grounds" or on the grounds that another country has a better claim to jurisdiction. Officials of NATO or European Union countries are automatically exempted from Belgian jurisdiction under the new law. Thus, the new law has aligned Belgium to the more restrictive universal jurisdiction laws of other European countries.[70]

Following the repeal of the universal jurisdiction law, the cases against Bush and other American officials, as well as those against Sharon and other Israeli officials, were dismissed by the Belgian Supreme Court. Without a doubt, the principle of universal jurisdiction had suffered a serious blow. That blow came from within—the decision of an apex domestic court. Another was to land from without—an international jurisdiction.

YOU CAN'T TOUCH SOVEREIGNS

The judgment of the International Court of Justice in the *Yerodia* case[71] was just as damaging to the doctrine of universal jurisdiction as the repeal of the Belgian law. Emanating as it did from the Peace Palace at The Hague, it was less political in its motivation and appropriately restrained. But the result was the same. The issue for decision in that case was not universal jurisdiction as such (though reference was made to it) but rather that of the immunity of certain individuals under international law. This, however, is legal sophistry. As noted earlier, immunity and universal jurisdiction are often linked in the contemporary legal and political sphere. Judicial challenges to immunity from prosecution of international crimes have often been inspired by the concept of universal jurisdiction.

At issue was the legality of a "international arrest warrant in *absentia*" issued on April 11, 2000, by a Belgian investigating judge in Brussels, against Yerodia Ndombasi, the then minister of foreign affairs of the Democratic Republic of Congo (DRC). The warrant was based on the Belgian law of 1999 and circulated internationally through the International Police

Organization (INTERPOL). It charged the Congolese diplomat with criminal responsibility for war crimes under the 1949 Geneva Conventions, and crimes against humanity, in particular hate speech that was reported by the media and allegedly incited the population to attack Tutsi residents in the Congolese capital of Kinsasha.

As the ICJ noted, and Belgium did not contest, the alleged acts on which the arrest warrant was based were committed outside Belgium, Yerodia was not a Belgian national at the time, and he was not in Belgian territory when the warrant was issued and circulated. Moreover, no Belgian nationals were victims of the attacks that reportedly resulted from Mr. Yerodia's statements. Yerodia was reassigned as minister of education in November 2000, and in April 2001 ceased to hold office as a minister altogether.

The Congolese government, which brought the case to the ICJ, urged the Court to rule that Belgium violated the rule of customary international law concerning the absolute inviolability and immunity from criminal process of incumbent foreign ministers; in so doing, it violated the principle of sovereign equality among States, and all states, including Belgium, were thereby precluded from executing the warrant. The DRC argued that Belgium be required to recall and cancel the arrest warrant and to inform the foreign authorities to whom the warrant was circulated that Belgium "renounces its request for their cooperation in executing the unlawful warrant."[72]

Belgium for its part argued that, although it accepted the immunity of serving foreign ministers from jurisdiction before foreign courts, such immunity applied only to acts done in the course of their official functions. Belgium asserted that there was no evidence that Yerodia was acting in an official capacity when he made statements alleged, and in any case the warrant was issued against him personally.

The International Court of Justice ruled that Ministers of Foreign Affairs enjoy full immunity from civil suit throughout the duration of their office when they are abroad. No distinction, the Court concluded, could be drawn between the "official" or "private" acts of such an official of state, or between acts done before the person assumed office and acts performed while in office.[73] It found that the jurisprudence of international criminal tribunals such as those for Rwanda and the former Yugoslavia, and ICC, which expressly state that sovereign immunity is no bar to prosecution, cannot be applied to national courts in this context, and that no exception to sovereign immunity exists in customary international law regarding national courts. Lest it be seen as providing tacit encouragement to impunity, the ICJ noted that "jurisdiction does not imply absence of immunity, while absence of immunity does not imply jurisdiction." It also clarified that "the *immunity* from jurisdiction enjoyed by incumbent ministers of foreign affairs does not mean that they enjoy *impunity* in respect of any crimes they might have committed, irrespective of their gravity. Immunity from criminal jurisdiction and individual criminal responsibility are quite separate concepts."[74]

Accordingly, the ICJ laid down some circumstances in which the immunity of a minister of foreign affairs would not shield such an official from prosecution: in the courts of their own countries; if the state they represent or have represented decided to waive that immunity; after a person ceases to hold such an office, a former minister of foreign affairs may be tried in the court of another state that has jurisdiction, for acts committed before or after his or her period in office, as well as for acts committed during the period in a private capacity; an incumbent or former minister of foreign affairs may be tried before international criminal tribunals established by the Security Council resolution under Chapter VII of the United Nations Charter, such as those for Rwanda and the former Yugoslavia and the permanent International Criminal Court.[75]

By a thirteen to three vote, the Court found that the issue and circulation of the arrest warrant was a violation of Belgium's legal obligation to respect the immunity and inviolability of a serving minister of foreign affairs under international law. By ten to six, it ruled that Belgium must cancel the warrant and so inform the authorities to whom it had been circulated.[76]

This decision, coming as it did from the apex judicial organ of the United Nations, an institution seen by virtually all state and non-state actors in international society as the last word in international law, was especially weighty. Although it dwelt on immunity, and did not address at significant length the issue of whether or not Belgium had jurisdiction, it nevertheless gave the advance of universal jurisdiction a decidedly frosty reception that has diminished the latter's conceptual appeal and influence.

The decision appeared to have had a dual purpose. First, although one can only speculate on this point, it was probably aimed at restraining the spirit of the Belgian law and discouraging radical judicial interpretations of international law by national courts and scholars. By delineating the situations where sovereigns were untouchable and where their immunities were forfeited, the ICJ, in a ruling that human rights advocates unsurprisingly view as retrogressive, acted as a quarterback for traditional notions of international law. Certainly, the decision was seen by dispassionate observers as reigning in a political/legal movement that was fast becoming a runaway train.[77]

Second, the decision had the effect, if not the motivation, of reasserting the ICJ's primacy in international law at a time when it appeared that the political spotlight—and the attendant financial resources—had shifted to the ad hoc international tribunals at The Hague and Arusha. As of 2000, when the UN General Assembly granted the first significant increase in the ICJ budget since 1946, the Court's annual budget was $10 million, while that of the war crimes tribunal for Yugoslavia was $100 million. Shifting from a cold war-imposed mode when it was derisively dismissed as "the case of the empty courtroom," the ICJ's docket exploded phenomenally in the 1990s.[78] Part of this stream of cases inevitably included questions of international humanitarian law as it concerned the rights and obligations of states, which was the preserve of the Court, in contrast to the criminal responsibility of individuals, which is the jurisdiction of international criminal tribunals such as Arusha and The Hague ("norm entrepreneurs" that swept unto the international society in the 1990s[79]).

Two separate opinions of the judges of the ICJ in the *Yerodia* case on the matter of universal jurisdiction appear to support a conclusion that it was the real issue simmering beneath the surface of the decision. It should be noted that the DRC did not make a specific claim on universal jurisdiction in its final submission to the Court, and so the court could not address it in its majority opinion. Judge Guillaume is particularly persuasive, and differs starkly in his conclusions on the status of universal jurisdiction in international law from that of Judge Abdul Koroma.

Judge Guillaume thought it useful to address in a direct manner the question of universal jurisdiction, in other words, whether the Belgian judge had jurisdiction to indict Yerodia.[80] Dismissing the Belgian claim to jurisdiction, Judge Guillaume rendered one of the most elegant and well-supported arguments against unbridled borderless justice, beginning by tracing the development of opposing views on universal jurisdiction. It is worth quoting at length:

> The primary aim of the criminal law is to enable punishment in each country of offences committed in the national territory. That territory is where evidence of the offence can most be gathered. That is where the offence generally produces its effects. Finally, that is where the punishment imposed can most naturally serve as an example. Thus, the Permanent Court of International Justice observed as far back as 1927 that "in systems of law the principle of the territorial character of law is fundamental."

> The question has however, always remained open whether states other than the territorial state have concurrent jurisdiction to prosecute offenders. A wide debate on this subject began as early as the foundation in Europe of the major modern states. Some writers, like Covarruvias and Grotius, pointed out that the presence on the territory of a state of a foreign criminal peacefully enjoying the fruits of his crimes was intolerable. They therefore maintained that it should be possible to prosecute perpetrators of certain particular serious crimes not only in the state on whose territory the crime was committed but also in the country where they sought refuge. In their view, that country was under an obligation to arrest, followed by extradition or prosecution ...

> Beginning in the eighteenth century however, this school of thought favouring universal punishment was challenged by another body of opinion, one opposed to such punishment and exemplified notably by Montesqieu, Voltaire and Jean-Jacques Rousseau. Their views found expression in terms of criminal law in the works of Beccaria, who stated in 1764 that "judges

are not the avengers of humankind in general....A crime is punishable only in the country where it was committed."[81]

Judge Guillaume noted treaty exceptions to the absence of universal jurisdiction,[82] as well as the limited practice of certain states, such as Germany, which has limited universal jurisdiction over genocide committed by a foreigner abroad. He declared: "... international laws know only one true case of universal jurisdiction: piracy," and as well that "universal jurisdiction *in absentia* as applied in the present case is unknown to international law."[83]

The president of the ICJ went on to link this understanding of the law and its development to a strong view of contemporary judicial policy:

"International criminal law has itself undergone considerable development.... It recognizes in many situations the possibility, or indeed the obligation, for a state other than one on whose territory the offense was committed to confer jurisdiction on its courts to prosecute the authors of certain crimes where they are present on its territory. International criminal courts have been created. But at no time has it been envisaged that jurisdiction should be conferred upon the courts of every state in the world to prosecute such crimes, whoever their authors and victims and irrespective of the place where the offender is to be found. To do this would, moreover, risk creating total judicial chaos. It would also be to encourage the arbitrary for the benefit of the powerful, purportedly acting as agent for an ill-defined 'international community.' Contrary to what is advocated by certain publicists, such a development would represent not an advance in the law but a step backward."[84]

Despite Judge Koroma's call in his own separate opinion that the ICJ decision in the *Yerodia* case not be seen as a rejection or validation of the principle of universal jurisdiction, the judgment was undoubtedly seen around the world precisely as a rejection of the theory, or at the least as strictly curtailing its scope. Judge Guillaume's separate opinion simply provided an intellectual explanation for the unspoken, "body language" of the majority ICJ ruling. Judge Koroma's separate opinion nonetheless points up how starkly divided lawyers—even two members of the International Court of Justice—and policy makers are on the subject. He argued:

"On the other hand, in my view, the issue and circulation of the arrest warrant show how seriously Belgium views its international obligation to combat international crimes. Belgium is entitled to invoke its criminal jurisdiction against anyone, save a Foreign Minister in office. It is unfortunate that the wrong case would appear to have been chosen in attempting to carry out what Belgium considers it international obligation.

... In my considered opinion, today, together with piracy, universal jurisdiction is available for certain crimes, such as war crimes and crimes against
humanity, including the slave trade and genocide."[85]

POLICY ISSUES IN UNIVERSAL JURISDICTION

In seeking to radically extend what Robert Jackson called the "global
covenant" the doctrine of universal jurisdiction, as represented by the
Belgian law, clearly has run into a serious obstacle. That stumbling block is
the nature of the international society. That we live in a society, not yet a
real community is reflected in Judge Guillaume's opinion when he refers to
"an ill-defined international community." That society continues to be one
of sovereign states, and there are clear limits to how far justice should be
not just borderless, but completely unregulated in its borderless nature. Even
the 1994 German legislation that authorizes the assertion of universal jurisdiction recognizes the contemporary nature of the international society of
sovereign states. The law states that, where an appropriate link does not exist
between Germany and the prospective defendant, "prosecution would violate the principle of noninterference, under which every state is required to
respect the sovereignty of other states." Wisely, Germany based its assertion
of jurisdiction on a realization Belgium would only come to a decade later.

In rejecting the immunity of serving state officials—a foundation of
intercourse in the international society—without the backing of positive
international law, Belgium's universal jurisdiction law was a recipe for potential disorder. Let us assume, for example, that Belgian authorities had
arrested Ariel Sharon, Yassir Arafat, or Donald Rumsfeld in the exercise
of universal jurisdiction. It is certain that their countries would have used
force to obtain their release or in reprisal. That such a scenario does little
to advance international law is self-evident. There are several supporters
of the universal jurisdiction doctrine who accept that, in the pure form in
which Belgium sought to assert it, the principle was liable to abuse. As the
numerous opportunistic suits brought against world leaders demonstrated,
the perfect became an enemy of the good. In addition to the total absence
of sustainable bases for jurisdiction in the Belgian law and its attempt to
assert jurisdiction in absentia, any private citizen could file a complaint
against anyone. How ridiculous the situation had become was poignantly
illustrated when a fringe political party in Belgium filed a complaint against
the country's then minister of foreign affairs, Louis Michel, for approving
arms sales to Nepal. As a Belgian law professor commented, "it was not
the government that was making foreign policy, but independent judges."[86]
And while the inevitable repeal of an unsustainable law was described as another lost battle in a "clash of civilizations" between Europe and the United
States, it was more accurately a clash between cosmopolitan and positivist
conceptions of international law and society.

Is there space for the doctrine of universal jurisdiction in international society? Certainly, there is. Were it otherwise, the doctrine would not exist in a number of treaties. Crimes like hostage taking cannot be effectively checked without some form of universal jurisdiction. But a universal jurisdiction that is based solely on the nature of the crime, and not on any other connections to a potential prosecuting state, will be exceedingly difficult to translate into state practice. Certainly, it remains important to discourage impunity with accountability. But every legal theory ought to be subject to empirical tests—and even to common sense standards. In this case, the practice of states is a clear indicator of the possibilities of universal jurisdiction. The exercise of such jurisdiction based solely on the nature of the crime will be difficult to attain when we consider the nature of international society.

This is why an effort by some eminent scholars and practitioners of international law to clarify this subject in the "Princeton Principles on Universal Jurisdiction" has not resolved the debate.[87] The Principles have essentially restated the sweeping viewpoints of scholastic activism on this thorny question, and avoid some of the more difficult issues. They seek to maintain universal jurisdiction on the basis of the nature of the crime and nothing else. They avoid taking a position on the assertion of jurisdiction *in absentia*, arguing that trials *in absentia* are acceptable in the civil law tradition of which Belgium is a part. The Princeton Principles do not recognize the substantive immunity of heads of state and government—complete immunity of sitting heads of state, with the exceptions laid down by the International Court of Justice in *Yerodia*—from prosecution for acts performed in their official capacity. It is unhelpful to juxtapose clear exceptions, such as the Nuremberg Charter and the statutes of the Rwanda and Yugoslavia tribunals and the permanent International Criminal Court, with the jurisdiction of national courts under customary international law. And while recognizing the great potential for politically motivated litigation, the principles propose no remedy. They could not have, having foregone an opportunity to do so by stipulating some connection between the offender and the prosecuting state. The postulations of the Princeton Principles are so starkly divergent from the subsequent decision of the International Court of Justice in the *Yerodia* case and the repeal of the Belgian law that some middle ground is simply not in sight. The competing tensions that engender hesitation on the parts of states to unreservedly embrace universal jurisdiction are real, just as the ICJ decision in *Yerodia* is a legal fact of life with weighty implications in the international political sphere. For these reasons, the influence the Princeton Principles were meant to have will likely remain illusory.

Thus, there appears to be qualified merit in Lord Browne Wilkinson's dissent from the Princeton Principles when he argues:

"I am strongly in favor of universal jurisdiction over serious international crimes if, by those words one means the exercise by an international court or by the courts of one state of jurisdiction over the nationals of another state with the prior consent of that latter state, i.e. in cases such as the ICC or the torture convention.

But the Princeton principles propose that individual national courts should exercise such jurisdiction against nationals of a state which has not agreed to such jurisdiction. Moreover the principles do not recognize any form of sovereign immunity....If the law were so established, states antipathetic to Western powers would be likely to seize both active and retired officials and military personnel of such Western powers and stage a show trial for alleged international crimes. Conversely, zealots in Western States might launch prosecution against for example, Islamic extremists for their terrorist activities. It is naïve to think that, in such cases, the natural state of the accused would stand by and watch the trial: resort to force would be more probable....I believe that the adoption of such universal jurisdiction without preserving the existing concepts of immunity would be more likely to damage than to advance the chances of international peace."[88]

The point where one would add a caveat to Lord Browne Wilkinson's dissent is his requirement of prior consent, without exception, of the state whose citizen is subject to prosecution in the courts of another state. In a world in which the moral dimension in international relations is stronger than it was once, a few states will occasionally summon political will to prosecute persons accused of violations of international humanitarian law. But such jurisdiction must be based on something more concrete than moral outrage. And, from the standpoint of international society, Lord Wilkinson is right when he worries about the potential consequences of attempting to bring to justice in foreign courts the high officials of another state.

His observations lead us to another fundamental weakness of the doctrine of universal jurisdiction: the justified concern that it can only be exercised against citizens of weaker nations by the courts of powerful states.[89] For if powerful states such as the United States can successfully resist the doctrine as we have seen, it follows that the citizens of states that do not have recourse to similar strategic leverage in the international society are in a weaker position should more powerful states decide to implement it. As Professor Shadrack Gutto has pithily observed, "What would happen if an African state like Djibouti would prosecute let us say a national of the United States for crimes against humanity? The prosecuting state would either be bombed or will not receive aid from the World Bank."[90]

Professor Gutto's comment is an allusion to the perspective that while attempts by courts in Western countries to exercise universal jurisdiction against officials of some great powers is a reflection of liberalism's desire to subject power to law, universal jurisdiction, when exercised against nationals of weak, developing countries, is also an instrument of hegemony. A classic illustration of this sensitivity is the case of Hissène Habré, the former President of Chad. The case also illustrates the argument made earlier in this chapter that universal jurisdiction exists only when it is anchored in a treaty or is firmly established customary international law.

In January 2000, a decade after Habré was deposed in a coup by his former chief of staff Idriss Déby and in the wake of the Pinochet case, a reperesentative group of seven victims of torture under Habré's regime filed a legal action against the former Chadian leader alleging that he violated the Torture Convention.[91] In 1992, a truth commission established by Déby published a report accusing the former Chadian leader of having used his security forces when he was in office to kill 40,000 people and tortured 200,000 victims.[92] The action was filed before the investigating magistrate of the Dakar regional court in Senegal, where Habré fled after his overthrow. Habré was subsequently indicted by the Court of Appeals in Dakar, but the court ruled that although Senegal had ratified the Torture Convention, Senegalese courts had no jurisdiction since the crimes were not committed in Senegal, the Torture Convention required ratifying states to adopt domestic legislation to give domestic courts competence to try cases brought under the Convention, and Senegal had not yet incorporated this treaty into domestic law. The Supreme Court of Senegal upheld the ruling.

On September 19, 2005, following a 4-year investigation of Habré by a Belgian investigating judge, Daniel Fransen, and despite the politico-legal setback Belgian attempts at universal jurisdiction had suffered at the hands of powerful states, Belgium issued an international arrest warrant for Hissene Habré and formally requested Senegal to extradite him. The Senegal authorities arrested Habré on November 15 and placed him in custody, but later released him after tense political wrangling inside the Senegalese government and a decision by the Senegalese court of appeal that it had no jurisdiction to rule on Belgium's request.[93] As a consequence of the potentially explosive political dimensions the Habré case was assuming, Senegal referred the Habré situation to the African Union, which formed a "Committee of Eminent African Jurists" to advise the continental body on the matter.

At its annual summit in July 2006, the African Union announced its decision that a Senegalese court, not one in Europe, should try Hissene Habré for the charges brought against him.[94] The Union's legal experts recommended that Senegal pass a law giving the country's courts clear jurisdiction to try Habré for his alleged crimes. The decision appeared to have been heavily influenced by Senegalese President Abdoulaye Wade, who had come under internal political pressure not to extradite Habré and had stated that "Africans must be tried in Africa."[95]

This politically sophisticated outcome points to several things about universal jurisdiction: it still had to be grounded in positive law and indeed added a requirement of enabling domestic legislation to the fact of a treaty in itself; the African Union demonstrated a clear awareness that universal jurisdiction has political implications for weak states; and Africa, under pressure from external and internal sources and for the first time, made a political decision to assume direct responsibility as a continent for the legal fate of one of its ex-dictators rather than encourage the hegemony of justice without borders. The outcome is a compromise from a clash of a cosmopolitan worldview and sovereignty. This perspective is buttressed by the well-known fact that Senegalese political authorities were initially reluctant to have Habré prosecuted, and interfered politically in the case in 2000 to ensure the outcomes that occurred.

With a careful eye to balancing the policy and legal tensions inherent in the concept of universal jurisdiction, Germany has also prosecuted a small number of individuals for war crimes, crimes against humanity, and genocide committed during the wars of the former Yugoslavia in the 1990s. In one such case, the Supreme Court of Düsseldorf in 1997 convicted Nikola Jorgic, a Bosnian Serb, on eleven counts of genocide and thirty counts of murder during the "ethnic cleansing" of Bosnian Muslims.[96] The Court established that in June 1992, Jorgic, the leader of one of the paramilitary groups in the Doboj region of Bosnia–Herzegovina, together with another person executed twenty-two citizens of Grabska (including disabled and elderly persons) who had gathered outdoors as a result of the fighting in the region. They forced three other Muslims to carry the victims to a mass grave, where their bodies were disposed of. The accused and his subordinates later forced fifty residents of another village from their homes, brutally abused them and shot six of them. In an appeal from the convict, the Federal High Court of Germany rejected the appeal in 1999. It confirmed, however, only one count of genocide involving thirty persons, and addressed the question of a German court's jurisdiction to try a national or Bosnia–Herzegovina.

The court ruled that its jurisdiction could not be questioned if legitimate grounds existed for the exercise of such jurisdiction under German law. Those grounds included: the provisions of Section 16, Article 220a of the German Penal Code, which conferred on German courts jurisdiction to prosecute certain international crimes including genocide, and the provision in the Genocide Convention (to which Germany became a party in 1954) that genocide is a crime which all nations should punish. That the prosecution of the International Criminal Tribunal for the former Yugoslavia declined to prosecute this case was another ground on which it asserted jurisdiction. Also pertinent, the German High Court ruled, was the fact that the convict had lived in Germany from 1969 to the beginning of 1992, when he returned to Bosnia but remained registered in Germany even after his departure. His German wife and his daughter still lived in Germany and he visited them even after the commission of his crimes, and he was arrested in Germany, which he had entered of his own volition.[97] Short of a scenario where the crime was committed in Germany, or the accused or the victims were German, there could hardly be a stronger example of the exercise of universal jurisdiction.

The situation, then, is that while universal jurisdiction exists in limited forms in treaties and in the national laws of some states, it has gone into relative decline at a more general level. Despite the doctrine's visibility and moral appeal, its absence and near-dormant state in the general practice of states is one more indication of how the nature of international society balances the tension between order and cosmopolitan notions of justice. The repeal of the Belgian law and the ICJ's *Yerodia* bear out the thesis that two conceptions of justice—cosmopolitan or human, on the one hand, and state or international, on the other—remain locked in competition. True, the existence of the concept of universal jurisdiction in customary international law demonstrates Hedley Bull's acknowledgment that even traditional notions of order cannot exist without justice, and human justice has made significant advances in the past century.

Nevertheless, consistent with the fundamental structure of international society, the sovereignty-based, positivist approach to international justice is not in real decline. This is not an argument in support of impunity for dictators. Rather it is an empirical statement based on an examination of the relationship between law and politics in a world of sovereign states. And what that analysis points up is that, because the "international community" is more of an aspiration than reality, there are limits to the globalization of justice. As far as justice for war crimes is concerned, the world society has not yet arrived.

5

Sierra Leone: Judging Charles Taylor

The dead cannot cry out for justice; It is the duty of the living to do so for them
—Lois McMaster Bujold, *Diplomatic Immunity*

HYBRID JUSTICE

Inspired by the use of international war crimes tribunals in the former Yugoslavia and Rwanda but with an eye on the shortcomings of these courts, the Special Court for Sierra Leone was established in 2002 to prosecute the "persons most responsible" for serious violations of international humanitarian law and Sierra Leonean law committed in Sierra Leone during its decade old conflict between the Government of Sierra Leone and the Revolutionary United Forces (RUF). Although that conflict began in 1991, the court's jurisdiction was to cover crimes committed since 1996, the year the warring parties signed the Abidjan Peace Agreement.

The creation of this war crimes tribunal was the first backlash against international justice, imposed as the latter was through the fiat of the United Nations Security Council in the Balkans and Rwanda in the early 1990s. Several years after the work of those two war crimes tribunals began, a view developed that their most important drawback was their physical and psychological distance from the societies where the crimes occurred. The two international courts, located in foreign countries, were thus not as relevant to people on the ground in the former Yugoslavia and Rwanda as the lofty rhetoric of societal reconstruction through legalism might have suggested.

The Hague and Arusha tribunals have no judges from the territories of the former Yugoslavia or Rwanda. Moreover, the two courts were considered slow and costly. The two courts had no sunset clauses at the time—although end-dates were later established for their work. The pace of trials in both war crimes tribunals was slow. And the Hague Court was widely seen as spending too much time and money indicting and trying "small fry" defendants, a strategic failure given that the international tribunals were established to focus on the "big fish."

The Sierra Leone Tribunal was the first mixed international court to have on its bench judges from the country where the crimes were committed, and have national law, not just international humanitarian law, as part of its remit. The Sierra Leone Tribunal is thus what has become known as a "hybrid" war crimes tribunal. This attempt at a bottom-up approach to international justice for Sierra Leone was spearheaded by the United States and Britain, in consultation with the United Nations and the government of Sierra Leone.

The Special Court is a treaty-based war crimes tribunal. It was established by an agreement negotiated and signed by the United Nations and the government of Sierra Leone. This meant that it was not fully anchored in either the national legal system of Sierra Leone or in international law, but rather was an amalgam of the two. This unique nature of the Court, while it was celebrated at the time as an improvement over the Hague and Arusha tribunals by engaging the sovereignty of Sierra Leone, has had important consequences for the Court's jurisdiction. The most important of them is that, though addressing a conflict that had widespread regional implications in West Africa, the Special Court has concurrent jurisdiction with and primacy over Sierra Leone's courts but does not have similar primacy over the courts of other countries.[1] This is because unlike the Hague and Arusha tribunals, it was not established under the peace enforcement powers of the Security Council in Chapter VII of the United Nations Charter.

Kofi Annan, the Secretary-General of the United Nations, pointed to this weakness and suggested how it could be remedied: "Lacking the power to assert its primacy over the national courts in Third States in connection with crimes committed in Sierra Leone, it also lacks the power to request the surrender of an accused from any third state and to induce the compliance of its authorities with any such request. In examining measures to enhance the deterrent powers of the Special Court, the Security Council may wish to consider endowing it with Chapter VII powers for the specific purpose of requesting the surrender of an accused from outside the jurisdiction of the Court."[2]

This gap in the jurisdiction of the Special Court was the first pointer that it could not be all things for all purposes—a court with both international and national status, in effect eating its cake and having it—without problems. The Security Council, apparently not wanting to endow the Special

Court with supranational characteristics similar to the Hague and Arusha tribunals, did not heed the Secretary-General's advice. This omission was to return to haunt the court in the case of its star defendant, the former Liberian president Charles Taylor.

Second, the Special Court was established while the war in Sierra Leone was still ongoing, on the basis of an invitation by Sierra Leonean president Tejan Kabbah to the United Nations. In a letter addressed to the Secretary-General and dated June 12, 2000, President Kabbah asked Annan to initiate a process whereby the UN would decide to set a special court for Sierra Leone.[3] Kabbah's letter requested a mixed international–national court which will meet international standards for the trial of criminal cases while at the same time having a mandate to administer a blend of international and domestic Sierra Leone law on Sierra Leone soil. It is noteworthy, however, that Kabbah had clearly envisaged "a strong and credible court that will meet the objectives of bringing justice and ensuring lasting peace"[4]—"*a court created by the UN Security Council*"[5] (emphasis added). A court created under the UN Security Council, Kabbah noted, "will have the advantage of strong enforcement powers that will call for cooperation from states in investigations, arrest, extradition and enforcement of sentence."[6]

Although this is not to say that a Security Council-created tribunal with wide enforcement powers, which was what Kabbah clearly wanted, would have ensured lasting peace any more than the hybrid court with weak enforcement powers that was ultimately created, it is clear that this problem was already on the minds of a number of key actors in the creation of the Special Court.

The Council, despite the requests by President Kabbah and Kofi Annan, was reluctant to deploy its interventionist powers in the judicial arena as it had previously done in Yugoslavia and Rwanda. But perhaps it should not be surprising. The legitimacy of both war crimes tribunals had been vigorously challenged not just in the political sphere, but in the legal one as well.[7] And the creation of such tribunals under the Security Council's enforcement powers had also been challenged by some of the states that were members of the Council in the early 1990s when the Hague and Arusha tribunals were created.[8]

Moreover, it can be speculated that another reason why Kabbah did not get the exact kind of war crimes tribunal he wanted was that from both legal and political legitimacy standpoints it might have been difficult for the Security Council to legislate into being a tribunal with both international law and Sierra Leonean law jurisdiction. Would the Council not have been accused by "colonialism" in legislating not just international law, but, in addition, how the domestic laws of a sovereign state would apply in legal trials for crimes? From this perspective, then, Kabbah might indeed have wanted to have it both ways, which was not a practical scenario.

Sierra Leone then negotiated to have as much influence as possible in the framework of the Special Court, including through the designation of its attorney general as "co-prosecutor" of the court. This proposal was not accepted by the UN during negotiations that created the Court. Nevertheless, it would appear that the fallout, even within the Security Council's ranks, from its creation of the Hague and Arusha tribunals, was the main reason for the Council's reticence in venturing yet again into the terrain of creating war crimes tribunals. This was a further swing of the pendulum away from the supranationalization of the legal framework for accountability for mass atrocities. It was against this backdrop that the Security Council adopted resolution 1315 of August 14, 2000, in which it requested the Secretary-General to negotiate with the Sierra Leonean government the creation of an "independent special court" to prosecute the perpetrators of mass atrocities in Sierra Leone's conflict.[9]

President Kabbah's idea of a war crimes tribunal was one that would prosecute the leaders of the RUF. In his letter to the UN Secretary-General he made clear that the purpose of the tribunal he was requesting "is to try and bring to credible justice those members of the Revolutionary United Front and their accomplices responsible for committing crimes against the people of Sierra Leone and for the taking of UN peacekeepers as hostages."[10]

This is of course not uncharacteristic of war crimes tribunals—that the "bad guys," in this case the RUF whose rebellion caused the prolonged civil war, and which remains notorious for the gruesome atrocities it committed against civilians including signature amputations of hands and limbs, should face justice having been defeated in the battlefield. But under the influence of the great powers such as Britain and the United States, the mandate of the Special Court was not restricted to the RUF but to crimes committed in the conflict by all sides. "The most responsible persons" would be prosecuted regardless of whether they fought on the side of the "angels" (the government forces) or the "demons" (the RUF).

While this balanced approach was reminiscent of the provisions of the statutes of the war crimes tribunals for Yugoslavia and Rwanda, the difference is that it was actually enforced in subsequent indictments and trials at the Special Court for Sierra Leone. The Hague Tribunal started out with indictments and prosecutions of mostly Serbs (who were seen as being politically responsible for the wars that followed the breakup of Yugoslavia), leading to resentment of the tribunal by Serbs who saw the tribunal as "victor's justice." It would later indict and prosecute Croats, Bosnian Muslims, and Kosovar Albanians. At the Arusha Tribunal, the perfect victor's justice appears to have been handed down, with only Hutus prosecuted so far and trials scheduled to end in 2008. This reality at that tribunal exists because there the forces of the current government in Rwanda defeated those of the extremist government that carried out the genocide and installed themselves as the government and so were in practice the victors. In Sierra Leone, it took the intervention of external forces of the Economic Community of West African States Monitoring Group (ECOMOG) led by Nigeria, the regional power, and British troops. In Yugoslavia, the conflict ended not because any side won, but because NATO intervened.

So the Special Court indicted not just the leaders of the RUF such as its head, Foday Sankoh, and his deputy, Sam "Mosquito" Bokary, but, to the consternation of many Sierra Leoneans, Sam Hinga Norman, a former Deputy Minister of Defence and leader of the Kamajor militia that contributed greatly to the eventual defeat of the RUF and was widely seen as a hero in the country.[11] This situation created significant political problems for President Kabbah. Further, the ECOMOG troops cannot be indicted by the Special Court because the statute of the Special Court provided that such troops did not come under the jurisdiction of the court but could only be prosecuted in their own countries. Unlike the NATO bombing campaign discussed in Chapter 3, here there was an explicit waiver of the jurisdiction of the war crimes tribunal over the regional enforcers (inspired, of course, by political considerations). In the Balkans the immunity of NATO forces was de facto, a political and practical one.

And in limiting its indictments to just 12 "most responsible" persons in number since it was established, the Special Court has realistically kept true to its ultimate mission as an instrument of political justice. Kept in check by the decision of its political masters that, although the Court's temporal jurisdiction is open-ended, its life span is limited to 3 years, renewable once, the Special Court has not fallen into the experience at the Hague Tribunal, and to a lesser extent the Arusha Tribunal of pursuing persons whose roles in the atrocities of armed conflict were not pivotal. The creation and the work of a truth and reconciliation commission alongside a war crime tribunal has also served to relieve the court of this burden and allowed a focused approach to prosecutions. Sankoh died while in custody at the tribunal, robbing the court of the opportunity of prosecuting the most important leader of the RUF who started the conflict. Bokary also died without having been arrested.

Importantly, the remit of the Special Court does not include the crime of genocide. This is because, while 75,000 Sierra Leoneans are estimated to have died in the conflict and many more became refugees in the West African subregion and beyond, the atrocities were random and not intended to destroy any particular group because of who they were.

CHARLES TAYLOR: FROM INDICTMENT TO EXILE AND TRIAL

It is the nature of war crimes justice, considering its political context, that every war crimes tribunal has its star trial and defendant. Just as Slobodan Milosevic was the most important and controversial defendant at The Hague and Jean Kambanda and Theoneste Bagosora were the main defendants at

Arusha, Charles Taylor, the former president of the West African state of Liberia, is the most important person to have been indicted by the Special Court for Sierra Leone. It is ironic that (a) he is not from Sierra Leone, (b) there has been no attempt to bring him to justice in his native Liberia, and (c) it has taken an international war crimes tribunal premised on a rejection of the principle of global justice to bring Taylor before the bar of justice. Put differently, the Taylor case has demonstrated the contradictions in the Special Court for Sierra Leone.

Charles Ghankay Taylor is an Americo-Liberian who took the name "Ghankay" during the war he began in 1989 in order to bolster his legitimacy among indigenous Liberians of the Gio ethnic group whom he used to prosecute the war in Liberia. In the early 1980s Taylor was a senior procurement officer in the Liberian government. After he was charged with embezzling nearly $1 million of government funds, he fled to the United States, but was arrested and detained in a high security prison in Boston in 1984 under an extradition treaty. But Taylor later escaped from jail in 1985 and left the United States. He later showed up in Libya, where he obtained guerrilla training and financial support for his plans to invade Liberia and take power by force of arms.

In December 1989, Taylor and a small band of revolutionaries attacked Liberia from across its border with Côte d'Ivoire. Samuel Doe, Liberia's leader at the time, was deeply unpopular. Taylor skillfully exploited ethnic tensions between Doe's Krahn ethnic group and the Gio and Mano to gather momentum for his rebellion.[12] The war was soon to claim more that 250,000 lives, leaving more than a million Liberian refugees and internally displaced.

Taylor was denied ultimate victory in the battlefield by the intervention of ECOMOG forces in 1990 at the behest of General Ibrahim Babangida, Nigeria's military president at the time, but he was elected president of Liberia in national elections held in 1997 in which he defeated former UN official Ellen Johnson Sirleaf. It was widely known that many Liberians voted for Taylor out of fear of a return to civil war if he lost at the ballot box. Taylor's expansionist ambitions were not confined to Liberia. Seeking to control and profit from Sierra Leone's diamond fields, Taylor is believed to have trained and financed the RUF in the Sierra Leonean conflict. It is for that reason that he was ultimately indicted by the Special Court.

In early June 2003, while some West African heads of state, including Charles Taylor were meeting in Accra, Ghana, to negotiate a peaceful settlement to the Liberian conflict which had reignited during Taylor's presidency, the chief prosecutor of the Special Court, David Crane, attempted to serve a previously sealed indictment and warrant of arrest against Charles Taylor on the Liberian leader. In what was interpreted as a slight on the African leaders and the peace talks they brokered, the war crimes tribunal sent the indictment to the Ghanaian authorities by email and then held a press conference in Freetown to announce it.[13] The attempt was unsuccessful, frustrated by the Ghanaian president John Kufuor, who frowned on the idea of a sitting African head of state being indicted for violations of international law while participating in peace talks on Ghanaian territory. The negotiations broke up and Taylor hurriedly returned to Monrovia with a presidential jet put at his disposal by Kufuor.

The previously secret indictment and warrant of arrest had been approved by Judge Bankole Thomas of the Special Court on March 7, 2003, while Taylor was still head of state of Liberia.[14] Taylor thus became the second sitting head of state, after Milosevic, to be indicted by a war crimes tribunal. From the inception of the Special Court in 2003, there had been intense speculation among observers of the court on whether or not it would indict Charles Taylor. The question had now been answered.

But the indictment and possible trial of Taylor raised the specter of further instability in Liberia and West Africa, for both Taylor's opponents and his own forces were mobilized by the development. The timing of the release of the indictment has been criticized by commentators who believed it complicated the search for peace in Liberia.[15] The indictment of Charles Taylor crystallized the tension between order and justice in a particularly stark manner: The day after the indictment was made public rebels opposed to Taylor attacked the Liberian capital of Monrovia and began a push that progressively jeopardized Taylor's hold on power. In this sense, although African leaders at the Accra peace talks had advised Taylor to resign for the sake of his country's stability, the indictment certainly weakened Taylor by delegitimizing him in the eyes of his opponents—a fundamental characteristic of political justice.

Predictably, Taylor and his supporters were stunned and enraged by the indictment, as were several African leaders. Taylor dismissed the indictment as politically motivated, with his aides describing Crane as "a little white boy from somewhere in America who still believes in colonialism and thinks he can come in and try a sitting African president."[16] Even the United States was embarrassed by the timing of Taylor's indictment. In the words of the *Economist*, "America, the court's biggest donor was not amused."[17] Crane was unperturbed and unrepentant, threatening to indict Libya's president, Muammar Qaddafi, for arming and training Taylor and Sankoh.[18] It can only be speculated what effect indicting the Libyan leader would have had on the strategic considerations of Arab states and Western powers, who were beginning a process of engagement with Qaddafi that ultimately led to the latter forswearing chemical weapons. Ultimately, the United States re-established diplomatic relations with Libya.[19] This was certainly a more beneficial strategic outcome for the international society than the single-minded pursuit of abstract notions of justice through allegations of vicarious criminal responsibility.

The indictment against Taylor charged the Liberian leader with seventeen counts of crimes against humanity and war crimes. He was accused of giving financial support, military training, and weapons to the RUF, led by Foday Sankoh, during the armed conflict in Sierra Leone in order "to obtain access to the mineral wealth of the Republic of Sierra Leone, and to destabilize the state."[20] Taylor is charged with participating in a "joint criminal enterprise" with Sankoh's RUF and the Armed Forces Ruling Council that ousted Kabbah's government in 1997[21]—to kill, maim, and rape civilian populations throughout Sierra Leone, as well as armed attacks against UN peacekeepers.[22]

Charles Taylor's slide into the political wilderness quickened after the controversial indictment against him was unveiled. With rebel troops closing in on him, his government weakened by sanctions imposed by the Security Council, and a U.S. warship parked on the Liberian coast after U.S. President Bush had taken the position that Taylor had to leave Liberia if peace was to have any chance there, Taylor resigned as head of state of Liberia in August 2003 and went into exile in Nigeria. The arrangement in which Nigeria offered him asylum was brokered by ECOWAS, the African Union, the UN, and the United States. It was one that put political expediency and the stability of Liberia ahead of justice, whether in Liberia or Sierra Leone—at least for the moment. Subsequent developments have borne out the wisdom of this approach.

On the day Taylor left Liberia, he was flanked at a press conference in Monrovia by key African leaders—President Olusegun Obasanjo of Nigeria, the then President Joachim Chissanno of Mozambique, who was chairman of the African Union, President John Kuffour of Ghana, who was also the chairman of ECOWAS, and President Thabo Mbeki of South Africa. Charles Taylor thus became the first leader in history whose flight into exile was a political and media spectacle watched by the whole world on CNN. Exuding defiance but visibly rattled, Taylor declared to the television cameras in a message clearly targeted at his political supporters in Liberia: "God willing, I will be back." The presence of the African leaders who came to see him off and escort him into exile was highly symbolic. It was at once a message of fraternal solidarity with their "brother" head of state and a political rejection of the legal reality of the indictment of Taylor by the war crimes tribunal. Reading the indictment as a rebuff to the peace process in which they had been engaged, their public solidarity with Taylor was a symbolic rejection of "international" or "global" (but in fact hegemonic) justice, a phenomenon African leaders are decidedly unenthusiastic about.[23]

There are several reasons for this perspective by African leaders. The first is a feeling that legalism is essentially foreign to African culture, which emphasizes mediation, conciliation, or traditional arbitration and restitution. Legalism is thus seen as a legacy of colonialism. Professor Bolaji Akinyemi, an astute scholar of international relations and a former Nigerian foreign minister, has described the tension between liberal legalism and the attitude of African leaders toward it as "a clash of civilizations."[24] Analyzing the implications of the saga of Taylor's indictment and eventual surrender for war crimes trial for Nigerian foreign policy and statecraft, Akinyemi has posited:

> The issue at stake should not be perceived as a conflict between the U.S. and Nigeria. It is much more serious than that. The competing versions of the strategic doctrine of the regional enforcer as played out in the Liberian case are in fact an illustration of a clash of civilizations. African civilization does not emphasize revenge. It emphasizes conciliation and forgiveness. This has been amply demonstrated in post-colonial attitudes toward former colonizers and in the most dramatic case, in the attitude of Nelson Mandela toward his persecutors.
>
> Western civilization on the other hand with its roots in "eye for an eye" syndrome emphasizes vengeance in the name of justice. While few African societies have blood feuds going back centuries, European culture is noted for such blood feuds. Getting this distinction right is important as Africa and the rest of the world squares off over Darfur and whatever African conflicts may be in the pipeline.[25]

Second, in a continental context in which conflict and mass atrocities have been frequent in the post-colonial era—though admittedly now on the decline—African leaders are reticent about real accountability for war crimes because they fear precedents that may return to haunt other members of their leadership club. Third, the attitude of African leaders to the contested ability of international law to breach the immunity of serving heads of state is not unique: Leaders everywhere else, from Pinochet to Milosevic to Saddam Hussein, are keen to assert the privilege of heads of states and government from prosecution. As we have seen in the discussion of the controversial concept of universal jurisdiction in Chapter 4, the leaders of powerful states in international society likewise resist any breach to their own immunities in any circumstance.

Fourth, the leaders and citizens of poor countries often see war crimes justice as an abstraction with little relevance to their daily lives. They are more interested in economic and social justice in the international society. Indeed, as we shall see later, despite having been hailed as a more grassroots kinds of justice than the Hague and Arusha tribunals, the Special Court subsequently faced similar skepticism among Sierra Leoneans.

It is against this backdrop that Taylor went into exile in Nigeria and was offered asylum with his large entourage in the Southern port city of Calabar. From day one of this arrangement, President Obasanjo had begun to resist pressure to hand Taylor over to the Special Court, although neither President Bush nor UN Secretary-General Annan spoke explicitly of a war crimes trial while welcoming the prospect of Taylor stepping down as president.[26] Indeed, at the press conference before Taylor's flight to asylum and exile, the Nigerian leader defiantly declared that he would not be "harassed" by anyone into surrendering Taylor to the Special Court. Taylor, standing beside Obasanjo, nodded in emphatic and solemn agreement.

Pressure on the Nigerian leader came from two sources, one domestic (mostly Nigerian civil society, especially human rights NGOs, bar associations, and academics), the other external (most especially, and increasingly the U.S. government, Western NGOs, and the European Parliament).[27] The Nigerian government's policy was that it would only hand Taylor back to Liberia if an elected government in that country requested his surrender to stand trial. For one thing, Nigeria possibly believed at the time it took this position that the prospect of a democratically elected government in Liberia making a trial of Taylor a priority issue was a distant one, given the sheer devastation of the country's basis infrastructure.[28] For another, implicit in this position is the one that Nigeria either did not recognize the Special Court's jurisdiction to try Taylor and believed his country's courts were the only ones competent to try him, or else Nigeria believed it should only hand Taylor to Liberia, which could then make the decision on whether to hand him over to the Special Court. The sequence of events in the case indicated that Nigeria's positions evolved from the former to the latter.

Nigeria's position was also noteworthy when we consider that the country is a member of the "Management Committee" of the Special Court, a group of states—most of which provided funding for the court—that was entrusted with oversight of the Special Court. But this has more to do with maintaining its wider strategic influence as a regional superpower, given its heavy investment of financial resources and peacekeeping forces in Sierra Leone and Liberia in the 1990s, than with a single-minded commitment to legalism. This is yet another indication of the weakness of the proposition that states are motivated by liberal ideas when they create or support war crimes tribunals.

Passions were also inflamed over Taylor's exile as it appeared the former Liberian leader violated the terms agreed between him and his Nigerian hosts—that he would not meddle in Liberian or regional politics. For Taylor still cast a long shadow over Liberia. In this practical sense, Taylor overplayed his hand and almost certainly accelerated his own eventual surrender and surrential.

Two major legal issues framed the political and diplomatic debates over Taylor's fate. The first, which is fairly straightforward, was that as noted earlier, the Special Court has no powers to enforce the cooperation of third states. This is why Taylor could stay in Nigeria for two and a half years, although, in all probability, had he gone into exile in another country in

Africa, few countries in the continent could have resisted the hegemonic pressures at play against him as Nigeria was able to for so long. Thus the soft underbelly of the hybrid nature of the Special Court, in terms of its institutional legal underpinning, was exposed, moving the issue almost completely to the political terrain. To partially remedy this, and wary that Taylor might return to Liberia following national elections there in November 2005, the UN Security Council adopted a resolution authorizing the UN peace keeping mission in Liberia to arrest Taylor and hand him over to the Special Court for Sierra Leone if he set foot in Liberia.

Secondly, and more controversially, Taylor challenged the legality of the charges against him because as a sitting head of state at the time, he was immune from the jurisdiction of the Special Court. This legal wrangle went to the heart of the very nature of the war crimes tribunal.

THE DIPLOMATIC IMMUNITIES

On July 23, 2003, Charles Taylor, acting through his counsel Terence Terry, filed a motion at the Special Court asking the war crimes tribunal to quash the indictment and arrest warrant against Taylor and declare both documents "invalid at their inception."[29] The motion was made "under Protest and without waiving of Immunity of a Head of State President Charles Taylor."[30] The appellate chamber of the Special Court, which decided the preliminary motion under the Court's procedural rules, heard oral arguments between October 30 and November 1, 2003, from Terry, on behalf of Taylor, and Desmond de Silva, Queens Counsel (QC) for the prosecution. As the issues of international law in the motion were considered so fundamental to the entire effort to prosecute Taylor, the court invited submissions from the international legal scholars Professor Diane Orentlicher and Professor Philippe Sands QC as *amici curiae* ("friends of the court"). The African Bar Association also made a friend-of-the-court submission.

Charles Taylor's lawyer argued in this motion that

a. Based on the judgment of the International Court of Justice (ICJ) in the *Yerodia* case,[31] Charles Taylor enjoyed absolute immunity from criminal prosecution because he was a serving head of state at the time he was indicted;

b. Exceptions from diplomatic immunities can only derive from other rules of international law such as Security Council resolutions under Chapter VII of the United Nations Charter;

c. The Special Court does not have Chapter VII powers, and so judicial orders from the Special Court have the quality of judicial orders from a national court;

  d. The indictment against Charles Taylor was invalid due to his personal
     immunity from criminal prosecution. Further, the timing of the dis-
     closure of the arrest warrant and indictment on June 12, 2003, was
     designed to frustrate Charles Taylor's peacemaking initiative in Ghana
     and caused prejudice to his functions as head of state.[32]

He further argued, apparently on the assumption that the Special Court
was a Sierra Leonean court, that the principle of sovereign equality prohibits
one state from exercising its authority on the territory of another; a state may
exceptionally prosecute acts committed on foreign territory by a foreigner
but only where the perpetrator is physically in the territory of the prosecuting
state; and the Special Court's attempt to serve the indictment and arrest
warrant on Charles Taylor in Ghana was a violation of the principle of
sovereign equality.[33]

The prosecution, in turn, argued among other points, that the Liberian
government was not a party to the case and all references to it should be
struck out; Taylor could not simultaneously refuse to appear before the
Special Court and use the processes of the Court by filing motions before it;
the *Yerodia* case concerns the immunities of an incumbent head of state from
the jurisdiction of the courts of another state; customary international law
permits international criminal tribunals to indict serving heads of state and
the Special Court is an international court established under international
law; and the lack of Chapter VII powers does not affect the Special Court's
jurisdiction over heads of state.[34] The prosecution cited the example of
the International Criminal Court (ICC), which does not have Chapter VII
powers but explicitly denies immunity to heads of state for international
crimes. Moreover, the prosecution argued, Charles Taylor was indicted in
accordance with the Special Court's Statute for crimes committed in Sierra
Leone and not the territory of another state, and the attempt to serve the
charges and arrest warrant in Ghana did not violate Ghana's sovereignty.

Further arguments between Taylor's counsel and the prosecution elab-
orated the heart of the matter—the exact nature of the Special Court and
thus whether it had jurisdiction to indict a sitting head of state. Thus Charles
Taylor' fate turned on interpretations of the *Yerodia* case, discussed at length
in Chapter 4. Taylor's lawyer distinguished the Special Court for Sierra
Leone form the Nuremberg and Tokyo tribunals, the International Criminal
Tribunal for the former Yugoslavia (ICTY) and the International Criminal
Tribunal for Rwanda (ICTR). The latter two war crimes tribunals were established by the enforcement powers of the Security Council under Chapter
VII of the UN Charter. They fell explicitly within the exceptions enumerated
by the ICJ in *Yerodia*. In a classic rendition of the tension between order
and justice, between sovereignty and the globalization of jurisdiction in international law, Taylor's lawyer concluded that "the emphatic nature of the

[*Yerodia*] decision and the size of the majority endorsing it send a clear signal that the main judicial organ of the United Nations does not wish to subject the stability of international relations to disturbances originating from the decentralized judicial investigations of crimes, no matter how abject they may be."[35]

Before reaching its decision, the Special Court gave significant weight to the friends-of-the-court arguments of Professors Philippe Sands and Diane Orentlicher and the African Bar Association. Perhaps not surprisingly, consistent with the positions of several academic writers in international law and those of civil society, those submissions supported the exercise of jurisdiction by the Special Court over Charles Taylor.

Sands submitted that, first, regarding international courts, such courts may exercise jurisdiction over a serving head of state for international crimes. He relied on "international practice and academic commentary" as well as the *Pinochet* cases and *Yerodia* for support for this view. Second, in respect of national courts a serving head of state is immune even in respect of international crimes.[36]

Third, Sands recognized that "the lawfulness of an arrest warrant depends on the Court's powers and attributes and the legal basis on which it was established."[37] He then argued that the Special Court is not part of the judiciary of Sierra Leone and is not a national court. "Rather," the law professor opined, "it is an international court established by treaty with a competence and jurisdiction that is similar to the ICTY, ICTR and ICC, and it has the characteristics associated with classical international organizations."[38]

Fourth, he argued that there is nothing in the agreement between Sierra Leone and the United Nations, or its Statute, to prevent the Court from exercising jurisdiction over offenses committed on Sierra Leonean territory by the Liberian head of state. Of interest, Sand also noted that the Special Court did not violate Ghana's sovereignty by transmitting the arrest warrant, but Ghana was not obliged to give effect to such a warrant, and a former head of state is not entitled to substantive immunity before an international war crimes tribunal.[39]

Professor Orentlicher anchored her opinion on the Special Court on the ground that there was an important distinction between the jurisdictional powers of international criminal courts and those of national courts. Since the Special Court was an international tribunal, it had jurisdiction over incumbent and former heads of state in accordance with its statute. She also asserted that, while substantive immunities shield the official conduct of former heads of states from the jurisdiction of the domestic courts of foreign states after such persons have left office, Taylor could not enjoy this type of immunity in respect of the crimes for which he had been indicted.[40]

In its decision, the Special Court first of all had to dispose of the technical question of whether an indicted person who was then not yet in custody and had not yet made an initial appearance before the court could bring a preliminary motion as Taylor did. The Special Court ruled that this case was not a normal one and exercised its "inherent power and discretion" to permit Taylor to make his application, notwithstanding that he had not appeared before the court.[41]

The Special Court then addressed the question of whether it was an international criminal tribunal. It ruled that although the Court was not explicitly established through the Security Council's Chapter VII powers, as had the Yugoslavia and Rwanda tribunals, the fact that the Council initiated the process of the Court's creation by adoption of resolution 1315, on the basis of which the UN and Sierra Leone established the Court by treaty, envisaged its status as international tribunal. The Court's appellate judges then went on to hold that "the absence of the so-called Chapter VII powers does not by itself define the legal status of the Special Court." The agreement between the United Nations and Sierra Leone was an agreement between *all* the members of the United Nations and Sierra Leone.[42] The judges then reaffirmed that the Special Court is an international criminal court and is neither a national court of Sierra Leone nor part of that country's judicial system.

On the preponderance of its constitutive instruments, let us assume, for the sake of argument, that the Court's ruling about its nature as an international court can be sustained, though it will surely be of interest that a court that was established as a "hybrid," "a treaty-based sui generis court of mixed jurisdiction and composition"[43] should now be straining to identify itself as a clearly *international* tribunal in order to be able to assert jurisdiction to indict a sitting head of state. That even its essential nature as an international tribunal can be contested is clear from the Secretary-General's explication of the nature of the court noted above. But it can be accepted that the manner in which its internal administrative law has actually developed, and the fact that it has primacy over Sierra Leonean courts (but not over the courts of other states), that it is certainly a cut above the Sierra Leonean judicial system.[44]

Does a status as an international criminal court, however, automatically confer jurisdiction to indict a sitting head of state, as the learned friends of the court have argued? In its decision, the Court recalled Article 6(2) of its Statute, which provides that "the official position of any accused persons, whether as Head of State or Government or as a responsible Government official, shall not relieve such a person of criminal responsibility nor mitigate punishment."[45] This provision is identical to those of the Yugoslavia and Rwanda tribunals, and similar to a provision of the International Criminal Court. The Court also recalled an identical provision in the Charter of the

International Military Tribunal (the Nuremberg Charter), which the General Assembly has accepted.[46]

The Special Court for Sierra Leone thus held that Taylor's position as a sitting head of state at the time of his indictment was not a bar to his being prosecuted by that court.[47] The Court subsumed itself under "certain international criminal courts" that the ICJ held could submit an incumbent Minister of Foreign Affairs to their jurisdiction in the *Yerodia* case. But the ICJ itself gave examples with the Yugoslavia and Rwanda tribunals, "*established pursuant to Security Council resolutions under Chapter VII of the United Nations Charter, and the future International Criminal Court created by the 1998 Rome Convention.*[48] (emphasis added)

The decision of the Special Court conferring on itself jurisdiction to indict Charles Taylor while he was a sitting head of state is not in accordance with international law, strictly interpreted. Being an international criminal court does not by that fact alone confer jurisdiction to do so, the desirable political goal of confronting impunity notwithstanding. Such a court must have specific jurisdiction, as enunciated by the ICJ, to breach what is otherwise an established norm of international law. The point that the tribunal was established by an agreement between Sierra Leone and all members of the United Nations under the UN Charter is also erroneous, for under the Charter, responsibility for international peace and security is vested not in the General Assembly, to which all members of the UN belong, but in the Security Council, of which most members of the organization are not members. Thus, even if we accept that in signing the Agreement Sierra Leone entered a treaty with all UN member states, that still does not confer authority for peace enforcement under Chapter VII.

The Special Court is neither a Security Council created court nor a treaty-based court of *widespread* jurisdiction. This is why comparing itself to the ICC is inapposite: that Court is based on a treaty to which, as of this writing, 100 countries have acceded. If the implication of the Special Court not having Chapter VII enforcement powers for its ability to apprehend suspects in foreign countries was obvious, so also should have been the limitations on its jurisdiction.

This legal controversy, in which a war crimes tribunal interprets its jurisdiction, rightly or wrongly in order to give effect to its political imperatives, is yet another reason why the timing of Charles Taylor's indictment was ill-considered. And it is why Akinyemi was on strong ground, legally speaking, when in early 2004 he argued that the Special Court should cancel the indictment and issue a fresh indictment and warrant of arrest now that Taylor was no longer a head of state.[49]

Professor Orentlicher concluded in her *amicus curiae* submission, correctly, that "although substantive immunities shield the official conduct of heads of state after such persons cease to hold office, this type of immunity is not available in respect of the crimes for which Taylor has been indicted."[50]

It is for precisely this reason that an indictment of Taylor after he had left office would have been a legally stronger move.

But war crimes justice is political justice. As noted earlier, indicting Charles Taylor probably hastened his resignation from office and exile, just as the indictment of Slobodan Milosevic quickened his political defenestration in Serbia and subsequent arrest and trial at The Hague. If Taylor had any hopes that, somehow, the indictment against him would be lifted in exchange for his resignation and exile in Nigeria, he was mistaken.[51] In any event, the legal position has been overtaken by factual and political developments in his home country of Liberia that were to bring Charles Taylor's exile in Nigeria to an abrupt end. Nevertheless, the issue of the legality of his indictment is bound to be at the center of Taylor's defense at his substantive trial.

ENDGAME

For as long as there was a transitional government in Liberia after Taylor's resignation, that government, headed by Liberian businessman Gyude Bryant could not request Taylor's surrender to it because it was not seen as having democratic legitimacy. Nigeria would not have granted such a request, with Obasanjo having made clear it would only respond to a request from an *elected* Liberian government. Bryant, however, explicitly supported bringing Taylor to justice at the Special Court in Sierra Leone.[52] But with the presidential elections held in Liberia in late October/November 2005 that were won by Ellen Johnson Sirleaf, the need to confront—and decide—the question of justice for Taylor became unavoidable. Sirleaf discussed the matter in a meeting she had with President Obasanjo soon after her inauguration in January 2006, but she clearly did not have much appetite for the topic.[53] This was no surprise, since the internal politics she inherited in Liberia as a new president were complex. While Taylor was no longer a dominant political force, he still cast a long shadow. Several successful candidates in the national elections, especially legislative elections, were close political and personal associates of Taylor's. These include the speaker of the House of Representatives, Edwin Snowe, and Taylor's estranged wife, Jewel Taylor, who was elected to the Liberian Senate after having left Taylor in Nigeria and returned to Liberia to begin a new political career. Both are still under an international travel ban imposed as part of UN sanctions.

Johnson Sirleaf, a Harvard-educated former banker and director of the United Nations Development Programme, has been both an affiliate and opponent of Taylor during her long political career.[54] Having initially supported Taylor's armed rebellion in the late 1980s, she eventually distanced herself from him after some of her personal friends became victims of atrocities committed by Taylor's militias.[55] In the 1997 presidential elections, she won 10 percent of the vote to Taylor's 75.

Thus in establishing her new government, Johnson Sirleaf has had to deal with the uncomfortable reality of the need to placate some of Taylor's supporters who played significant roles in the crimes of Liberia's not-so-distant past. As the newly-elected Liberian leader—the first woman ever to have been elected president of an African country—put it: "I don't go around and say, 'This is a political compromise.' But everybody knows when I make a certain appointment that it's not an appointment from my heart."[56] One of the ways through which she has sought to face Liberia's past is by establishing a Truth and Reconciliation Commission to investigate war crimes.

Given that Liberia was still in such a fragile state, with electricity and other essential infrastructure destroyed by war, Johnson Sirleaf feared a possible backlash on the country's stability if she moved too quickly to seek a war crimes trial for Charles Taylor. Moreover, Taylor threw the support of his political supporters in Liberia behind Johnson Sirleaf during the runoff elections between her and the other leading contender, George Weah, after the first ballot proved inconclusive.[57]

But juxtaposed against this reality was another—the strong, hegemonic pressure being applied by Western governments whose financial, political, and security support was crucial if she was going to have a chance to deliver on her campaign promises to give the citizens of her blighted country a better life. Those interests, especially the U.S. government, wanted Taylor immediately handed over to the Special Court for Sierra Leone for trial. "There is no doubt in my mind that Mr. Taylor has to have his day in court," she told a journalist. "And he has the right to self-defense. But the timing is the issue, because, don't forget, Mr. Taylor still has operatives in this country."[58]

In the meantime, for Obasanjo and Nigeria, hosts to an exile arrangement that was unpopular among Nigerians from day one, the ostensible moment of decision—a democratically elected government in Liberia—had arrived. Who would make the first move? From Obasanjo's perspective, it would have to be the Liberian government. In March 2006, Johnson Sirleaf formally requested Nigeria to hand Charles Taylor over for trial at the Special Court.[59] Taylor's spokesman in Nigeria, Sylvester Paasewe, immediately reacted to the Liberian request, branding it "an indecent proposal" engineered by the United States.

Johnson Sirleaf's reluctance in making the request—and the fact that she was responding to external pressure—were palpably evident in the circumstances surrounding the affair, leading to some buck-passing by the Liberian and Nigerian governments. Visiting the United States, where she addressed both the United Nations Security Council and a joint session of the U.S. Congress, Johnson Sirleaf said it was "unfair" to force her to act against Taylor when the international community should have acted sooner to help Liberia free itself from his long reach;[60] but she commended Nigeria for hosting Taylor and U.S. president George Bush for "forcing a tyrant into exile."[61]

Two related issues arose—first, the role of other African heads of state in a decision on Taylor's fate and, second, whether Taylor was to be surrendered directly to the Special Court in Sierra Leone or to Liberia. In her request, Johnson Sirleaf had asked Obasanjo to consult African leaders, as they had helped broker the deal that sent Taylor into exile in Nigeria. This was a delicate situation that was quickly interpreted by some human rights campaigners as "changing the goal posts."[62] Although this was probably just a formality, and it does not appear that the other African leaders consulted by Obasanjo (the chairman of the African Union, President Denis Sassou-Nguesso of the Republic of Congo and his ECOWAS counterpart, President Mamadou Tandja of Niger) expressed or could impose any objection, it was delicate because Taylor's aides claimed in media interviews that African leaders had agreed in 2003 to quash the indictment against Taylor as part of the package of his resignation and exile.[63] While there is no independent confirmation of the veracity of this claim, canceling Taylor's indictment after it had been made public would have been a near-impossible task since that would have required a decision by the judges of the Special Court at the request of the Court's chief prosecutor. African states, including Sierra Leone, had little control over the prosecutorial policy decisions of the Special Court. The American prosecutor David Crane, whose pursuit of Taylor was infused with messianic zeal, was hardly likely to capitulate to such pressure if any had been applied. It is possible, however—but one can only speculate—that similar strategic policy pressures from non-African sources might have informed his apparent decision not to follow through on his threat to indict the Libyan leader Muammar Qaddafi.

There is greater plausibility to the claim that the African leaders agreed that Taylor would *not* be handed over to the Special Court in any event and that Nigeria would ensure this outcome.[64] It is from this perspective that some analysts have interpreted Obasanjo's subsequent statement that he would only hand Taylor over to an elected Liberian government on the latter's request as either a strategic miscalculation, and/or a statement made in response to pressures and in the belief that that scenario was an extremely unlikely one.[65] Here it is important to recall that the pressures the Nigerian government faced were not just external, but internal as well, except one has to say that the civil society organizations in Nigeria calling for his trial were acting as agents of external forces. But the antipathy of the Nigerian populace toward Taylor was quite genuine, given that many Nigerian soldiers of the ECOMOG force died in combat, mostly with Taylor's forces, and those forces also killed two Nigerian journalists, killings believed to have been executed on Taylor's direct orders.[66]

The second question, to *whom* Taylor should be surrendered, was also a delicate one for both Johnson Sirleaf and Obasanjo. The Liberian president clearly dreaded the prospect of having Taylor on Liberian territory. She emphasized in her public comments that she was not seeking Taylor's extradition to Liberia because the former Liberian leader had not been charged for any crimes by the authorities of his own country.[67] Obasanjo, who apparently believed that only the courts in Liberia could or should try Taylor, could not afford to lose face by caving in to pressure and sending Taylor directly to Sierra Leone. He needed the face-saving fiction of surrendering Taylor to his own country.

But before this conundrum could be resolved, and as Obasanjo set out on a visit the United States, where he was scheduled to meet with President Bush at the end of March 2006—a meeting that had Taylor as a major agenda item—the former Liberian leader made a dramatic escape from his villa in Calabar.[68] Within the discreet circles of law enforcement and the intelligence channels between United States and Nigeria the diplomatic equivalent of pandemonium erupted. Panic spread inside Liberia, with rumors of an imminent coup by forces sympathetic to Taylor.[69] Obasanjo, apparently shocked, placed Nigeria's borders in full alert. White House officials dropped hints that the Obasanjo–Bush meeting might be cancelled if Taylor was not found, summoned Nigeria's ambassador in Washington, George Obiozor, for an explanation, and stressed Nigeria's responsibility to apprehend Taylor and hand him over for trial.[70]

After a dramatic twenty-four hours, Taylor was reportedly arrested in the early hours of March 29 at border post in Northern Nigeria, from which he was attempting to escape from the country in a sports utility vehicle with diplomatic number plates.[71] This fortuitous development saved Nigeria's government from further embarrassment, Obasanjo's meeting with U.S. President went ahead as scheduled, with the mood at the White House "drastically changed" according to President Obasanjo at a press conference at Ritz Carlton Hotel in Washington, DC.[72]

The incident underscored how significant a part of American foreign policy toward Africa—and that of Nigeria—the war crimes trial of Charles Taylor had become. This is part of a larger view of the Bush administration, which has ranged itself against certain "international outlaws" such as Taylor, Saddam Hussein, and individuals suspected as having committed atrocities in Darfur, Sudan.[73] However, some critics have asserted that America's resolve to put Taylor on trial for war crimes had far less to do with liberal legalism that as an act of vengeance for his favoring China over the United States in granting concessions to exploit Liberia's offshore oil.[74]

Although Obasanjo condemned insinuations that Nigerian security agents actually connived to let Taylor "escape" as uncharitable criticism, a speculative school of thought holds tenaciously to that theory.[75] The theory holds that international diplomatic pressure was becoming too much for both Johnson Sirleaf and Nigeria to bear, yet the Nigerians were also under the pressure of their "undertakings" not to surrender Charles Taylor for trial, and so the way out was that "Nigeria should look the other way while Taylor makes the necessary arrangements that he needed to make" to find an alternative sanctuary.[76] From this perspective, the timing of Obasanjo's visit to Washington, DC, before the "escape" had been fully executed was a strategic blunder.[77] But, seen another way, Obasanjo, under additional domestic political pressures imposed by his apparent desire at the time to have the Nigerian constitution amended to give him a third 4-year term in office, needed the meeting with Bush for his own reasons, and this consideration might have been enough to "sacrifice" Taylor.

Immediately after his capture, Taylor was transported by Nigeria to Liberia, where he was handed over to the United Nations peacekeeping troops who promptly flew him to Sierra Leone. There the eleven counts of his indictment—now reduced from the original seventeen[78]—were read to him by officials of the Special Court, who took him into custody. Where 3 years earlier a dapper and defiant Taylor had predicted his triumphant return, he now returned to his country only briefly, unshaven and in handcuffs, on the way to his trial in another country.

One reporter has opined that "the trial is sure to resonate on a continent where dictators have ruled with ruthless impunity. From Idi Amin, the soldier whose murderous rule in Uganda gave way to comfortable exile in Saudi Arabia, to Haile Mengistu Mariam, whose 14-year Communist rule in Ethiopia brought political purges that killed more than a million people but who is now living quietly in Zimbabwe, African leaders who brutalize their citizens have faced few consequences."[79]

This analysis, though no doubt accurate, does not present the whole picture. For Taylor, unsavory a character as he is, is part of a dying breed in African politics. We must confront the question of why Liberians themselves, and even more so the victims of Taylor's atrocities, and Sierra Leoneans as well, are not baying for a war crimes trial of the former Liberian leader.[80] The case of Charles Taylor is seen by some Sierra Leoneans as an abstract diversion with little practical resonance.[81] It is either the case represents a collective failure of Africans and their leadership or perhaps it suggests that the whole concept of war crimes trials in foreign courts is a hegemonic idea that is having a hard time taking root in a continent with a somewhat different approach and more basic problems.

Meanwhile, the greatest contradiction of the Special Court for Sierra Leone was soon to unfold—the prospect that Taylor would not face trial in Sierra Leone. Believing that a trial there would constitute in itself a threat to regional peace and security, the Special Court and the government of Sierra Leone requested the government of the Netherlands and the International Criminal Court for their cooperation toward a trial of Taylor by a panel of the Special Court sitting in a courtroom in the International Criminal Court (ICC) at The Hague.[82]

This approach was technically feasible, for the rules of the Special Court allow for a trial chamber of the court to sit away from the Court's location in Sierra Leone.[83] But, given the tangled nature of the Court, a resolution of the Security Council would have to be adopted to underpin this scenario.[84] On June 16, 2006, the Security Council voted unanimously to adopt its resolution 1688 under Chapter VII of the UN Charter, authorizing Taylor's transfer to the Hague to stand trial.[85] In a tacit acknowledgment of the significance of not holding Taylor's trial in Africa, the Council noted in its resolution that it was not possible to try Taylor at the International Criminal Tribunal for Rwanda at Arusha, Tanzania, because that tribunal was fully occupied with its caseload in order to wind down its work, and that no other international criminal tribunals exist in Africa where Taylor could be tried.

Thus the Council has had to intervene, *à la carte,* to prop up this "hybrid" war crimes tribunal that was envisaged as an answer to pure international criminal tribunals. Netherlands agreed in principle to host the trial in the premises of the ICC, but only on the condition that another country should be willing to provide a prison for Taylor if he is convicted after his trial, or host him if he is acquitted.[86] Requests to the governments of Austria, Sweden, and Denmark to host Taylor upon his conviction or acquittal met with rejections.[87] Taylor opposed the idea of his being tried in The Hague.[88] Finally, on June 15 Britain, which was a driving force in obtaining a Security Council endorsement for a trial of Taylor at the Hague, also offered to provide a British jail for Taylor if he was convicted.[89] This offer cleared the way for the adoption of resolution 1688 the next day.

Trying Taylor at The Hague is a prudent option on the face of it, as it would seem to increase the chances of a secure trial for Charles Taylor. But it is fraught with problems—and political contradictions. First, it smacks of an abdication of responsibility by the Special Court and the Sierra Leonean government. It is odd that having caught its priced "big fish," the court balked at the prospect of confronting his power and influence and sought safety in Europe. If Charles Taylor was really as powerful as he is projected to be, why bother to indict him? Indicting political leaders for war crimes is always a political choice, and thus a "pardon"—a decision *not* to prosecute—might also have been made. Solomon Barewa, Sierra Leone's vice president, has justified holding Taylor's trial elsewhere in order to spare his country the trauma of revisiting the atrocities of the civil war.[90] This reasoning appears weak, because the other trials taking place at the Special Court are doing precisely that—revisiting the horrors of the war.

Second, as some Sierra Leoneans and several African and non-African civil society organizations have noted, trying Taylor at The Hague weakens the relevance and resonance his trial might have had for Africa in terms of serving as an object lesson on the consequences of warlordism.[91] It is more likely to reinforce a view of international war crimes justice as a concept that rides on the back of hegemonic power in the international society while speaking the language of liberal legalism as a motivation for the pursuit of war criminals. It certainly renders inchoate any claims the Special Court might have laid to being an improvement on the Hague and Arusha tribunals. The crisis of legitimacy that international war crimes justice is facing thus continues, and the handling of the Taylor case has done nothing to diminish it.

Third, it is often assumed that a trial at The Hague is a trial that automatically meets high standards in procedure and security—or at least higher standards than in Africa. As the troubled trial and eventual death of Slobodan Milosevic demonstrated, coupled with the suicide of another accused, Milan Babic at the Hague Tribunal, war crimes trials everywhere face certain challenges whenever high political figures are the ones in the dock. The great powers that pushed so hard for the apprehension and trial of Charles Taylor could have supported his trial in Sierra Leone with a heavy detachment of security personnel. As John Leigh, Sierra Leone's former ambassador to the United States has argued, "the benefits of trying Mr. Taylor in Freetown far outweigh the costs of activating internationally trained security forces to help maintain short-term stability in the [West African] region."[92] Fourth, the cost of judicial logistics – flying judges and witnesses and other participants in the trial – to The Hague will be enormous. It is hoped that adequate financial provision will be made in the budget of the Special Court for this unanticipated development.

In conclusion, all of this is not to say that Charles Taylor should not be brought to justice. He should. I make the point, however, that it is just one of several policy options. And it is important to point to the contradictions in the process that underscore the nature of war crimes trials as political justice. Indeed, in this lies perhaps the most important—and beneficial—outcome of prosecuting Charles Taylor—removing him and the threat he represents from the political space in Liberia and the wider West African sub-region. As one Liberian analyst put it—correctly, one believes—"A lot of people are still sitting on the fence. Once they have a clear idea where Taylor is and what's likely to happen to him, they're likely to really turn their backs on that period and move forward."[93]

6

The Politics of the International Criminal Court

> We believe that states, not international institutions are primarily responsible
> for ensuring justice in the international system
> > —Marc Grossman, U.S. Under Secretary of State

The establishment of a permanent International Criminal Court (ICC) by a treaty signed by 120 states at a diplomatic conference in Rome in 1998 is a remarkable development that at first sight would appear to presage "global justice," "justice for all," or an end to impunity. But it is nonetheless a phase in the struggle between universalist notions of justice, on the one hand, and international society conceptions of international order based on sovereignty, on the other. In other words, the ICC is not "the end of history" (to borrow Francis Fukuyama's memorable phrase) in international criminal justice.

This chapter will attempt to analyze the political dynamics and implications for the international society of the ICC. There are four aspects of the ICC with important political/strategic ramifications that will be addressed here. These are (1) the framework of the ICC—the importance of the consensual nature of the establishment of the Court and the implications thereby for the institution's legitimacy, and the "balance of power" between the Court and the sovereign states that are parties to its statute as expressed in the "complementarity" of the Court's jurisdiction; (2) the United States' opposition to the ICC; (3) the political and legal ramifications of the as-yet undefined crime of aggression in the Rome Statute of the ICC; and (4) Africa and the ICC.

FROM NUREMBERG TO ROME

As the Nuremberg and Tokyo trials wound down in the late 1940s and the Genocide Convention was adopted in 1948, the outlines of the cold war were already clear in the division of Germany into East and West. The establishment of a standing international criminal court, a longstanding aspiration even in the 1950s and what many would have considered a natural outcome of the Nuremberg and Tokyo trials, inevitably fell hostage to the global strategic politics of the times. There was initial enthusiasm for the idea of a permanent international criminal court. It was one of the first questions taken up by the International Law Commission (ILC) of the United Nations, a group of eminent jurists elected in their individual capacities and charged with the task of developing and codifying international law, when the Commission was set up in 1947. The Commission was divided on the question, but ultimately voted by large majorities that the establishment of such a court was both desirable and possible. It adopted a Draft Code of Offences against the Peace and Security of Mankind in 1954, but the UN General Assembly had by then transferred the question of a permanent court to enforce the Code to a committee of experts, the Committee on International Criminal Jurisdiction. The Committee met in Geneva in August 1951 and prepared a first draft of the statute for such a court by the end of its meeting.[1] But the political debates of the day had already crept into this effort. There were divergent interpretations of the criminality of apartheid, the legality of the threat or use of nuclear weapons, and the use of force by states in the context of defining crimes against peace.[2]

Thus the heady euphoria inspired by Nuremberg and Tokyo was short-lived. The reason was that, with the exception of France (the only power that supported the creation of such a court), the great powers did not want to establish a standing international court before which defendants from all nations, including theirs, could be held impartially to account for violations of international humanitarian law.[3] This absence of political will was evident in the argument that three practical requirements for such a court—a clearly defined set of crimes, jurisdiction, and arrangements for enforcement—could not realistically be achieved at once, and going ahead to create a standing court without these elements would ultimately do international law more harm than good.[4] Thus Britain, the Soviet Union, and the United States rejected arguments advanced by Ricardo Alfaro, the rapporteur of the ILC, in favor of a permanent international criminal court.[5] But it was not just the great powers, anxious to protect their prerogatives, who opposed the court's creation. There were other states that were against the idea on more philosophical grounds. Brazil and Poland were to be counted here.

Brazil was not persuaded that the Nuremberg and Tokyo tribunals, being coercive impositions on conquered states, were evidence of the practicability of international criminal justice. Poland argued that giving an international penal tribunal competence to punish the international crimes would violate the sovereignty of states. The hope of universalists for a supranational judicial authority that would adjudicate crimes that offended the conscience of mankind went into abeyance in the United Nations. It was to be revived a full 40 years later.

As the cold war thawed in the late 1980s and relations warmed between the communist Eastern and capitalist Western bloc of states, reopening the consideration of the question of such a court became a distinct possibility. In 1989, Trinidad and Tobago and a group of fellow Caribbean states in the UN General Assembly proposed that the International Law Commission reopen consideration of an international criminal court. But the impetus for their request was a desire for a court that would try narcotic drug traffickers who posed a serious threat to the Caribbean states. It is interesting, then, that drug trafficking ended up not being included in the Rome Statute. Rather, the focus returned to violations of international humanitarian law.[6] Other geopolitical events such as the 1991 Gulf War against Iraq and the creation of the ICTY led some of the great powers to revisit their earlier assumptions about a standing international criminal court.

In 1994, the ILC completed a draft statute for the court and submitted it to the General Assembly. The Assembly established a Preparatory Committee on the Establishment of an International Criminal Court in 1995, with all member states of the United Nations as members. The Committee had the task of reviewing the ILC Draft Statute of 1994 and preparing the text of a convention for a court for consideration of a conference of plenipotentiaries. Over the next 3 years the Committee worked hard to prepare a treaty that would command wide acceptance among states leading up to the diplomatic conference.

A UN diplomatic conference was held in Rome from June 15 to July 17, 1998. It was much more than a normal diplomatic event, drawing hundreds of civil society organizations in addition to 160 states and numerous international organizations. A palpable sense of history was in the air. Five weeks of frenetic negotiations later, the Rome Statute of the International Criminal Court was adopted after 120 states voted to create what has been optimistically described as "the last great international institution of the twentieth century."[7] Seven states voted against the Rome Statute, with twenty-one others abstaining. Among the dissenting states was the United States, which was an active participant throughout the negotiations and drafting process. Although the vote was not recorded, China, India, Iraq, Israel, Libya, Qatar, and Yemen are believed to have voted against the court's creation.

The success of Rome and the establishment of the ICC more generally can be attributed mainly to a coalition of states known as the "like-minded" group of about sixty states that included most of the European states. The role of civil society organizations was also a major contributory factor. Expectations of a drawn out ratification process, one in which attaining the minimum threshold of sixty ratifications would take several years, were ultimately confounded. The ICC treaty was ratified by sixty-six states by April 2002 and went into operation in July 2002.[8] Although the momentum of ratifications has slowed, as of this writing 100 states had ratified the Rome Statute—roughly one half of all member states of the UN. Of these, twenty-seven are African states, twelve are Asian, fifteen Eastern European states, twenty-one states in the Latin American and Caribbean region, and twenty-five Western European and other states.

THE POLITICAL FRAMEWORK OF THE ICC

The ICC is the product of a major ideological or conceptual battle in international relations between visions of cosmopolitan world society and those of international society that favor interstate cooperation, but one predicated on sovereignty. Both sides have claimed victory, but the institution in its current form is a compromise from that battle. This is the most important point of departure in assessing the ICC. A serious assessment cannot ignore this level of analysis—that of the realm of struggle between opposing normative visions in international relations.

That this battle is real and was present in the minds of protagonists is evident in the exultant and optimistic commentary of the cosmopolitan group, the more muted wariness of the advocates of an international order in which sovereignty remains ascendant, and the determined opposition of the United States for which sovereignty is nothing short of sacrosanct. ICC supporters such as Antonio Cassese expect it to become "the central pillar in the world community for upholding the fundamental dictates of humanity."[9] Leila Nadya Sadat adopts the metaphor of "revolution" and "counter-revolution" to describe the deep significance of the Court and the opposition to it. She admits that, despite the conceptual and potential practical shift the ICC represents, many aspects of the Rome Statute "reflect the constraints of classical international law that did not yield to the forces of innovation and revolution at Rome."[10] Observing the unsurprising nature of this fact, Sadat also agrees that "if state sovereignty (and particularly its expression as nationalism) is often blamed for the violent conduct of world affairs, international governance is not necessarily looked upon as a superior alternative."[11]

One concurs with this observation, which leads me to clarify my view on the ICC before proceeding further. First, the ICC is an important institution in international affairs. It has the potential to fill the gap left by the reality that although credible national prosecutions are to be preferred to top-down, international approaches, in some cases national jurisdictions are unable or unwilling to investigate or prosecute mass atrocities. Second, the ICC's potential value should not result in a failure to see the political nature of the court (which is the purpose of this chapter to demonstrate). Third, the establishment of the ICC is an important advance for the cosmopolitan conception of international justice, although as Sadat accepts, that worldview did not ultimately prevail in Rome to the extent its advocates had hoped. This is a *political* reality, and from it flows another—that some proponents of the ICC see the institution as a prelude of sorts to a world government. This would be an unhealthy outcome, for the concept of a world government, while it appeals to utopians, is one that enjoys little consensus and requires a type of centralization of police powers that poses its own unique dangers of dictatorship.[12] This is why the most essential aspect of the ICC framework is the fact that it will *complement*, not supplant, the jurisdiction of states. How this will work out in practice remains to be seen, but the likely implication is that the universalist vision and cosmopolitan ambition of some of the court's proponents will be circumscribed by the nature of the international society.

At the Rome conference and the negotiations that preceded it states were keen to avoid extensive intrusions into their sovereignty, although transnational civil society lobbied for an outcome in which the court would have jurisdictional primacy over states parties. The defining reality of the ICC is well summed up by Spyros Economides: "What was supposed to be a major departure from the traditional conduct of international relations was colored by that very same method of conducting international relations."[13] Thus states constructed a regime that denied the ICC enforcement powers to compel states to cooperate with the court's requests for judicial cooperation and assistance.

Under the complementarity principle, the ICC cannot accept jurisdiction over a case that it is being investigated or prosecuted by the state on whose territory the crime occurred unless that state is "unwilling or unable to genuinely carry out the investigation or prosecution," or where the state with jurisdiction has investigated the case and decides not to prosecute, unless the decision stems from an unwillingness or inability to prosecute.[14] In determining unwillingness on the part of a state, however, the ICC will consider whether the national proceedings are designed to shield the person from the ICC's jurisdiction, there has been a kind of delay that indicates the absence of intent to bring the concerned person to justice, or the national proceedings were not independent or impartial.[15]

The ICC is thus essentially a substitute for national jurisdiction. It is a centralized institution that rests on the foundations of decentralized power in the international society, unlike the UN ad hoc tribunals, and thus is a contradiction in terms. Despite the apparent victory the court's creation represents for the solidarist or universalist worldview, at the heart of the ICC lies the paradox that it was created to render human justice in a world of states, on which the court will depend to a very large degree. It will not be free from their influence. One way in which that control will be exercised is the Assembly of States Parties that has ratified the Rome Statute. This is the organ that elects the judges, the prosecutor, and the registrar of the court, approves its budget, and generally has something of an institutional oversight and policy role in the same manner in which the UN Security Council is the political parent of the ad hoc international tribunals for Rwanda and the former Yugoslavia. Another potential source of political influence will be countries that are not party to the Rome Treaty, particularly the United States. Through their absence these countries will deny the court the universality it seeks by limiting its reach.

Maintaining its independence as a judicial institution while keeping the states parties that are its political masters happy, and pushing the limits of how states and intrastate entities define their strategic interests vis-à-vis the court's mandate, will require a balancing act. It is noteworthy that the prosecutor of the ICC is inclined to pursue violations of international humanitarian law from a much wider perspective than the existing UN and other ad hoc tribunals. The prosecutor will investigate financial transactions that are linked to crimes; for example, the purchase of arms that are used to commit mass atrocities may well be crucial to establishing criminal responsibilities.[16] This is often one aspect of international crimes that is defined *out* of the quest to end impunity, for the merchants and economic benefactors of the global weapons trade are frequently the very states that most loudly profess their commitment to peace, justice, and the rule of law. To illustrate, let us say that state X has a weapons manufacturing and trading conglomerate that employs thousands of people. It supplies weapons for the prosecution of a conflict in, say, Africa or Asia. Massive violations of humanitarian law are committed in this conflict, and Government X has signed on to the ICC. Present in this scenario are power, diplomacy, money, and crass existential realities combined. How does the ICC proceed to investigate this situation?

The court's prosecutor has a number of options: (1) He could take discrete diplomatic steps to obtain jurisdiction, such as receiving a referral from a state party, the Security Council, or a submission from a nonstate entity, in which some aspects of the "situation" (such as the linkage between atrocities and the arms sales by state X) are implicitly excluded from the purview of investigations, which would be limited to the acts of one or more parties to the conflict; (2) He could proceed in a more radical fashion, commencing an investigation on his own initiative, including the arms sales, which would draw an angry response from (powerful) state X and yield unpleasant practical consequences of any number of permutations.

This dilemma can only be addressed by ensuring that it is the "criminals," and not their supporters and structures that feel threatened. The roots of the problem are left unaddressed and the "fight against impunity" continues as other "criminals" take the place vacated by the ones sanctioned with international prosecutions. In a sea of conflicting interests, the ICC must seek its own interests, and institutional survival and strengthening will be among them. For these reasons, the ICC will be a court where the weak states in the international society will supply the defendants. Those states, however, do not have a monopoly either on the use of force or on violations of international humanitarian law. But I will return to this point later.

The complementarity provisions of the Rome Statute include an explicit emphasis in its preamble that "the International Criminal Court established under this statute shall be complementary to national criminal jurisdictions." They are the most important in a framework that ripples with a constant tension between universalism and sovereignty, resulting in a court with *international*, but not *universal* jurisdiction. That a universal cosmopolitan justice is the Court's ultimate goal is explicitly clear from a policy statement by the Court's president, the Canadian judge Phillipe Kirsch, who prior to his election to that position was the Chairman of the Preparatory Commission on the ICC established after the adoption of the Rome Statute. "Universal ratification of the Rome Statute," Judge Kirsch said, "remains an essential long-term objective of the Court. Universality is necessary to establish a truly global reach in the fight against impunity."[17]

The "balance of power" between the ICC and sovereign states is a delicate one that came out just about right. A court in whose architecture the prosecutor's initiative was completely yoked to the political whims of states would not have advanced the cause of enforcing the rights of individuals against the genocides, crimes against humanity, and war crimes by which those rights are frequently violated. A carefully calibrated prosecutorial independence, with embedded checks, is essential for any international criminal tribunal. This balance, at least in theory (how things will work out in practice remain to be seen), was achieved in the Rome Statute. First, the complementarity principle is not defined in the Rome Statute. Whereas in the ad hoc international criminals for the former Yugoslavia and Rwanda the states have concurrent jurisdiction with the international tribunals but the latter have primacy, in the ICC it is clear that the ICC's jurisdiction is subsidiary. Yet, the Rome Statute gives the ICC the power to make a determination of inadmissibility of a case before it where a state asserts its national jurisdiction.[18] This is an important qualification to a state's ability to assert its jurisdiction, for the determination of how genuine or valid a state's judicial process is in each case is to be made by the ICC, not the national authority.

Moreover, the ICC has wide political or policy discretion in considering what cases to pursue. Complementarity has substantive (the subordination of the ICC's role to national courts), procedural (the Rome Statute's provisions on admissibility of cases), and "political" or "prudential" components (policy choices about what kinds of cases should be heard by the ICC, rather than national courts).[19] The Rome treaty in its preamble made clear that the ICC will deal with "the most serious crimes of concern to the international community as a whole." This test will thus be a factor that comes into play. But the Rome Statute admits of the thoroughly political context of international criminal justice and allows for a political analysis, by implication, in Article fifty-three, which deals with the initiation of an investigation. That provision requires the ICC prosecutor, in deciding whether to initiate an investigation, to consider whether the information available to the prosecutor provides a reasonable basis to believe that a crime within the Court's jurisdiction has been or is being committed; the case is or would be admissible under Article 17; and, taking into account the gravity of the crime and the interest of victims, there are nonetheless substantial reasons to believe that an investigation would not serve the interests of justice.

In practice, an examination of those interests will include a "situation analysis" of political issues such as the existence and implications of peace negotiations and processes, the potential political/military destabilization that a prosecution by the Court might engender, and whether or not a truth and reconciliation commission exists, is envisaged, and might better address the situation.[20] While it is of course important to be professional and impartial, the ICC is keenly aware that it is operating in international and national political contexts, and so must gather and analyze information that is essentially political.[21] It is also worth noting that the interests of victims and the political possibilities mentioned above may occasionally converge. This might be especially so where the payment of substantial reparations to victims is part of this mix.

Second, built into the Rome Statue is a tripartite system of balances between the ICC prosecutor, its judges, and the Security Council in the initiation or continuation of investigations. The Rome Statute empowers the ICC prosecutor to initiate investigations at his own instance on the basis of information on crimes within the Court's jurisdiction.[22] But such an investigation must be authorized by a three-judge pretrial panel, which will review the request for authorization and the supporting material that accompanies it, and grant or deny authorization to the prosecutor to commence an investigation.[23] This provision supplies the checks and balances that assuaged the fears of both the human rights community during the negotiations of the Statute that the process might yield an impotent prosecutor controlled completely by the Security Council, and several states that feared a rampaging prosecutor and wanted to see his prerogatives filtered through some form of judicial control. For the human rights community and the like-minded group, this independence of the prosecutor, textured though it ultimately was, was their bottom line in the negotiations.

The United States, on the other hand was adamantly opposed to a prosecutor with the power to initiate prosecutions without Security Council approval. This will be discussed in the section on the United States and the ICC. In practice, it is unlikely that the pretrial panel of judges will prevent the initiation of an investigation by the chief prosecutor absent solid reasons to do so. In the ICTY and ICTR, charges preferred by the chief prosecutor have to be confirmed by a single judge and there have been very few instances where that initiative was fettered by a refusal to confirm. But, given the wider geography covered by the ICC, a hands-off approach by the authorizing panel cannot be taken for granted.

It may be for these reasons that ICC chief prosecutor Luis Moreno Ocampo of Argentina has tactically opted for now to follow another path to taking on cases, that of the referral by a state party to the Rome Statute.[24] The exception is Sudan, where the situation in Darfur was referred to the court by the UN Security Council. This is a safe route that puts more conservative forces at ease by placing the burden of requesting an international judicial process on sovereign states. There is no requirement that the requesting state should be that in which the crimes referred occurred, although this would normally be the case. I will examine possible political motivations behind referrals when I discuss Africa and the ICC.

The Security Council, charged as it is with responsibility for international peace and security in the UN Charter, could not logically be absent from the ICC's framework. The Council can also refer a situation in which one or more of the relevant crimes have occurred to the Court under Chapter VII of the UN Charter.[25] In that case the principle of universal jurisdiction is applicable because there are no geographical limits to the Council's remit. Perhaps even more important from a political standpoint, the Security Council can request a deferral of the commencement of an investigation by the ICC with a resolution to that effect adopted under its peace enforcement powers in Chapter VII of the UN Charter.[26] And in that case the investigation or prosecution must be deferred for 12 months, with the request renewable under the same conditions.

Few things are more indicative of the political stakes in the ICC than this provision. The provision for Security Council power to request a suspension of proceedings (the Rome Statute does not say how many times such a request can be renewed) is the "Singapore compromise" between the members of the Council that wanted a stronger role for it and states that believed it was important to preserve some distance between the Court and the UN although an institutional link between the two organizations was recognized as helpful for the ICC.[27] Britain's agreement to this compromise proposal was critical to its adoption in the Rome Statute. China and France were also strongly opposed to the extent of the prosecutor's powers. India wanted the Court statute to include a ban on nuclear weapons, and Sri Lanka wanted the inclusion of terrorism as one of the core crimes. Many Arab countries (with the exception of Egypt, an American ally) opposed the very creation of the Court, fearing it would serve Western agendas.[28] It is doubtful that subsequent events in Iraq gave them any reason to alter their positions. But if a court could not be avoided, they wanted one that would serve *their* interests: creating a loophole to attack Israel's occupation policies in the West Bank and Gaza. And, notably, most Asian states were and have remained skeptical of the ICC. They remain the region with the lowest ratio of ratification of the Rome treaty.

The ICC's strongest attribute is that, unlike the international criminal tribunals for the former Yugoslavia and Rwanda, it was the direct outcome of a treaty negotiated and agreed between sovereign states. To that extent, its democratic legitimacy cannot be seriously questioned. As we have seen, those states have maintained their primacy in the distribution of competences between them and the Court. But they have, at the same time, created an institution that bridges an important gap in the normative architecture of international law. To the extent they have given up a bit of sovereignty in the process, it is by mutual consent, and no one can legitimately quarrel with that.

This democratic legitimacy runs into problems only to the extent that the Rome Statute seeks to confer on the Court jurisdiction over states not parties to the statute or which have not otherwise accepted its jurisdiction—a matter that will be discussed in greater detail later. One cannot agree, then, with Leila Sadat's caveat to the Statute's legitimacy. She argues that to the extent the Rome conference was a "quasi-legislative mechanism by which the international community 'legislated' by non-unanimous vote, the political legitimacy of the norm rests not on any classic theory of contract between absolute sovereigns (treaty-making) but on some other grounds." These "other grounds" should have been specified. Unanimity has never been the basis for democratic legitimacy, neither in any liberal democracy nor in any international multilateral organization. Majorities or a broad consensus are what count. To that extent, the Rome conference was a democratic process, barring the caveats I have noted regarding the extent of the court's jurisdiction. Just as concerns exist about "imperial overstretch" by the great powers, so is it appropriate to caution against what could be termed "universalist overreach" by the ICC.

One important fact that diminishes the legitimacy of the ICC, and ultimately its effectiveness in achieving its stated aim of internalizing human rights norms in states, is its centralization at The Hague.[29] The "legitimacy deficit" imposed by the distance and insularity of top-down models of international criminal jurisdiction is one whose consequences have been analyzed by this writer as well as others.[30] Thus the suggestion that the ICC's legitimacy and relevance would have benefited from a decentralized structure, while recognizing the need for the court, is well founded.[31]

We can now turn to the political, diplomatic, and legal battle that has largely defined the ICC, that of its relationship, or the lack of one, with the United States, the sole superpower in the world today.

THE UNITED STATES AND THE ICC

All we need from the United States is benign neglect. Is that asking for too much?

International Criminal Court official, *The Economist*

Official policy in the United States toward the establishment of an *independent*, permanent international penal tribunal has always been at best ambivalent and at most, as now, that of visceral opposition. The reasons for this are not hard to see. Several lawyers and diplomats who work or have worked for the executive arm of the U.S. government have carefully considered the pros and cons of U.S. participation in such a court, seeking assurances that will protect American strategic interests. They were generally supportive of the Court if the necessary safeguards for their national interest were obtained. But often, that level of engagement is disconnected from the less informed "main street USA" in which a majority of politicians are reflexively opposed to subjecting U.S. citizens to such a sensitive act of international governance as international criminal justice under *any* circumstances. And, on such major matters of national interest at least, it is these elected political leaders, not the diplomats who negotiate on America's behalf, who influence the foreign policy decisions of the President of the United States who has constitutional responsibility for foreign relations. The story of the United States' active engagement in the ICC process leading up to the Rome Conference, where it faced a humbling diplomatic defeat, is not the objective of this section. Rather, I intend to undertake a brief review and analysis of the reasons why the United States voted against the Rome treaty and the various political and legal steps it has taken in that context.

To begin with, the fundamental ambivalence I have referred to is evident in the fact that the kind of court the United States wanted was precisely the kind that a majority of other states did not—an *explicitly* politically controlled one. This ambivalence and eventual opposition is rooted in an attitude of historical exceptionalism, a fundamental commitment to its sovereignty, and a view of international law that flows from that worldview. How the last two factors are *interpreted*—a matter of style, if not of substance—largely depends on which American political party occupies the White House at any given time. But a significant pointer to the reality that the interpretation of U.S. attitudes to international law is more a matter of style (or rhetoric) than substance is the fact that in recent years foreign policy and military actions which are controversial in international law have been taken by Democratic and Republican presidents—the NATO bombing of Kosovo in 1999 and the invasion of Iraq in 2003 are the most famous examples. Both military interventions were undertaken in the course of "upholding our values."[32] Similarly, there has been more or less bipartisan consistency of opposition to U.S. participation in an independent ICC under Presidents Bill Clinton and George W. Bush.

To understand the U.S. position on the ICC at a normative level it is helpful to refer to Robert Jackson's discussion of "national responsibility" as one of four traditions in theories of international relations.[33] According to Jackson, the national responsibility is one in which values such as national self-interest, national security, and national welfare are the guiding lights of state action. The normative basis of this approach is that the state—however formed—is prior to any international associations it may form or join, and its citizens can have a prior claim to defining the responsibilities of their national leaders, who are actually their servants: "According to that domestic-focused way of thinking, international law and international organization are instrumental arrangements which are justified by how well they serve the national interests of states. This is the thinking that inclines many Americans to believe that their laws always trump international law when they come in conflict...."[34]

As Jackson explains, this idea of national responsibility is rooted in classical realism, which is nevertheless based on values and value judgment—contrary to much conventional thinking, one might add. But the values on which the idea of national responsibility is based are certainly not those of liberal internationalism. Jackson argues that "National responsibility is an authentic morality, however, and should not be confused with narrow self-interest. Realism as classically understood is an ethical theory: it conceives of the state as a moral community; it involves defending the national interest, which is a moral idea. The national interest is one of the most important justifications of pluralist world politics, perhaps the most important...."[35]

Similarly, Jason Ralph has illuminated the basis of American opposition to the ICC, this time from the perspective of the cultural dimensions of the country's democracy. The cultural value of that method of governance, by which the United States was born, also defines in the eyes of Americans who they are, and has led it to be distrustful of any institution that threatens to subject the country's actions to the decisions of foreign judges in ways that are not controllable by Washington. The fundamental reason for this policy position is that the United States interprets the internationalization of democracy as the idea of an international society of democratic (sovereign) states, and not that of a world society without borders represented by an independent prosecutor for the ICC.[36]

Against this backdrop, we can now proceed to examine—and perhaps better understand—the "clash of the titans" in the politics of the International Criminal Court. As the Rome Conference drew to an end, David Scheffer, then U.S. Ambassador at Large for War Crimes Issues and head of the American delegation, rose and made a final intervention. He was clearly faced with a looming defeat for the key U.S. proposals for an amendment of the draft statute before the vote. "I deeply regret, Mr. Chairman," Scheffer said, "that we face the end of this Conference and the past 4 years of work with such profound misgivings and objections as we have today," and noted that the Rome Statute would create "a court that we and others warned of in the opening days—strong on paper but weak in reality."[37] He proposed an amendment that would effectively place U.S. troops beyond the Court's jurisdiction, but the United States lost the vote 113 to 17, with 25 abstentions.[38]

Despite its disagreements with the Rome Statute, the Clinton administration continued negotiations in the Preparatory Commission established after the Rome Conference, hoping to obtain concessions that would make U.S. participation in the Court possible. By mid-2000, however, its efforts became complicated by a piece of draft legislation in the U.S. Congress that rendered the possibility of U.S. participation a lost cause. The "American Servicemembers Protection Act," popularly known as the "Hague Invasion Act" was introduced by Senator Jesse Helms (Republican—North Carolina) in the U.S. Senate on May 10, 2001, and introduced in the House of Representatives by Representative Tom Delay (Republican—Texas) the same day. Adopted by Congress and signed into law by President Bush on August 2, 2002, the legislation prohibits cooperation with the ICC, the exercise of jurisdiction by the Court over U.S. citizens and "Allied Persons," and the provision of U.S. military aid to any country that has ratified the ICC Treaty, but exempted NATO countries and key non-NATO American Allies.[39] It required the UN Security Council to grant immunity from prosecution by the ICC to American personnel in UN peacekeeping operations. Most dramatically, it authorized the U.S. president to "use all means necessary and appropriate" (a phrase that encompasses the use of force) to obtain the release of members of the U.S. armed forces detained or imprisoned by or on behalf of the ICC.

The Clinton administration had signed the Rome Statute just before leaving office in December 2000 but announced that the treaty would not be submitted to the Senate for ratification.[40] The Bush administration subsequently "unsigned" the treaty by a letter to UN Secretary-General on May 6, 2002, nullifying the earlier U.S. signature.[41] These measures were followed up by a diplomatic campaign to sign bilateral agreements with individual states exempting U.S. citizens from the possibility of ICC prosecution for crimes committed on their territories.[42] As of this writing, the United States has signed Bilateral Immunity Agreements (BIAs), dubbed "bilateral impunity agreements" by critics, with 100 countries. These agreements have been signed in the context of Article 98(2) of the Rome Statue. Article 98(2) provides that the ICC cannot request for surrender or assistance which would require the requested state to act inconsistently with its treaty obligations to a third state. It was included in the Rome Statute at American insistence. Among the 100 states that have signed bilateral immunity agreements, several are from the developing world, heavily dependent on U.S. aid, and those among them that are candidates for future membership of NATO were threatened with shaky prospects for their candidacy should they fail to sign on the dotted line.[43]

Even traditional Western allies have not been immune from U.S. pressure. Although the United States has not as of this writing concluded a bilateral immunity agreement with Britain, it emerged from proceedings in the British House of Lords, where Lord Wallace of Saltaire raised the question in 2002, that the matter had indeed been discussed between the two allies. Lord Wallace pointedly asked whether the British intended to sign a BIA with the United States on the jurisdiction of the ICC. Baroness Symons of Vernham Dean, Minister of Trade, confirmed that "preliminary discussions" had taken place, but that the government would ensure that any agreement that emerges will be consistent with Britain's obligations under the Rome Statute.[44] She justified the discussions on the basis of a perceived need to keep the United States engaged in international peacekeeping operations. Canada and the Netherlands, on the other hand, reportedly rebuffed American pressure to sign similar agreements.[45] In October 2004 in Iraq, the dichotomy of Britain's position on the ICC and that of the United States came into sharp focus when British forces were temporarily deployed to an American sector in Basra to fight under American command. British critics opposed the arrangement partly out of a belief that it exposed their troops to possible investigation by the ICC in a scenario where they were accused of war crimes for acts done under American military command.

U.S. diplomats have noted, in defense of the pressure they have applied on other countries to signed Article 98 agreements, that countries in Europe that were recently admitted into the European Union declined to sign the agreements precisely because they faced a similar threat to their candidacies for EU membership by the Union's older members.[46] This, in other words, is a *tu quoque* defense.

In the UN Security Council the U.S. government threatened to shut down UN peacekeeping missions by vetoing their renewal if U.S. troops were not granted immunity by the Council. It backed up its threats by vetoing the renewal of a UN peacekeeping operation in Bosnia–Herzegovina on June 30, 2002, overriding opposition from the European Union, NATO, and the Bosnian government.[47] Kofi Annan sent a letter to U.S. Secretary of State Colin Powell criticizing the U.S. demands as a threat to the legitimacy of the Security Council that "flies in the face of international treaty law." In short order, the European parliament adopted a resolution in which it "deeply deplored" the U.S. veto, noted that the "Hague Invasion Act" went well beyond the exercise of the U.S.'s sovereign right not to participate in the ICC, and noted that the legislation denied the U.S. itself the very military intelligence and cooperation it needed to fight terrorism.[48]

Nevertheless, on July 12, following two weeks on debate, the Council balked in the face of U.S. demands and adopted resolution 1422 (2002) that granted immunity to U.S. members of UN peacekeeping missions and those of other nonstate parties to the ICC for 12 months. Legalism had precipitated, yet again, tensions between cosmopolitan notions of justice and international order. It was certainly possible that the closure of the UN mission, or the possible unraveling of other peace operations as a result of the double standards in liability of peacekeepers from different countries to criminal prosecution, could have led to renewed conflict in these conflict zones. In a trenchant criticism of resolution 1422, Kai Ambos, a German participant in the negotiations of the Rome Statute, commented on its anomalous nature:

> In light of the Council's resolution, the [ICC] becomes itself a threat to peace, because only under this condition can the Security Council adopt a resolution under Chapter VII of the UN Charter. Let us pause to assess this truly grotesque logic: a resolution as it was adopted by the Security Council on July 12th presupposes that the ICC must be labelled as a threat to the peace, which can only be averted by granting immunity before the Court![49]

When the United States sought a renewal of the immunity upon the expiry of its 12-month time frame in 2003, it ran into the determined opposition of several members of the Security Council and Secretary-General Annan.[50] "Blanket exemption is wrong," Annan wrote. "It is of dubious judicial value, and I don't think it should be encouraged by the Council."[51] For the states that were wavering once again in the face American pressure, Annan's letter was a welcome intervention that tipped their views firmly into opposition mode. The letter was also one instance of a clear departure from the epiphenomenal status that realists grant to international institutions. With the Secretary-General having gone on record on the legality of the exemptions, it is doubtful that the members of the Security Council would have liked to be caught on the wrong side of the law as it were. It is a demonstration as well of the limits of power in its relation to international law and how the latter feeds back to international relations.

Meanwhile, China was threatening to veto the renewal resolution, and more than forty countries requested a public debate on it. A major scandal had erupted in this period as abuses of Iraqi prisoners by U.S. troops in Baghdad's Abu Ghraib prison were revealed, further undercutting U.S. ability to sway the debate. China pointedly noted that it could not support a resolution that could shield U.S. troops from culpability for abuses such as those at Abu Ghraib.[52] Faced with the backlash from Iraq, China's opposition, and that of Annan, the United States withdrew the draft resolution. Of China's opposition, U.S. officials noted that the Asian power, which had similarly voted against the ICC treaty and had previously supported U.S. efforts to limit its reach, was really engaged in brinksmanship on other issues. "They don't care about the ICC," one diplomat reportedly said. "It all has to do with Taiwan."[53] A solidarist international community? Not so. The divergent and shifting tendencies demonstrate the dominance of Hedley

Bull's concept of an anarchical society, one in which the cosmopolitan and realist perspectives coexist in a state of constant friction.

I now turn to other substantive bases for U.S. opposition to the ICC's jurisdiction. The Rome Statute provides that when a person commits a crime under the statute, the state where the crime was committed *or* the state of nationality of the offender would have to assent to the trial of the offender by the ICC.[54] This means that the court can prosecute a national of a state not party to the Rome Treaty, where the offender is a national of the nonstate party but the state on whose territory the crimes is committed gives its consent to prosecution by the court. Scheffer had attempted to change this provision to require the agreement of the state of territorial state *and* that of the nationality of the defendant, but failed. This is the most important reason why the United States is adamantly opposed to the ICC, for the American position is that it cannot allow its citizens to be prosecuted by an international tribunal under a treaty to which it is not a party. Interestingly, the United States has agreements with the Hague and Arusha tribunals that allow for the surrender of U.S. citizens as well as those of other countries from that country.

U.S. resistance to the ICC's jurisdiction stands on two legs. One is political, the other legal. Its overall political response is that of the peculiarity of the U.S. role in the international order. Given U.S. troop deployments in various trouble spots around the world and its position as the lone superpower, the U.S. position is that American troops offer a tempting target for malicious, politically motivated prosecution by the ICC. American troops are deployed in about 140 countries, mostly in Europe and Asia. Because America shoulders unequal responsibility, its argument is that it should not be liable to equal accountability. Despite the arguments put forward by supporters of the court—the remote prospect of an American being indicted by the Court, and the option of relying on the complementarity principle to try its own national in that scenario—the U.S. remains unmoved. America's distrust of the good faith of other nations is understandable, because its role in world politics has earned it deep resentment in some quarters. And there are those who oppose America simply on ideological grounds. These foes would exploit any loophole to embarrass or humiliate it. As of mid-2004 more than 100 complaints had been filed at the ICC against Americans.[55] In a telling point, *The Christian Science Monitor*, justifying U.S. wariness of the ICC, wrote: ". . . the chief prosecutor, Luis Moreno-Ocampo, wants to go after corporate officials who do business with nations that have committed mass atrocities."[56] This is another classic illustration of the anarchical nature of the international society and the self-interest that motivates its members. The *Monitor* editorial is a pointer to a national interest in shielding the amoral activities of some corporations from international scrutiny. It is all the more telling coming from a newspaper that has long espoused liberal ideals at home and abroad.

Let us now examine six politico-legal reasons for U.S. opposition to the ICC. First, if U.S. determination to put its nationals beyond the reach of the ICC on the basis of political inequality before the law is unacceptable to many, the *legal* basis for its position, dispassionately examined, is on rather solid ground. The United States maintains that the exercising of jurisdiction over its nationals by the ICC would violate the international law principle that a treaty cannot bind a state that is not a party to it without that state's consent.[57] This rule of customary international law is codified in Article 34 of the Vienna Convention on the Law of Treaties.[58] While the United States is not a party to this Convention, it can find justification in the customary law norm. Although this position is opposed by some commentators[59] on the basis of the well-known principle that a state has jurisdiction over crimes committed on its territory regardless of the offender's nationality, the U.S. position is well founded for the following reasons. First, a multilateral treaty is a democratic process of international society. It is profoundly undemocratic to seek to bind by a treaty agreed by mutual consent of states one that has chosen *not* to be party to such a treaty. Second, the principle of territorial jurisdiction of a state would be applicable if that state chose to try an offender under its domestic laws. The United States does not dispute this legal fact of life.[60] But that is not the case here. The Rome Statute empowers parties to it to hand over to an *international* court a national of a nonstate party for trial over a *treaty*-based crime. The U.S. position hinges on this subtle but fundamental point. It argues that absent state consent or a UN Security Council mandate, an international organization to which it does not belong, has no such legal powers. This position would hold true not just for the United States, but for any other nonstate party as well. The ICC provision in question is an attempt to import into the Court's remit the controversial doctrine of universal jurisdiction. Of course, in the international society, in which dispersed power is a fact of life, this universalist overreach has greater implications for international order in the case of United States, which is better placed to rebuff such an intrusion on its sovereignty than a weaker nation. But the ICC statute is on weak ground here all the same.

It has been argued that "defenders of this position have attempted to analogize the establishment of the court to the creation of a mechanism to settle inter-state disputes," and that the argument confuses the concepts of state responsibility and individual responsibility.[61] This very argument itself is a somewhat limp one, for the exercise of treaty-making power by a state does not depend on whether the subjects of that treaty are states or individuals. The bottom line is that treaties are entered into by states in the exercise of their sovereignty, which encompasses their citizens. Individuals do not make treaties in international law. Thus, we can see that Article 12 of the Rome Statute clashes with a standing principle in international law and to that extent cannot bind a nonstate party.

The second reason for the U.S. antagonism toward the ICC is simply because, as noted earlier, it wanted a political court dominated by the Security Council, where the United States would be reassured by the comfort of its veto power. It did not achieve this outcome, though the political constraints on the Court as it was actually established, made to assuage U.S. anxieties, are obvious. Put simply, the United States does not wish to be bound by externally enforced international law on issues that involve the use of force. This position is reinforced by America's view of its national identity, based in turn on what Paul Kahn has described as "its myth of popular sovereignty."[62] From this perspective the prosecution of *one* American soldier would be one too many. As Scheffer told a journalist in the hallways of the Rome Conference, "bland assurances of the unlikelihood of any given outcome simply don't move the mail back where I come from."[63] Scheffer was evidently committed to the ICC project, but his hands were tied by the domestic political reality in his country. The conservative Senator Jesse Helms, who headed the U.S. Senate Foreign Relations Committee that handles treaty ratification, had warned that absent a complete U.S. veto over what cases the Court would take up, the Rome Statute would be 'dead on arrival' at the U.S. Senate if it is submitted for ratification.[64]

A third U.S. objection was that a 10-year "opt-out" clause was not included in the Rome Statute, whereby a state party can opt out of the Court's jurisdiction for war crimes and crimes against humanity. The United States made this proposal because it is more likely to be accused of war crimes and crimes against humanity, as an active military power, than the crime of genocide. An obvious reason for this position, other than the U.S. strategic design to create a court weak enough to conform to its national interest, is that of the significant differences between America's "forward-leaning" war-fighting doctrines in relation to international humanitarian law, and those of several other countries.[65] One example of this divergence in doctrines of military necessary is American military doctrine regarding the targeting of electrical power systems during a war.[66] U.S. military doctrine considers the bombardment of national power systems an essential component of an effective military engagement. But this kind of military activity effectively targets civilian populations, an "unspoken but known result" of such bombardment.[67] This is the concept of collateral damage—civilian deaths as an unavoidable consequence of war. In the modern world in which armies no longer charge at each other across expansive open fields, but powerful states bomb their adversaries from high altitudes with "precision bombs" that are not always so precise, debate rages about the necessity and proportionality of this kind of targeting.

That civilians should not be military targets is a well-accepted notion in customary international law. Yet the bombing of electrical power grids was systematically utilized in the 1991 Gulf War. The argument for bombing electric grids is that they are potent sources of support for the armies of the adversary. But the humanitarian perspective is that bombing electrical grids usually has a greater impact on civilian life and population than on military objectives. In other words, collateral damage is so severe that such military activity could amount to a direct targeting of civilians. This dilemma of war is captured when, say, an American bomber pilot about to drop a precision bomb in this age of virtual warfare and "embedded" journalists, and looking at his presumed target on the monitor of his cockpit, brags: "I've got the target on my nose." Meanwhile, the pictures of the destruction his bombing has wrought as shown in graphic detail on our television sets are not what would be called military targets. Rather, the images are frequently ones of civilian casualties in hospital wards.

Protocol I Additional to the 1949 Geneva Conventions, which codified the nature of noncombatant immunity, provides that civilian populations as well as individual civilians should not be the object of attack and that acts or threats of violence, the primary purpose of which is to spread terror among the civilian population, are prohibited.[68] Even more to the point of the present discussion, the Protocol has offered a clear definition of what would amount to indiscriminate attacks, including: "Those which may be expected to cause incidental loss of civilian life, injury to civilians, damage to civilian objects, or a combination thereof, which would be excessive in relation to the concrete and direct military advantage anticipated."[69]

The United States has not ratified Protocol I, citing "fundamental and irreconcilable flaws."[70] U.S. military manuals in international law adopt language that is similar and sometimes identical to Protocol I.[71] The United States was a major influence behind the formulation of Protocol I and signed it on the first day it was opened for signature. But the Reagan administration subsequently received internal advice that the Protocol was inimical to U.S. strategic interests and declined to forward it to the Senate for consent and ratification.[72] An important reason for the U.S. position on Protocol I is that in customary international law the primary duty to protect the civilian populace rests with the defending nation, and not with the attacking one, which has a secondary duty.[73] The U.S. views Protocol I as seeking to shift that burden to the attacker, irrespective of the defending nation's actions.[74] Even weak states violate the laws of armed conflict, particularly when faced with superior firepower in a "David versus Goliath" situation, by using civilians as human shields. In such cases civilians, including women and children, are placed in the direct path of weaponry and at military installations in order to increase the numbers of civilian casualties and score propaganda points. This was the case, for example, in Iraq during the U.S. invasion of that country in 2003.

Some commentators have found the U.S. rejection of the ICC on the basis of its non-inclusion of a 10-year opt-out clause for war crimes *and* crimes against humanity puzzling, because the Rome Statute includes a 7-year opt-out clause in relation to war crimes.[75] But if the U.S. delegation in Rome believed that, while the prospect of its committing genocide is remote, it could very well be accused of crimes against humanity, it was not far off the mark. The prisoner abuse scandal at the Abu Ghraib prison in Iraq triggered impassioned debates about whether the treatment of Iraqi prisoners was tantamount to torture (a crime against humanity in the Rome Statute[76]). This is a classic example of U.S. actions over which international humanitarian law could implicate the superpower (Iraq is not, however, a party to the ICC treaty). At the least, the acts of sensory deprivation and the photographing of nude prisoners with U.S. troops in menacing positions over them could be interpreted as "inhumane acts intentionally causing great suffering or serious injury to body or to mental and physical health"—a crime against humanity under the Rome Statute.[77] Seen from this perspective, the U.S. position and its self-interested motivation become clearer. One problem with the U.S. proposal in Rome was that, from the standpoint of an effective and workable treaty, the position is a self-defeating one, for it would apply not just to the United States, but to all other parties to the Statute. A law from whose jurisdiction (or large parts thereof) its subjects can opt out for prolonged periods is obviously one of very limited effectiveness.

Fourth, the United States also rejected the Rome Statute because it includes the crime of aggression as one of the core crimes over which the Court has jurisdiction. This crime, however, has not yet been defined, and jurisdiction will commence if agreement is reached by state parties to the Rome Statute at a review conference to be convened 7 years after the Rome Statute entered into force.[78] Aggression will be more substantively reviewed in a moment, but the point here is to note the basis of U.S. opposition to its inclusion: that aggression is a matter that ought to dwell within the purview of the UN Security Council and not the ICC. The world's preeminent military power, and the basis on which it undertakes the use of force, should not, in its own view, be subjected to the judgment of the rest of the international society. One man's "just war" could be "aggression" in the definition of another. The U.S. preemptive invasion of Iraq in 2003 is the illustration of why the inclusion of aggression in the Rome Statute would be problematic for the United States If the U.S. response to the inclusion of aggression was predictable, perhaps more intriguing is its rejection of the Rome treaty because it includes provisions that countenance a possible future expansion of the crimes within its remit to include terrorism and drug trafficking[79]— a fifth reason for its rejection of the Rome treaty. The explicit desire to bring the crimes within the ambit of the ICC is spelt out in the Final Act of the Rome Conference that adopted the Rome Statute.[80] The impetus for a political decision to reconsider the Statute in the future in this context of drug trafficking arose from the fact that the initiative of the Caribbean states which led to the creation of the ICC was motivated by a desire to create an international framework of accountability to fight transnational drug trafficking. It was thus ironic that the Rome treaty developed in other directions and omitted this issue.

As for terrorism, the prospect of an international enforcement mechanism for this crime has roots going as far back as 1937, when the League of Nations adopted a convention against terrorism and prepared a draft statute for an international criminal tribunal.[81] India was the only country that ratified the convention, which never became law. The U.S. opposition to the ICC because it might conceivably acquire jurisdiction over terrorism is contradictory. The terrorist attack on the United States on September 11, 2001, has turned the conflict between extremist political Islam and the West into an existential one. There are a number of international treaties, based on a limited form of universal jurisdiction, and several of them actively promoted by the United States, that are aimed at fighting terrorism.[82] Although these treaties permit states to prosecute or extradite offenders, the reality is that the judicial systems of several state parties are simply too weak to cope with the political and security pressures that accompany these kinds of criminal trials. This point becomes even more germane when we consider the terrorist bombings of U.S. embassies in Kenya and Tanzania in 1998, and terrorist bombings in other countries in recent years. Henry Kissinger has aptly observed: "Terror has no fixed address; it has attacked from Bali to Singapore, Riyadh, Istanbul, Moscow, Madrid, Tunis, New York and Washington."[83] The United States alone and by itself, would find if difficult, if not impossible, to win the "war on terror." Its military power notwithstanding, the limitations of that power and its intelligence capabilities have become painfully apparent in recent years in light of 9/11 and the situation in Iraq. This reality, then, suggests the need for an international framework of legal accountability for these transnational crimes in addition to national ones. If ever there was a type of crime deserving the jurisdiction of an international penal tribunal, it is that of terrorist crimes.

Finally, the United States has argued that it cannot join the ICC because the Rome Statute prohibits reservations. There is no legal requirement in international law that a treaty must provide for reservations, but the provision is unusual when viewed in light of practice. As Sadat and Carden have observed, perhaps a more interesting question is why this was done.[84] Clearly, the states parties believed that, especially given the delicate compromises that had already been made between national jurisdiction, international jurisdiction by the Court, and the role of the Security Council, allowing reservations to the Rome Statute would have simply rendered the Court stillborn. And they were right, in this writer's view. The statute includes a provision whereby a state party to it can withdraw—which safeguards the element of freedom of association for any party.

Was the bar to reservations a sufficiently weighty reason to justify U.S. nonparticipation? The question is academic, as the United States has the sovereign right to choose what international institutions it may or may not join. A detailed discussion of international law regarding reservations to treaties is beyond the scope of this work. Suffice to note that reservations are a complex matter, and the International Court of Justice, in the *Reservations to the Genocide Convention* case,[85] stipulated that reservations must be consistent with a treaty purpose. Knowing what is known about the U.S. position on the ICC, it would be unrealistic to contemplate a U.S. reservation that would have been in conformity with the purpose of the Court.

To conclude this review of the United States and the International Criminal Court, the six main reasons why the United States wants no part of the ICC in a sense amount to one: the United States, while espousing the rule of law abroad, does not wish to see its military power and strategic scope for maneuver fettered by that notion and does not want to suffer the "indignity" of seeing its service personnel being tried in an international court. It supports ad hoc international criminal justice by special courts and tribunals on an ad hoc basis, but is fundamentally opposed to the cosmopolitan aspirations of a standing court with global reach. For better or worse, that decision is well within its rights as a sovereign state. In the frequently emotional tenor of the ICC debate this fact is frequently forgotten.

There are those who wistfully believe that this situation exists because President George Bush is widely seen as distrustful of international institutions. But it should not be forgotten that America's positions were staked out at the Rome negotiations during the presidency of William Jefferson Clinton who had earlier lent his voice at the UN General Assembly in 1997 in the hope that the world would one day have a permanent International Criminal Court. Even as his government signed the Rome treaty just before he left office, it appeared as if the signature was appended more to justify years of efforts expended by the U.S. negotiating team, led by the dedicated David Scheffer, than for any other reason. Even had the signature not been subsequently "unsigned" by President Bush, the treaty would have been one of several others that the United States had signed without ratifying. The chances that *any* U.S. government will join the ICC are bleak. The story demonstrates once again the strength of the international society approach toward international war crimes justice. That approach looks at how states actually behave, not only at what they say or how we wish them to act.

Going a bit further along what states actually do, a clear majority within the society of states *decided* to establish the ICC in its current form over U.S. objections. That is also a significant development in international relations. It demonstrated that, subject to the protection of their sovereignty through the complementarity principle, those states share a value of international cooperation for international justice through a mechanism that the United States did not. The key to the defeat of the U.S. position in Rome was the united front of the European states, several of who have positioned themselves in world politics as champions of human rights and liberal justice and have greater experience with supranational human rights oversight.

These states project military power in the international realm mostly in the context of consensually agreed peacekeeping operations, and rarely in a unilateral manner.[86] This is a reflection of the "soft power" of those states compared to the "hard power" of the United States. Clearly, the United States overrated its own power in relation to the court, believing during the Rome negotiations that a court without U.S. participation in terms of political muscle and financing was doomed to failure. There is no evidence that this will be the case—that the Court will go the way of the League of Nations. Should the ICC fail, it will more probably be attributable more to a failure by its states parties to live up to their obligations in the area of judicial cooperation with the Court than to America's absence from the Court.

AGGRESSION

> Aggression is remarkable because it is the only crime that states can commit against other states: everything else is, as it were, a misdemeanour.
>
> Michael Walzer, *Just and Unjust Wars*

Aggression was unquestionably the most controversial topic at the Rome Conference. This is no surprise. Attempts to subject to judicial parameters the most political, sovereignty-laden question in international relations—the use of force by states—has always generated tensions.

The crime of aggression was included in the Rome Statute at the tail end of the Rome Conference. It was written into the treaty at the insistence of the European Union and about thirty nations that are members of the Non-Aligned Movement.[87] The European nations supported it because, as noted earlier, their foreign policy in the twenty-first century has relied more on "soft power" than on "hard power." Britain is an exception, considering its active military engagements in the Falklands, the 1991 Gulf War, and the 2003 Iraq War. The states of the Non-Aligned Movement saw its inclusion as a means to equalize the international juridical playing field between weak and powerful states. Several NGOs, including the Lawyers Committee for Human Rights and the American Bar Association, opposed adding aggression to the list of core crimes with the ICC's remit while others were in favor. The strength of differences of opinion was such that agreement could not be reached on the meaning of aggression within the five-week Rome Conference, and the matter was considered best postponed to the future.

The International Military Tribunal at Nuremberg was the first international tribunal to try individuals for the crime of waging aggressive war, described in the Nuremberg Charter as "crimes against peace." The irony is that it was the American chief prosecutor Robert Jackson that insisted on criminalizing aggression at Nuremberg. But this was possible largely because the Nuremberg Tribunal was a victor's court. Between then and now, agreement on the definition of the crime of aggression, let alone a *prosecution*, has been fraught with difficulty. Aggression was the center-piece of the Nuremberg Trials, for it was Hitler's aggressive wars against his neighbors that led to World War II. Jackson pushed for that legal strategy at negotiations before the trials began and sought an expansive definition of the crime, while Soviet chief prosecutor Ion Nikitchenko argued for a more restrictive definition.[88]

The Nuremberg Charter defined crimes against peace as "namely plan-ning, preparation, initiation or waging of a war of aggression, or a war in violation of international treaties, agreements or assurances, or partic-ipation in a common plan or conspiracy" to accomplish these aims.[89] At Nuremberg, defendants had been deemed leaders or accomplices with per-sonal knowledge of a plan for aggression and active participation in planning or waging aggressive war before they could be convicted.[90] For the first time, making war—an act of state—was criminalized and individuals deemed to constitute the policy-making organs of a state and its military high command were held individually accountable for what the Nuremberg judgment char-acterized as "the supreme international crime." But the precise meaning of "aggression" or "aggressive war" was not elucidated either by the Nurem-berg Charter or by the judgment of the IMT.[91] A slight definitional advance was made at the U.S.-conducted war crimes trials that followed the IMT trial and were prosecuted by the American attorney and later by the law professor Telford Taylor. Those trials were based both in the Nuremberg Charter and the Control Council Law No. 10, of which the latter included *invasions* as a crime against peace.[92]

In 1974 the UN General Assembly finally arrived at a definition of aggression by consensus—remarkable, considering that the cold war still dominated international politics at the time. General Assembly resolution 3314 defined aggression as "the use of armed forces by a state against the sovereignty, territorial integrity or political independence of another state, or in any other manner inconsistent with the Charter of the United Nations, as set out in this definition."[93] It then listed various acts of aggression that were prohibited, including armed invasions or attacks, military occupations or annexations, military bombardments and blockades, and the use by one state of mercenary troops against another state.[94] The resolution stipulated that a determination of whether aggression had been committed in a given case would depend on "all the circumstances of each particular case." A final decision would be made by the Security Council, which had primary responsibility for international peace and security under the UN Charter.

While this definition represented significant progress in the quest for clarity, the limitations of General Assembly resolution 3314 are (1) it was considered more as a political guidance to the Security Council than as a legal basis for judicial prosecutions; (2) the definition was spelt out by a

General Assembly resolution and so does not have the binding force of law; and (3) the definition is a state-centric one, fails to address individual responsibility in acts of aggression, and thus was a step back from the Nuremberg and Tokyo judgments.[95] Moreover it appears that the evolution of the contemporary international society, when *individuals* can hire mercenaries to overthrow governments by force of arms or wage war against states, was not envisaged in this definition.

What realistic hope, then, can we have that the ICC will be able to define—let alone punish—aggression? Aggression is a highly political crime, and sanctions or other enforcement action in response to it appears far more possible in the political context of the UN Security Council or individual or collective self-defense than in a judicial forum like the ICC. This is so in spite of the effort to "lift the veil" of statehood and hold to account the individuals responsible for aggressive war. True, the argument is a good one that resolution 3314 provides a reasonable basis to begin the ICC's definitional quest because that resolution specifies the acts that constitute aggression.[96] Still, it does not address all the realities of current international politics or even the normative hurdles it has to scale.

Since 1945 the only act of aggression that the member states of the UN have been able to confront unanimously was Iraq's invasion of Kuwait. Several others have arguably been committed. And we have seen the fate of all the attempts to abolish war in the twentieth century, including the Kellogg-Briand Pact. The ICC will not effectively advance its cause, moral or institutional, by squandering its political capital on the pursuit of a resolution of the age-old question of aggression. As the Lawyer's Committee for Human Rights has argued, focusing the court's jurisdiction in its early years would garner it far more credibility.[97] Moreover, individuals who plan and launch aggressive wars invariably commit other crimes within the Rome Statute for which they can be brought to justice. Saddam Hussein of Iraq provides an excellent illustration of this point. It should also be noted that there is no definition of aggression in customary international law, and aggression has never been the subject of a multilateral treaty, a requirement that the International Law Commission suggested for crimes over which the ICC could assert jurisdiction.[98] The relationship between the ICC and the Security Council would have to be worked out before aggression can be defined by the Court.

That aggression is a high crime is not disputed. That it should be "punished" is not questioned. The real question is *how*? The political philosopher Michael Walzer, who has argued strongly for the punishment of aggression, recognizes that a military repulsion of aggression is a prerequisite to the possibility of punishment.[99] As noted earlier, this is relatively easy when the aggressor state is a weak one, and stronger states can defeat its ambitions should they choose to do so. Even that is a big if: Political will is a vital ingredient for such a response, and that depends on political interest. This suggests the inevitability of the specter of victor's justice, which is the basis on which the Nuremberg Tribunal was able to try the Nazis for aggression. Even Walzer, the moral philosopher that he is, recognizes the complex realities of international society in relation to aggression.[100] Although he recognizes the rights of individuals in that society, he nevertheless realizes that aggression, which in his view is the only justification there can be for war, can best be dealt with by a military response. That response, which he terms "resistance," is first and foremost the duty of the victim of aggression, but there is a parallel obligation on the part of other states to come to the victim's defense—collective self-defense, from which Kuwait benefited in 1991 in the face of Iraqi aggression. Secondly, Walzer posits that a way must be found to punish aggressor *states*, although individuals are almost always responsible for aggression, and concedes that whether it is the state, or particular individuals that should be punished is a difficult question to answer. Thirdly, he recognizes *imminent* aggression as a crime, and thus, by analogy, preemptive war can be justified where the imminence of danger is real, immediate, and present. This, of course, is the rub: defining what constitutes imminent aggression that can justify preemptive war. Walzer offers that "The boastful ranting to which political leaders are often prone isn't in itself threatening; 'injury' must be offered in some material sense as well. Nor does the kind of military preparation that is a feature of the classic arms race count as a threat unless it violates some tacitly agreed-upon limit. What lawyers call 'hostile acts short of war,' even if these involve violence, are not too quickly to be taken as signs of an intent to make war. . . . Finally, provocations are not the same as threats."[101]

He then argues that "The line between legitimate and illegitimate first strikes is not going to be drawn at the point of imminent attack but at the point of sufficient threat. The phrase is necessarily vague. I mean it to cover three things: a manifest intent to injure, a degree of active participation that makes that intent a positive danger, and a general situation in which waiting, or doing anything other than fighting, greatly magnifies the risk."[102]

Walzer wrote nearly 30 years ago—presciently, as it were, but with no more effective solutions for the problems that face the international society today regarding aggression. With this in mind, and with the "war on terror," the situation in the Middle East, and other international trends, it would be surprising if the states parties of the ICC were to agree in the future on a definition of, *and prosecute*, aggression. The inherent tension between a necessary role for the Security Council, which is a political body, and the perspective of a judicial institution such as the ICC will be extremely difficult to resolve. Agreement on adding terrorism and drug trafficking would be a more likely compromise.

AFRICA AND THE ICC

Africa is important for the ICC. And the ICC is important for Africa. Africa is important for the ICC not because it has a monopoly of mass atrocities—Asia, Latin America, and Europe have such situations as well—but because it happens to have some of the weakest states in the international society. Asia has the smallest number of ratifications of the Rome Statute by region. Next to Africa, Europe has the highest—in the full knowledge that the likelihood of European defendants at the ICC is slim. Asia, although a developing region, is economically more independent than Africa and is thus better able to resist the hegemonic pressures that the ICC represents.

But the ICC also represents an opportunity for Africa. It is possible that African states could utilize the ICC to develop the rule of law in the continent. This could be a logical consequence of the democratization process that began in the 1990s, although regional judicial institutions, decentralization, or regionalization of the ICC's structure would have been better placed to perform this role. As of this writing the ICC has received two referrals from two African states, Uganda and the Democratic Republic of Congo, and one referral by the Security Council in relation to the crimes in Darfur, Sudan.

In the DRC, individuals who are part of the current transitional government of President Joseph Kabila are under investigation for violations of international humanitarian law. To demonstrate the court's effectiveness in a speedy manner, the prosecutor of the ICC is believed to have indicated his interest in the recent conflict in that country and encouraged a referral to him of a "situation." The referral originally covered the Ituri region where mass atrocities occurred in 2002 and resulted in the intervention of a peacekeeping force formed by a number of European countries. However, the referral was subsequently expanded to cover the whole country. In March 2006, the ICC arrested Thomas Lupanga, leader of the Union of Congolese Patriots, one the armed groups in the country. Charged with the war crime of enlisting children under the age of 15 years as child soldiers and using them in hostilities, Lupanga is the first person to be arrested and transferred to The Hague on the basis of a warrant of arrest issued by the ICC.

In Uganda, President Yoweri Museveni adroitly sought to turn the tables on the Lords Resistance Army (LRA), a rebel movement that has fought the Ugandan government for more than a decade in Northern Uganda, by referring a case against the group to the ICC, giving the ICC its very first case. But the involvement of the ICC has generated internal tensions in Uganda.[103] An amnesty process is favored by the citizens and local civil society groups, who fear that ICC investigations could provoke renewed military attacks in civilians by the LRA. The people of Northern Uganda appear to want peace at any price and deeply resent the ICC investigations, which they view as a confluence of an opportunistic maneuver by President Museveni and the ICC's need to justify its existence by taking on the first case that was referred to it. This raises the question of whether, given the requirement of the ICC prosecutor to weigh the need and impact of prosecutions in particular, this approach is actually "in the interest of justice."[104]

Moreover, there are concerns that the court will investigate only the LRA and sidestep the government, whose Ugandan Peoples Defence Forces are similarly suspected of committing atrocities. The ICC will be under pressure to investigate these alleged crimes as well, but may either find them not of sufficient gravity for a prosecution by the ICC prosecutor, or Uganda is likely to assert the complementarity principle and claim primary jurisdiction. In the latter case the Ugandan authorities would be justified, as it cannot reasonably be argued that Uganda's national judicial system has collapsed and it is nonfunctional or otherwise unable to undertake such prosecutions.[105] On the other hand, defenders of the Uganda ICC referral argue that it has in fact helped bring the conflict closer to solution by isolating the LRA, influencing Sudan to cut off its support for the rebel army, and forced the rebels to seek a negotiated settlement of the conflict.[106]

The most controversial test case for the ICC in Africa is undoubtedly that of prosecuting war crimes committed in Darfur, Sudan. The conflict in that region between the Arab Janjaweed militia, supported by the central Sudanese government in Khartom and black Africa rebel groups, has resulted in the deaths of 200,000 people and nearly 2 million refugees. Out of this anarchical response of the international society, which wrangled over whether the crimes in Darfur constitute genocide, consensus emerged that the instigators of the crimes in Darfur should face trial. But even that consensus soon became hostage to disagreement and almost disintegrated. Debate ensued over the options for a trial of Darfur atrocities. European states insisted on giving jurisdiction for such trials to the International Criminal Court through a Security Council referral,[107] as recommended by the UN's Commission of Inquiry, while the United States (in light of its opposition to the ICC) and the African Union proposed a UN-financed African ad hoc tribunal to be based in Arusha, Tanzania, where the UN war crimes tribunal for Rwanda was already based.[108] The United States was unable to muster enough support for its preferred option and the Council ultimately voted in favor of the ICC option, but not without inserting a clause exempting American personnel from the Court's jurisdiction.[109]

UN Security Council resolution 1593, adopted on March 31, 2005, and by which the Council referred the Darfur situation was referred to the ICC prosecutor, was adopted with eleven out of the fifteen members of the Council in favor, none against, and four abstentions—Algeria, Brazil, China, and the United States. The United States would almost certainly have vetoed the resolution if it did not contain a jurisdictional exemption clause for its nationals. Not surprisingly, Sudan made a strong statement against the resolution, but could not prevent it. Sudan's ambassador to the United Nations, Elfatih Mohamed Ahmed Erwa, pointed out the contradiction inherent in the Council granting exemption from jurisdiction to states that were not parties to the Rome Statute while Sudan itself was not a party to the statute. The resolution, he said, did not settle the question of accountability in

Darfur, but 'exposed the fact that the ICC was intended for developing and weak countries and was a tool to exercise cultural superiority.'[110] He condemned the Council's failure to consider the African position on the forum for a trial of the war crimes in Darfur, including a Nigerian proposal that the trials should be conducted in an African country by a continental court or an international tribunal sitting in the continent.

Other contradictions include the major one that the diplomatic and political muscle of the United States, a country that has strongly opposed the ICC, will be necessary if the ICC is ever going to bring the perpetrators of the massacres in Darfur to justice.[111] It is indicative of a certain shift in the U.S. position on the ICC—from that of a total objection to it and having nothing to do with the institution to one of mutual coexistence provided Americans are exempt from its jurisdiction—that the U.S. sponsored, 1 year later, another resolution by the Security Council that imposed sanctions on four individuals suspected of leadership roles in the atrocities in Darfur.[112]

This resolution from which China, Russia, and the Arab state of Qatar abstained on various grounds, including that it would have a negative effect on peace talks that were taking place in the Nigerian capital of Abuja at the time (the United States argued that the targeted sanctions would actually strengthen the political/diplomatic process), appears to be a certain prelude to future war crimes trials of these individuals at the ICC. This position of the United States had as much to do with the groundswell of domestic pressure it was under from the American public to do something about the killings in Darfur as it might have with a moralistic abhorrence of the ethnic cleansing in Darfur, on which Washington has consistently been more outspoken that other regions of the international society.

The International Criminal Court, then, is as much a political as a legal institution. The process of its creation was one in which politics and law played a role. It was an exercise in plenipotentiary treaty-making by the political and diplomatic representatives of states, and, as we have seen, all parties were fully aware that their decisions and negotiating positions had political implications. It is precisely because of those implications that the United States and some other states have opted not to join the Court. But the delegates also argued their positions on the basis of international law, demonstrating the impact of international norms on international politics.[113] On balance, though, politics clearly prevailed. This should surprise no one, for virtually all law is indeed political insofar as it comes into being through political acts aimed at ordering national or international society.

From the outset the ICC has become as much a political symbol as a legal one. Insofar as the United States will not join the Court in the foreseeable future, it is indicative of a deeply divergent view of world politics—and its legalization—between Europe, on the one hand, and America, China, and other non-ICC states on the other. And typical of the nature of the international society, even between the United States and China, which are both nonmembers of the international court, a divergence has emerged in their respective approaches to the carnage in Sudan, with critics accusing China of being guided by its economic interests in Sudan.[114] The government in Khartoum, pressured by the global spotlight on the crimes committed in Darfur by its proxies and soldiers, has sought to exploit the complementarity provision of the Rome Statute and thus block cooperation with the court's investigations by creating special Sudanese courts ostensibly aimed at prosecuting the persons responsible for the massacres.[115] This effort is likely to be judged a halfhearted one actually designed to shield the real suspects from prosecution by the ICC, and it is an open question whether the diplomatic efforts to resolve the Darfur conflict on the ground will lead the ICC prosecutor Luis Moreno Ocampo to conclude that prosecutions for crimes in Darfur are *not* in the interests of justice.

The universalist aspirations of the ICC, though, will not be realized, stymied as it will be by the international society's anarchical nature. The fact that the United States and a number of states in war zones—Iraq, for instance—are not members of the ICC has important implications for the Court's potential reach. One of those is that national or mixed national–international tribunals, and even on the odd occasion the pure Yugoslavia- or Rwanda-type tribunals directly created by the UN Security Council, will be used in future in such places.

And, despite the arguments for such a court in the international society's architecture, it's centralization in The Hague will deny it of an important component of legitimacy—psychological proximity and impact on the societies its work hopes to affect—as seen from the experience of the UN ad hoc tribunals for Yugoslavia and Rwanda. That a number of states have passed domestic legislation to place their laws in line with the Rome Statute is not the same as internalizing human rights norms. The latter outcome has much to do with the socialization of norms outside legal circles, such as in domestic politics, and is best achieved in the context of physical interaction, and even more so by domestic rather than international jurisdiction.

At the very least the ICC should have some form of regional branches in Africa, Asia, and Latin America, with a preponderance of judges from those regions sitting on each regional court and with The Hague as its European headquarters or a type of appellate chamber. It is often forgotten that Nuremberg, hallowed as it is in the minds of many human rights activists, achieved political impact in Germany largely because it sat in that country amid the ruins of war, and even then its impact was not immediate but took a generation to ossify.

The ICC is also hegemonic to the extent it will affect the internal sovereign choices of political communities, despite complementarity. Whether this is good or bad I cannot be certain. It is perhaps too early to say which way that principle will turn out. Madeline Morris is on strong ground when she observes: "Because of the array of overlapping but also divergent interests at stake, the meaning of the ICC's complementarity with national courts is neither obvious nor inconsequential."[116] The weak states for which the ICC will have hegemonic outcomes have allowed those outcomes by their inability to put their house in order, and so, of course, an outside influence will necessarily step into the breach, with consequences that are not automatic one way or another. The situation in Northern Uganda, where the ICC appears to be intent on prosecutions in the face of a clear alternative preference by the domestic community, is cause to be wary.

In conclusion, while the ICC fills a certain gap that would have been better plugged by domestic societies, it is important not to have expectations of the institution that would be unrealistic, such as that it will wipe out man's inhumanity to man. It will investigate, prosecute, and punish *some* warlords, which would be a function common to all criminal law. But it will not end wars or evil.

Iraq: Chronicle of a Trial Foretold

I am Saddam Hussein, the president of Iraq
—Saddam Hussein at his trial

VISIONS OF JUSTICE

Long before the American invasion of Iraq in 2003, before the occupation and the fruitless search for weapons of mass destruction (WMD), visions of the trial of Saddam Hussein had possessed several Western leaders. Prophetically, the prediction was made by George Herbert Walker Bush, the forty-first president of the United States whose son, George W., would a decade later become the forty-third president.[1] Iraq's invasion of neighboring Kuwait in 1990 was the trigger. That aggression by Iraq resulted in international military intervention by a U.S.-led coalition that was sanctioned by the UN Security Council and ultimately defeated Iraq and liberated Kuwait in early 1991.

In 1990 Saddam, president of Iraq, also took hundreds of citizens of Western and other states hostage. The United Nations Secretary-General Javier Perez de Cuellar dispatched Kofi Annan, then the financial controller of the world body, on a diplomatic mission to negotiate their release. Other Western leaders mooted the idea of putting Saddam on trial whenever the Gulf War to liberate Kuwait was over. Margaret Thatcher, the prime minister of Great Britain, was, in fact, the first world leader to have broached the subject in a television interview she gave on September 1, 1990.[2] In all cases, these leaders invoked the Nuremberg precedent.

In early 1991, news that Iraqi troops had massacred Kurds in northern Iraq, gassing them with chemical weapons, provoked international outrage that led the German foreign minister, Hans Dietrich Genscher, to propose the establishment of an international court to try the Iraqi leader at a meeting of the European Commission. His proposal was strongly supported by his colleagues in the European Council of Ministers. The Council sent a letter to de Cuellar asking him to "examine the question of the personal responsibility of the Iraqi leaders in the tragedy that is unfolding, in particular on the basis of the Convention against Genocide, and the possibility of trying them before an international court."[3]

While the UN Secretary-General responded to the European proposal with some interest, it was not followed through. The hard-fought but ultimately successful effort to build a coalition in the UN to defeat Saddam Hussein and liberate Iraq from the occupation of Iraqi forces took center stage. The Gulf War, which began on January 17, 1991, after Iraq missed a UN Security Council deadline to withdraw from Kuwait, ended on February 28, 1991. President Bush and Lt. General Colin Powell, the then chairman of the U.S. Joint Chiefs of Staff, made a tactical decision not to undertake "regime change" in Iraq in the wake of the Iraqis' surrender. With Saddam left in power, though defeated, the prospect of putting him on trial was practically foreclosed. The Security Council then adopted resolution 687 on April 3, 1991, imposing obligations on Iraq to disarm and destroy its arsenal of chemical and biological weapons, and not to obtain or develop nuclear weapons. A system of weapons inspections was established by the Security Council to monitor Iraq's compliance with resolution 687, but ended in 1998 in the face of noncooperation by the Iraqi government.

Early in the presidency of Bush W., the terrorist attack of 9/11 against the United States fundamentally altered the American government's foreign and national security policy. The government adopted a policy of preemptive military strikes against high-risk enemies in the exercise of the right of self-defense. This policy was naturally controversial, as critics considered it at odds with the UN Charter. The Charter permits the use of force by a state under its Article 51, which states that nothing in the Charter "shall impair the inherent right of individual or collective self-defense if an armed attack occurs against a member of the United Nations." Was the doctrine of preemption envisaged in this provision? Or had the evolution of international society arrived at a point where a second look at Article 51 was needed? While the U.S. war against Afghanistan, which was the base of the Al Qaeda terrorist organization, was a response to an actual attack, the American government began to build a case that Iraq, specifically its leader, was a clear and present danger with plans to attack the United States with weapons of mass destruction and therefore deserved a preemptive military response.

The Bush administration took the position that it was not going to subject the national security of the United States to disputes of interpretation law by waiting for the country's enemies to attack it again.[4] With authorization for the use of force granted by Congress, the executive branch of the U.S. government, arguing that Saddam's Iraq was a clear and present danger, went ahead with its plans for the invasion of Iraq. In March 2003, Bush ordered the invasion of Iraq by U.S. troops, backed mostly by Britain. From the standpoint of international law, the question was whether the United States could lawfully invade Iraq without a resolution that explicitly permitted the use of force. The UN Security Council had in November 2002 unanimously adopted resolution 1441, which stated that Iraq "has been and remains in breach of its obligations under relevant resolutions, including resolution 687 (1991)." The resolution gave Iraq 30 days to comply with an enhanced inspection regime by declaring in full its biological, chemical, and nuclear weapons.

The International Atomic Energy Agency (IAEA) was to report failure to comply, on receipt of which report the Council would meet to "consider the situation and the need for full compliance with all the relevant Council resolutions." Resolution 1441 warned that Iraq "will face serious consequences as a result of its continued violations of its obligations." Subsequent reports by the head of the UN weapons inspectors, Hans Blix, and IAEA director-general Mohammed El-Baradei did not confirm that Iraq had the weapons in question, but the U.S. argued that its own intelligence operations reported the existence of such weapons.[5] Thus did America launch the invasion of Iraq. While several international lawyers argued that the United States needed a follow-up resolution to 1441 authorizing the use of force,[6] the coalition argued that authorization to use force was implicitly authorized in the "serious consequences" phrase in 1441, combined with earlier resolutions 678 and 687 and so no further resolution was needed.[7]

The Iraq War of 2003, like that of 1991, was a short war. Beginning on March 20, 2003, and ending on May 1 of the same year, it was only a week longer than the Gulf War. Saddam's forces were routed by the U.S.-led coalition, and the erstwhile dictator went into hiding as his troops surrendered and the United States established a Coalition Provisional Authority to govern Iraq as an Occupying Power. After several months on the run, Saddam was eventually captured by U.S. forces on December 13, 2003. The arguments about the legality or otherwise of the U.S. invasion of Iraq notwithstanding, the role of the U.S.-led coalition as an Occupying Power in Iraq under the Geneva Conventions and its power or that of bodies established by it to make laws (including the establishment of a war crimes tribunal to prosecute Saddam Hussein) are legal facts of life. Thus we can now turn to the main focus of this chapter—the mixture of politics, law, and strategy in the subsequent trial of Saddam Hussein.

FORUM SHOPPING: AN INTERNATIONAL OR NATIONAL TRIBUNAL?

The political leaders and international lawyers who in the early 1990s foreshadowed a war crimes trial of Saddam Hussein had in mind an international tribunal, established by treaty and made up of judges of various nationalities, for international crimes such as "crimes against peace and the security of mankind."[8] This scenario, however, envisaged problems such as the difficulty of physically bringing Saddam to justice (it was suggested, for example, that he could be tried in absentia—an option that would have been in violation of international human rights standards) and the political risks and technical difficulties negotiating a treaty could bring.[9] The imaginative forays of the Security Council into war crimes court creation for the Balkans and Rwanda were still a few years away.

As soon as those precedents were established, however, diplomats such as David Scheffer, senior advisor in the U.S. Mission to the United Nations and later U.S. ambassador at large for war crimes issues, spoke frequently about trying Saddam before a tribunal established by the UN Security Council. But in the 1990s, it was unlikely that the obstacles to getting agreement among the five major powers on the Council and getting hold of Saddam could have been surmounted.

Thus, when Saddam was captured by U.S. forces on December 13, 2003, 6 months after his army had been routed and his country occupied by U.S. and British forces, many observers expected that Saddam would be prosecuted by an international tribunal created by the United Nations. Although, in invading Iraq without a second resolution of the Security Council after resolution 1441, the war bitterly divided the UN, some observers hoped that a UN imprimatur on the Saddam trial would "legitimize" the war and the dictator's ouster. It was not to be. Whether the U.S.-led coalition, which insists it did not violate international law, believed it needed such a blessing is of course open to question.

There are several technical, political, and strategic reasons why the forum in which Saddam would be tried was a matter on which the United Nations, the Occupation Powers, and the newly emerging Iraqi leadership and Iraqis in general had strong positions. The most important of these factors was the death penalty. For Iraqis, there was no question of trying Saddam *without* a death penalty as the maximum sentence if he was convicted. The United States, which also has the death penalty provision in its statute books, was sympathetic to its use in this particular trial, although it had suspended capital punishment in Iraq while the Coalition Provisional Authority (CPA) ruled the country.[10] For the United Nations, Kofi Annan pronounced the world body's position in a number of media encounters that the UN would not sponsor or actively participate in a trial of Saddam that could hand down capital punishment.[11]

This was a matter of policy for the UN. The situation was in some ways a reenactment of the tension in the Security Council that accompanied its establishment of the International Criminal Tribunal for Rwanda in 1994. Rwanda, which has the death penalty in its domestic laws and had requested the Security Council to create an international court to prosecute the architects of the 1994 genocide in that country, wanted a tribunal that could mete out similar punishment.[12] The European states in the Council were opposed to the death penalty while the United States supported it. There was no question, from the European standpoint, of creating an international war crimes court with capital punishment. The Hague Tribunal for the former Yugoslavia did not have it, and no international war crimes tribunal created ever since—from the Special Court for Sierra Leone to the permanent International Criminal Court—has a death penalty provision. Life imprisonment is the maximum sentence these courts can hand down. With passions running high after the Rwandan genocide and a need to see its idea of justice prevail, Rwanda took the extreme step of voting against the Security Council resolution that established the international tribunal it had requested.[13] This was exactly how Iraqis felt about the death penalty for a brutal dictator who routinely dispensed death to anyone that opposed his rule.[14]

Leaving aside the death penalty debate, there are other reasons why it was appropriate—indeed necessary—to try Saddam Hussein in an Iraqi court, drawing on lessons from the Hague, Arusha, and Sierra Leone tribunals.[15] In the particular circumstances of Iraq, the best justice for Saddam was always going to be local justice administered by a court owned and run by Iraqis, but one that strove to meet minimum standards of fairness.

A UN tribunal, composed of international judges, even were it to have sat inside Iraq, would not have been the most appropriate forum for the trial of Saddam. This is not because international justice is bad or wrong. It is neither. But that approach ought not to be utilized simply for its own sake in circumstances where it would be counterproductive and better alternatives exist. War crimes trials are inherently imperfect. As we have seen from the trial of Slobodan Milosevic, the Rwanda genocide trials at Arusha, and the Sierra Leone Tribunal, UN-mandated courts are not immune from shortcomings.[16]

Certainly, these tribunals have made great strides as well, but the model of justice they represent has an important limitation that would have greatly diluted the impact of Saddam's trial were that model to have been adopted in any form. That fundamental weakness is the absence of local ownership of the inspiration or process of justice for crimes that have distorted the very fiber of a society. The citizens, though most affected by the crimes in question, would be standing on the outside looking in on the process. Although, as I will discuss in the conclusion to this work, there were good reasons why the tribunals for Yugoslavia and Rwanda had to be international efforts, this psychological distance from the judicial process of trials for crimes committed against them, their relatives and friends and society is what has happened to the people of the former Yugoslavia and Rwanda.[17]

The Iraqi judiciary is relatively weak and inexperienced from the perspective of international standards of judicial trials, for a robust judiciary in the kind of dictatorship that Saddam Hussein maintained in Iraq would be a contradiction in terms. The need for international assistance was thus acute, and we shall see below that there were valid concerns about fairness of the trials of Saddam Hussein and other Iraqi Ba'ath Party leaders. Nevertheless, it remains the case that the greatest historical impact of a trial of Saddam was only going to be achieved by one conducted by an Iraqi court, in Arabic (with simultaneous interpretation into English), under Iraqi laws and elements of international humanitarian law drafted into national legislation. The challenge for the international society, to the extent they are interested in such an outcome and did not feel absolutely compelled on grounds of principle or politics to avoid the trial, was to provide the support necessary for such an outcome. In an appraisal of the trial of Milosevic at The Hague, Gary Bass notes the absence of this kind of impact at a critical moment in which Milosevic was confronted in the courtroom with damning evidence supplied by one of his former subordinates. "It's a message that can only be put across in Serbian," Bass quotes a senior official of the Hague Tribunal as saying.[18]

Again, a mixed national–international court would not have worked well for the trial of Saddam. First, in practice there would be jostling behind the scenes for dominance by its "national" and "international" staff and judges. This would affect unity of purpose. Second, such a model would not necessarily guarantee Iraqi ownership of the process, if the experience of the Special Court for Sierra Leone, where there is a strong perception of "foreign" control, is any guide.

Against this backdrop, it is not surprising that on May 26, 2004, the coalition authorities, in the context of their role as an Occupying Power under the Geneva conventions, promulgated the statute of the Iraqi Special Tribunal for Crimes Against Humanity ("Iraqi Special Tribunal" or "IST"), a national war crimes tribunal to try Saddam Hussein and other erstwhile leaders of the Ba'ath Party. The Iraqi Special Tribunal has jurisdiction to try the crimes of genocide, crimes against humanity, war crimes, and violations of certain Iraqi laws listed in its statute.[19] Its temporal remit extends over crimes by any Iraqi national or resident committed between July 17, 1968 (when the Ba'ath Party came to power) and May 1, 2003, when the hostilities of the U.S.-led war officially ended. The crimes in question may have been committed in Iraq or elsewhere in connection with the Iraqi invasion of Kuwait in 1990 or its war with Iran from 1980 to 1988.[20]

The tribunal's investigative and trial judges, prosecutors, and chief administrator have to be Iraqis.[21] But its statute requires the tribunal's chief investigative judge to appoint foreign advisors or observers to provide investigative judges (who are separate from the trial judges) with technical advice on investigations and prosecutions and to monitor the observance of due process standards.[22] In appointing such advisors, the chief investigative judge can request assistance from the United Nations.[23] However, it is clear from the statute that the Iraqi tribunal will be run by Iraqis and there is no direct role for the UN.

THE TRIAL

Judge: "Are you Saddam Hussein?"
Defendant: "Yes, I am Saddam Hussein, president of Iraq."

The scene was a courtroom used by the Iraqi tribunal. Ironically, the venue was one of Saddam's former palaces, now converted to "Camp Victory," the American headquarters near the Baghdad airport. The date was July 1, 2004, and Saddam Hussein was making his initial appearance before the war crimes tribunal. He was charged with crimes against humanity. The charges against him included massacres of Kurdish Iraqis with chemical weapons in Halabja in 1988, the forced deportations and displacement of Kurds from Kirkuk and other areas during the "Anfal Campaign" from 1986 to 1988, killings of religious figures in Iraq since 1974, suppression of the 1991 Kurdish and Shiite uprisings (Saddam is a Sunni Iraqi), and the 1990 invasion of Kuwait.[24] The charges were to be prosecuted separately in subsequent mini-trials.

When the investigative judge read out Saddam's occupation as "former president of Iraq," another dialogue ensued:

Saddam Hussein: "President of Iraq, current, present, chosen by the people. Who are you?"
Judge: I will introduce myself in due course. I am the investigative judge of the Central Criminal Court."
Saddam: "Let me understand. What law formed this court?"
Judge: "This law was by the Coalition authority."
Saddam: "So you are an Iraqi who represents the Coalition forces?"
Judge: "No, I'm an Iraqi representing Iraq."
Saddam: "You should not work under a law enacted by what you call Coalition authorities. They are occupation authorities, invasion forces."

Like Milosevic at The Hague, Saddam Hussein questioned the legitimacy of the war crimes tribunal before he was arraigned, calling it a "theatre" set up to help the U.S. president win elections, and rejected the charges against him. Thus began the opening of what was to be a frequently chaotic trial of the former Iraqi dictator. A few days before the arraignment of Saddam, the Coalition forces had transferred sovereignty to an interim government of Iraq headed by Iyad Allawi, a medical doctor and former Iraqi exile in London. "Legal custody" of Saddam Hussein was also transferred to the interim government, although American troops continued to guard the former Iraqi leader.

Saddam Hussein was not accompanied by any lawyer and refused to sign papers indicating that he had been read his rights. His lawyers began to serve notice in the media that he could not possibly get a fair hearing because their client was denied legal representation at his preliminary hearing and had been ousted by "an illegitimate invasion."[25] Meanwhile, soon after the arraignment of Saddam, but before his substantive trial, the interim government reinstated the death penalty in Iraq.

The actual trial of Saddam was still more than a year away, to begin in late 2005. But a number of teething problems dogged the trial process. Some of those problems were technical, such as the matter of not availing the defendant of a defense lawyer at his initial appearance before the tribunal. The other main technical problem the Saddam trial faced was the Iraqi judges' lack of familiarity with international humanitarian law.[26] Although they were well versed in Iraqi law, the real resonance of the trial of Saddam Hussein, although taking place in an Iraqi court, lies in the serial violations of international humanitarian law of which he stands accused. This situation led to substantial delays before the substantive trial could begin, as the Iraqi judges received training from their counterparts in Britain and America on subjects ranging from plea-bargaining to witness protection and prioritizing prosecutions.[27]

American support for the tribunal, including investigations and the collection and collation of evidence of war crimes in Iraq was directed by Pierre-Richard Prosper, the U.S. ambassador for war crimes issues from 2001 to 2005. In an indication that even international judges in UN war crimes tribunals were not in a much better position that the Iraqi judges when they began war crimes trials at the Hague Tribunal, Gabrielle Kirk McDonald, a former judge at the Hague Tribunal, reassured the Iraqis: "Ten years ago, we were exactly where you were, starting a tribunal with no experience," she said. "You'll design your own court as you want it."[28]

Other problems had to do with shortcomings in the Iraqi tribunal statute in addition to its death penalty provision. The standard of proof required for conviction was not "beyond reasonable doubt," and it appeared that it was technically possible that confessions obtained through coercion could be used as evidence in the tribunal. For all these reasons,

Western human rights organizations have declined to support the tribunal. Most notably, organizations such as Human Rights Watch refused to turn over to the Iraqi tribunal witness statements it obtained from victims of Saddam Hussein's oppression while preparing for the trial of the ousted leader—no doubt because they had hoped he would be tried by an international court, or at least by a court that would not have the death penalty.

This decision on noncooperation with the Iraqi tribunal was made without consulting the Iraqi victims who gave their testimony to human rights investigators in the hope that they were playing a concrete role in bringing Saddam to justice and establishing the rule of law in Iraq.[29] This position can be interpreted as a political one, for it is doubtful if the Iraqis who gave these statements would have objected to their testimony being transmitted to the Iraqi tribunal with or without the death penalty. Indeed, whatever positions international lawyers and others hold on the death penalty, from the perspective of most Iraqis, an Iraqi tribunal without the death penalty would have had a negative impact on public opinion in that country, thus denying the tribunal's work of essential public support. Some of the Iraqi judges on the war crimes tribunal were not in favor of the death penalty or were ambivalent about it, but have admitted as much.[30]

The death penalty, whatever may be its philosophical defects, and there are several, is a sovereign choice. The problems it has caused for the Iraqi war crimes court are just one facet of the clash between a globalizing cosmopolitan approach and sovereignty in the application of justice for war crimes. Some analysts have concluded that the real motive behind the refusal of many countries and organizations to lend a helping hand in the Iraq Trials—even to the point of withholding evidence—is a desire to punish the United States for what they view as its unilateral decision to effect regime change in Iraq,[31] the "you-break-it-you-own-it" syndrome.

Saddam's trial was further delayed because of the difficulties the tribunal's twenty-one investigative judges faced in compiling charges for crimes that spanned three decades, the difficulties in obtaining physical evidence from mass graves across a country where several parts of it were still engulfed by terrorist and sectarian insurrections against occupation forces, and the difficulty in obtaining defense lawyers for the twelve defendants.[32]

Saddam's trial proper began on October 19, 2005. The Iraqi lawyer Khali al-Duleimi led his defense, working with former American attorney general Ramsey Clark. He had eight codefendants including his half brother and former chief of Iraqi intelligence, Barzan Ibrahim al-Tikriti, and Taha Yassim Ramadan, former vice president of Iraq. He and his codefendants were charged in this particular trial with the massacre of 148 Shia Iraqis in the village of Dujail in 1982 as a reaction to a plot to assassinate Saddam. Further complications, several of them with political undertones, accompanied the trial. Saddam incessantly railed at the occupation of Iraq by "foreign invaders," hurled insults at the judges, repeatedly demanded adjournments, staged a walkout with his codefendants at one point, and then threw a hunger strike into the bargain—all of which led to the presiding judge being replaced with another who would impose better order on the proceedings.[33]

Further, one judge in the trial, a court official, and two defense lawyers were assassinated, and, outside the secure confines of the trial, the security situation in the wider Iraqi society deteriorated almost to the point of a civil war between the country's ethnic and religious groups who had been held together by fear in Saddam's secular dictatorship. Despite the chaos, however, the trial has improved in its process and has tried to adhere to international standards.[34]

Indeed, the journalist John Simpson of the British Broadcasting Corporation (BBC), who has covered Iraq and Saddam for many years, has argued that "simply because Saddam Hussein's trial is different from the court practices of, say, Britain and France, does not make it farcical."[35] But one disagrees with his position that it is better for the trial and for the judges to wear Saddam down with politeness than treat him roughly and risk turning him into a martyr (Simpson notes, in a gentle irony, that "in the old days the statue of justice outside the law faculty at Baghdad University was a figure of Saddam himself, holding a sword and scales").[36] The reason why a firm treatment of Saddam, not gentle coddling, is necessary in the courtroom of his trial is that nothing will prevent the former Iraqi leader from arguing his fundamental position that his trial is illegitimate, and that the invasion that ousted him is illegal. As with all war crimes trials of political leaders, firm judicial control of the trial process is not without its risks. A standard one is the propensity of war crimes defendants to go on hunger strikes, leading to judgment calls by the judge as to whether or not to appoint a defense team not chosen by the defendant. This scenario was frequent in the Arusha tribunal prosecuting the architects of Rwanda's genocide, and has replayed itself in the trial of Saddam Hussein.[37] This should not lead to exaggerated concerns about fairness, for such acts as hunger strikes and walkouts by defendants are political acts calculated to undermine the essence of the proceedings. Thus, in any such trial, someone will have to be in charge of the trial or the courtroom in real terms. It will be either the judge, which should be the case, or, if he fails to assert his or her authority in an effective manner, the defendant.[38]

We could not reasonably expect that a trial of a figure like Saddam Hussein would not be turned—by both Saddam and his opponents—into a politically charged process. Even before the substantive trial began, blatant political interference by the interim government of Iyad Allawi occurred. Ahead of national elections scheduled for January 2005, in which Allawi was a candidate for the position of prime minister, he sought to accelerate the opening of the trial of Saddam even before prosecutors and court officials were fully prepared.[39]

Allawi's first move was to dismiss Salem Chalabi, the tribunal's chief administrator. The court administrator also happened to be a younger brother of Ahmad Chalabi, a leading figure in the Iraqi exile movement before the Iraq War who was also Allawi's political opponent as the two jockeyed for power in post-Saddam Iraq. The 43-year-old Salem Chalabi, who was educated at top American universities—Yale, Columbia, and Northwestern—and holds degrees in law and international affairs, was later charged as a suspect in the murder of Haithem Fadhil, director-general of the Iraqi finance ministry, and fled Iraq.[40]

The interim prime minister then tried, without success, to have the trial of Saddam begin in November, a few weeks before the national elections and nearly a year earlier than the minimum time court officials believed they would be ready with a trial-ready case.[41] Amer Bakri, a member of Allawi's political party, the Iraqi National Accord, was appointed to replace Chalabi.[42] Chalabi charged that Allawi was seeking to gain popularity ahead of the elections and drop charges against Ba'ath Party officials whom Allawi, a former Ba'athist before he fell out with Saddam and fled into exile in Britain, saw as a potential political allies. "Show trials followed by speedy executions may help the interim government in the short term, but will be counterproductive for the development of democracy and the rule of law in Iraq in the long term," Chalabi declared in a statement from exile in London.[43]

Although Allawi denied that he was exerting political influence on the judicial process and argued that the pace of the process was "too slow," it was obvious he was doing exactly that. In a BBC television news interview broadcast on December 14, 2004—a day before campaigns for the January 2005 elections were set to begin—he announced that the trial of Ba'ath party leaders would begin the following week. The prosecutor-general of the Iraqi Special Tribunal was still undergoing intensive training at the time Allawi made his announcement, and several defendants were yet to meet their lawyers. Clearly, Allawi, who had nearly been axed to death by Saddam's agents while he was in exile, was eager for both political profit and vengeance from the war crimes trial of Saddam. Ultimately, however, he failed in his bid to become the country's elected prime minister, and the trial began several months later.

THE STRATEGIC FRAMEWORK

The demystification of Saddam Hussein has taken place in three phases. The first was the controversial invasion and regime change. Second came his capture in Tikrit when, after months in hiding, the former Iraqi leader crawled out of a hole in the ground, blinking in the sunlight, into the waiting hands of American soldiers. His trial is the third and final phase. Saddam's trial is not so much about justice and human rights as it is about the strategic goals of the coalition that ousted him. In other words, it is not about justice as policy, but justice as strategy. The paradox is that the trial will have a salutary effect in the long term.[44] While some of his fellow Sunni Iraqis who felt a loss of power at his fall may resent his trial, and whatever may be the current and long-term problems the occupation of Iraq by foreign troops may face, most Iraqis, who lived in dread of the dictator, are happy to see him on trial.

If we consider that the United States gave the former dictator forty-eight hours to abdicate his position and leave his country in order to avoid an invasion of Iraq, the political and strategic context of war crimes of leaders who have fallen from Olympian heights, with blood on their hands, becomes clear. In the most unlikely event that Saddam had taken up U.S. President Bush's offer, he might have enjoyed a quiet life in exile, his crimes against humanity notwithstanding.

There were many strategic factors that compelled a choice of forum for Saddam's trial—a national Iraqi war crimes tribunal. The most important one was that the United States wished to maintain control of the trial *framework* through the Iraqi governments that have been created as a result of Saddam's ouster and are thus beholden to the Americans. This is so even though the Iraqi Special Tribunal is independent of the Iraqi government. From a strategic standpoint, that desire is logical. The United States did not spend hundreds of billions of dollars to oust Saddam, in a war of strenuously contested legality, only to share control of the trial framework with countries or international organizations that did not support the war. America would have still been influential in the trial of Saddam in *any* forum—a national, international, or hybrid tribunal. Better, then, to work with Iraqis, who could claim ownership of the process. In that scenario, both America's strategic goals and those of the Iraqi opponents of Saddam's regime would be achieved—along with significant public support from a populace that broadly hated and feared Saddam even as they have mixed feelings about the invasion and occupation.

Saddam could also not have been tried in the International Criminal Court, except through referral of the case to that court by the UN Security Council, as neither the United States nor Iraq is a party to the Rome Statute of the ICC. To take that route would have amounted, from America's standpoint, to unnecessarily endorsing a court it had rejected when this, unlike the situation with war crimes in Darfur, was a situation well within the superpower's control. Moreover, the Rome Statute came into effect only in 2002, well after most of the important crimes in which Saddam is charged had been committed. The court's jurisdiction cannot be retroactive. Further, using the ICC would have opened the door to the extension of that court's reach to U.S. soldiers in Iraq.[45]

For reasons discussed earlier, a UN tribunal was not a practical option. Even before the war of 2003, the United States had already begun to question the performance of the ad hoc tribunal for the Balkans and Rwanda, with the U.S. diplomat Prosper calling for the completion of their work by 2008.[46] Thus U.S. policy had already begun to shift from top-down international prosecutions to the establishment of accountability for war crimes by national courts.[47]

The timing of Saddam Hussein's arraignment on July 1, 2004, just 2 days after the formal handover of sovereignty to the Iraqi interim government, was strategic. It was calculated to demonstrate the sovereignty of Iraq's interim government and give it credibility in the face of questions about its surefootedness. And yet, the substantive trial could not have begun before national elections in January 2005 (also for political reasons), even if the case file was trial-ready, which it was not. For a trial before the elections that ushered in a democratic government would have tipped the elections in favor of Allawi and the dominant parties in the interim government, which would not have been a level playing field.

Some international lawyers have also noted another strategic benefit for the United States in using an Iraqi court to try Saddam: avoiding contradictions on the question of aggression.[48] Article 14 of the statute of the Iraqi tribunal provides that the tribunal can prosecute persons who have committed certain crimes *under Iraqi law* (emphasis added). One of those offenses is "the abuse of position and the pursuit of policies that may lead to the threat of war or the use of the armed forces of Iraq against an Arab country, in accordance with Article 1 of Law Number 7 of 1958."[49] This is the crime of aggression, defined from a domestic law perspective.[50] It has been argued that, given the controversial legal basis of the U.S. invasion, the provision was included under the Iraqi domestic law in the Iraqi tribunal statute "to keep the spotlight solely on Saddam" and avoid the possibility of its interpretation against the U.S. war against Iraq.[51] This approach can also be explained by America's position on the legalization of the crime of aggression more broadly, as was evident in its position at the negotiations on the International Criminal Court.

The reversals that confronted the coalition's de-Ba'athification policy in Iraq provide an additional strategic context in which the trial of Saddam can be seen. Legal verdicts against the Iraqi dictator and his aides that firmly establish their crimes, based on reasonably credible judicial proceedings, will provide important future historical justification for the controversial actions of Western powers that led to his downfall. The question is—whose history will this be. This, too, is part of the intricate mix of policy and strategy that surrounds the trial of Saddam Hussein.

The trial of Saddam can be seen as a return to Nuremberg and Tokyo 60 years ago—the justice of the victor—or as a swing of the pendulum back from international war crimes trials with supranational jurisdictions to national ones that put ownership of such trials where it should belong—in the hands of the citizens of the state whose leaders have abused their position by committing mass atrocities. In fact, it is both, and whichever aspect of this bifurcated reality will be dominant in history will depend significantly on the consistency with which the Iraqi tribunal carries out the trials of Saddam and his associates to completion. As noted earlier, the indications are that the Iraqi judges are intent on doing the best job possible in difficult circumstances.

Those circumstances include the chaotic sectarian violence in Iraq.[52] The historical and societal outcome of Saddam's trial may well depend on the establishment of security in Iraq. It is only in a secure environment that the trial of Saddam can stimulate a culture of the rule of law. If real order is not secured in Iraq and the country disintegrates into a sectarian civil war between its Shia and Sunni groups, the impact of Saddam's trial would be quite limited, devoid of the larger societal context that can give it relevance.

The atrocities committed against Iraqis and Kuwaitis by the Iraqi army and security apparatus under Saddam Hussein's command is not in question. The challenge that faces the prosecutors of the Iraqi tribunal is to prove Saddam's guilt to the standards of legal justice. In most Western legal systems, that standard is proof beyond a reasonable doubt. In Iraqi criminal procedure and law, it is "proof to a moral certainty."[53] Saddam admitted in his trial that he signed the order for the execution of the 148 men and boys from the Shiite village of Dujail,[54] but argued that he had no knowledge of the killings. The Iraqi tribunal has charged him with genocide for the massacres of Iraqi Kurds in 1988, in which 50,000 civilians were killed. The Dujail trial, in which a verdict is expected was scheduled for October 2006, was a rocky trial run, but it is the genocide trial that will commence afterward that many observers believe will address the most grievous crimes.[55] The death penalty appears to be a sure fate for Saddam, an admirer of the Soviet dictator Josef Stalin, who hoped, like his famous role model, to die peacefully in his bed.[56]

8

International Justice: Not Yet the End of History

Justice and power must be brought together, so that whatever is just may be powerful, and whatever is powerful may be just

—Blaise Pascal

I set out in this book to interpret the phenomenon of war crimes trials and tribunals in international law and politics from the perspective not of liberal legalism, which is the conventional wisdom, but through that of a pluralist international society of states which have common institutions, rules, and shared values, but also conflicting and contrasting tendencies, as articulated by Hedley Bull. In that process I have sought to establish, through an empirical review of the trends in international justice for war crimes from World War I to the present day, first that a purist approach to justice (totally impartial, and before which all are equal) creates basic tensions between justice and order in the international society. Thus war crimes justice can go only as far as it can serve ends that are set by politics, creating new or legitimizing existing international or national orders. This political nature of war crimes justice and the selective, unequal justice it hands down derives from the fact that the international order consists of unequal sovereigns, although, in a formal sense, all states are equal.

The tensions created by this set of facts arise from the concept of sovereignty. Contrary to popular perceptions about the "end" of sovereignty in a globalizing world, sovereignty is not in decline. It has become contextualized, in the sense that it is no longer absolute. States, for example, do not have a right to commit genocide against their citizens because they are sovereign. In short, one agrees with scholars of international law and relations who have argued that the states system—and sovereignty—are not in serious decline. Rather, the loss of sovereignty is more apparent than real because "no institution—private, regional, or international—can compete with the nation-state's authority, which it obtains through direct legitimacy conferred by popular majority vote or, at least, by consent."[1] What has emerged is a contextualized form of sovereignty whereby states relinquish total control over affairs that affect them in order to advance their strategic interests, but without taking away in essence their ability to dominate their territory.[2] Or, as Anne-Marie Slaughter has posited, sovereignty has become "disaggregated."[3]

I conclude in this work, based on the analysis in the previous chapters, that, owing to the tenacity of the concept of sovereignty and the inequality of sovereigns in the international order despite the phenomenon of globalization, the desire and attempts at moving from the *internationalization* of justice for war crimes (which relates to standards and is consistent with international society) to its *globalization*, which relates to jurisdiction (that is to say, power to judge, perhaps vested in a world society or a world government) over war crimes, has failed.

It has failed because the globalization of jurisdiction attacks the fundamental nature of the international society, which is that there is no overarching sovereign therein, but a multiplicity of sovereigns—nearly 200 of them, to be exact. It has failed because the inequality of those sovereigns means that some are in a better position than others to guard their juridical sovereignty, and that ability arises from other aspects of international relations, of which international law is only a part. Other aspects include economics, technology, and military power.

Thus globalization may work to a large extent in the area of economics, but not in the arena of justice for war crimes. There are two main reasons for this. First, as Nicholas Wheeler has aptly observed, human rights goes to the heart of the relationship between governments and their citizens, and "poses the conflict between order and justice in its starkest form for the society of states."[4] Second, and just as important, economic globalization is supposedly a win-win proposition. The conflation of internationalization and globalization is what has led to exaggerated claims about "global" justice. That is why the backlash to "justice without borders" or universal jurisdiction over human rights crimes (legal globalization), jurisdiction that has direct political implications for order in the international society, has been far more profound than globalization in the economic sphere.

Even economic globalization—and the globalization of law relative to economic activity—is not without conflict.[5] To illustrate, the United States resisted, on national security grounds, attempts by the China National

Offshore Oil Corporation (CNOOC), a Chinese state-controlled oil company, to acquire the American oil firm Unocal[6]; the U.S. Congress blocked an initiative by President Bush to grant Dubai Ports World, a company based in the United Arab Emirates (an ally of the United States in the Gulf), a concession to manage American ports—again on national security grounds[7]—and France resisted, on grounds of economic nationalism, attempts by a British steel company Mittal Steel to buy a French steel company Acelor in what was on the face of it a straightforward economic transaction in a "global village."

The hope for a truly cosmopolitan global justice was based on a predominantly liberal–legalist, and thus, mistaken interpretation of the Nuremberg trial as a historical event and its legacy in world politics, which led to the unrealistic visions of an all-powerful permanent International Criminal Court. When that court was eventually created, by states exercising their sovereignty in the context of an international society, the nature of that society reasserted itself by making the court's jurisdiction complementary, not supranational, to that of states. The creation of such a court, however, was evidence of an advanced international society.

We arrived at this point via the international war crimes tribunals for the former Yugoslavia and Rwanda, which were established because the possibilities created by the end of the cold war—the existence of which prevented international action in response to the Cambodian genocide in the mid-1970s—allowed states to respond imaginatively, if belatedly, with United Nations Security Council-created courts. These courts were also established in the manner in which they were because, in the heat of the moment, there was insufficient time to negotiate and sign treaties between member states of the UN. Hence the mandates of those courts were limited to narrow geographies (the territories of ex-Yugoslavia, Rwanda, and neighboring states, and so on).

But the source and authority of those courts were entirely international, and in that fact their limitations quickly became apparent, for there was a major disconnect between them and the societies they were set up to help transform by rendering political justice, thus limiting their impact. Lack of local ownership led to charges of hegemony. Even weak states realized this and began to seek to assert their sovereignty. This led to the "hybrid" war crimes courts in Sierra Leone and Cambodia, and (for the reasons discussed in Chapter 7) the completely national Iraqi Special Tribunal for Crimes Against Humanity. Legal justice was, in the end, recognized to be more appropriately an attribute of sovereignty to be exercised as a general rule by sovereign states, and, in rare exceptions such as treaties or state failure, by international bodies.

International trials and tribunals have nevertheless made lasting, positive contributions, even if the challenges, legal and political, to their legitimacy have made the UN Security Council somewhat diffident about using them in the future. Although they have been remote from their supposed "clients" (the victims of the crimes and peoples of the states for which these tribunals were created), that they have removed the likes of Slobodan Milosevic, Rwanda's Jean Kambanda, and Liberia's Charles Taylor from the political space of these countries is remarkable and will create space for these societies to develop away from the culture of extremism that results in genocides, crimes against humanity, and war crimes. It will take another generation before this benefit becomes clearer, as was the case with Nuremberg and Tokyo.

In any case, despite their shortcomings, there were good reasons why these tribunals and their supranational enforcement powers were necessary: former Yugoslavia and Rwanda in the mid-1990s were societies that had experienced a total breakdown of the rule of law. They either were unable, or incapable, to render justice for violations of international humanitarian law. No court in the territories of the former Yugoslavia would have prosecuted any of the senior figures in the region—Serb, Croat, Muslim, or Kosovar for the crimes they committed and inspired. Rwanda, with its judiciary decimated by the 1994 genocide, could not cope with the demands of justice. With the architects of genocide having fled to several different countries in Africa, Europe, and North America, only the long arm of international law, through these international courts, could have brought these individuals to trial.[8]

Nevertheless, in a demonstration of the truism that justice remains at its core the responsibility of sovereign states, Rwanda created local *gacaca*, or peoples' courts, to confront the task of justice for thousands of more ordinary suspects and their victims. The Hague and Arusha tribunals have been slow. More than a decade on, it is clear they will not be able to prosecute all their indictees (about 80 for the Arusha Tribunal and about 130 for the Hague Court) before they end trials in 2008 and wind down. And, if they were allowed to stay open indefinitely, it would make a mockery of the term "ad hoc tribunals" they were created to be.

Thus the Extraordinary Chambers of Bosnia and Herzegovina were established with the support of the Western powers to take up the load of prosecuting war criminals that the Hague Tribunal would not be able to prosecute. And the Arusha Tribunal and Rwandan authorities have been negotiating the handover of cases from the international war crimes tribunal to Rwanda's national courts, although the maintenance of the death penalty in Rwanda remains a sticking point in these negotiations.[9] This is an indirect positive influence of international war crimes tribunals. Their defects eventually generated pressure on sovereign states to build their own judiciaries in order to be in a position to assume their sovereign responsibility of handing down justice for crimes committed in their territories.

But the problem of the willingness to prosecute still exists, for, as noted in Chapter 3, few states are eager to prosecute war crimes committed by their agents, especially when it involves their political leadership. International tribunals will remain necessary to handle some cases that fall through this crack in the architecture of justice for violations of international humanitarian law. The International Criminal Court, which was created by a treaty, will likely serve this occasional function, as the UN Security Council is unlikely to establish further war crimes tribunals under its peace enforcement powers.

Against this background, I offer the following prescriptive conclusions. First, in an international society with no overarching sovereign, the problem of power and selectivity inherent in international justice for war crimes can only be solved through the evolution of domestic democratic processes and institutions in powerful countries. The electorate in these countries, unwilling as they will be to surrender their troops and leaders to international accountability, can vote for the imposition of such accountability at home by domestic judicial institutions. While such accountability is already possible in theory, in practice it is not, for few electorates, whether in developed or developing countries, have a full grasp of the issues involved in crimes like genocide, crimes against humanity, and war crimes, especially when they are committed against "others" in other countries or territories. This perspective is endowed with the "democratic legitimacy" that international courts are often said to lack—which also applies to the point I made in Chapter 6 that a non-signatory to the Rome Statute of the International Criminal Court should not be brought under its jurisdiction, directly or indirectly.

Domestic courts may also by themselves assert accountability for war crimes or respect for the international legal regime governing such crimes where a basis exists in domestic law. There is perhaps no greater demonstration of this possibility inside the polity of great powers than the momentous decision of the United States Supreme Court in *Hamdan v Rumsfeld*.[10] In a ruling with major implications for the relationship between the politico-military power of the United States and the constraining influence of international law, the court decided that (a) the military commissions in which the U.S. administration planned to prosecute terrorist suspects were unconstitutional as they did not conform to the standards of the Uniform Code of Military Justice and were not authorized by an Act of Congress, and (b) that the provisions of Common Article 3 of the Third Geneva Convention of 1949 on the treatment of prisoners of war applied to America's war against terrorism and the detention of Al Qaeda terrorist suspects within that context. Hamdan had argued that the procedures under which he would be tried in the military commissions violate basic tenets of military and international law, including the right of a defendant to see and hear the evidence against him. The high court also ruled, in what was interpreted by some reports as an "escape clause," that the U.S. president could seek authorizing legislation from Congress regarding the military commissions.

For a country that consistently treats international law as subordinate to its constitution, the Supreme Court ruling is unarguably binding. The ruling's impact was made more forceful not only because the U.S. ratified the Geneva Conventions, but also because Common Article 3 is part of American law enacted by Congress in its War Crimes Act of 1996. In the debate that followed *Hamdan*, American scholars and legal experts agreed that—in what would surely be an ultimate act of sovereignty in relation to international law, more so than the "unsigning" of the as-of-then unratified Rome Statute of the International Criminal Court by the U.S. administration in 2001—the U.S. Congress can pass legislation rejecting the application of the Geneva Conventions in its domestic law.[11]

But, in a demonstration of the subtle influence of international law, these scholars also agree that in the context of the international society, such an act of defiance would be deeply damaging to the United States, not least because it could expose American troops captured abroad to barbaric treatment that would be justified on the grounds of America's own repudiation of the Geneva Conventions.[12] This illustrates the point I made in Chapter 1 about the nature of established international law. Although weaker than domestic law that is backed up by sovereign prerogatives of enforcement, international law derives its influence not always from positivism, but also from other factors such as reciprocity and peer pressure. All these factors make it likely that should the executive branch of the U.S. government seek and obtain legal authorization for the military commissions from the legislature, such authorization is unlikely to include a fundamental departure from the standards laid down in Common Article 3.

Even this approach will encounter problems, however, for it will always depend on the independence of particular judges. In the international sphere, justice is always political because "there is no formal separation between law and politics in the international society."[13] But it is not altogether accurate to assume, as is popularly done, that "in the domestic arena, judicial bodies are not only apolitical in and of themselves, ... established by legal process and stand solely concerned with the application of law, but in normal circumstances they stand entirely apart from the political arena."[14] In the United States, an overwhelming majority of judges are elected, and while this might appear admirably democratic, the frequent pandering to interests that helps ensure that candidates are elected clashes with the expectation that judges should be impartial.[15]

The Nigerian columnist Edwin Madunagu has also argued that in the domestic sphere "Law and politics can never be divorced. This is not just because their relationship is dialectical (mutually reinforcing) but also, and more importantly that politics gave birth to law, and explains it in a way that no other discipline or human activity can."[16] Although the mix of politics and law in the domestic sphere does indeed create a potential obstacle to the proposals in the first conclusion above, in that relationship also rests the hope of its realization, for a political movement that prioritizes accountability for war crimes can lead to laws and more effective judicial enforcement of accountability. Another alternative is to exercise democratic voting power to bring about governments that recognize that obeying international law may be in their own self-interest.

Second, we have seen that international war crimes justice is hegemonic, that even weak states resent this, and this is partly why the pendulum of justice for war crimes has swung away from unalloyed supranational jurisdiction back to the domestic sphere—or at least, a mixture of the two. Another major reason for this shift is the political philosophy of the U.S. government under President Bush as a result of its opposition to the International Criminal Court. In this sense, the rise of international law and tribunals that Nuremberg engendered, leading to hopes of "the end of history" in which international law and international justice will reign supreme, has imploded.

The question, in response to the unarguably hegemonic nature of international war crimes trials, is—what exactly can, or should, the weak states of the developing countries that supply defendants to international war crimes tribunals do about it? The answer is to create credible institutions of conflict resolution that render warlords redundant, and/or establish judicial accountability mechanisms that are strong and credible enough to be respected and left alone in the knowledge that they will function reasonably well. It is well and good, for example, to say that African problems should be solved by Africans. This is a laudable objective and is already well underway, as the successful African effort to negotiate a peace agreement for the conflict in Sudan's Darfur region in the Nigerian capital of Abuja attests.

It is also true that African culture is uncomfortable with legalism. But formal retributive justice dispensed by courts is now so entrenched in the domestic legal systems of African states that an exclusive reversal to precolonial, culture-based systems of justice is unlikely. And it remains necessary to address the question of political environments that produce the likes of Charles Taylor and other warlords. It appears unhelpful to Africa—and its commitment to its independence—when the continent's leaders avoid addressing frontally the question of accountability, which is essential for the continent's development. While one can only respect the wisdom inherent in the cultural approach of conciliation, might it not be that it creates a comfort zone that spawns warlords that commit mass atrocities? It is too early to assert that the African Union's decision that former Chadian president Hissene Habré should be tried in Senegal rather than Belgium is a definitive trend toward home-grown legalism. But it is certainly a preferable policy stance. In Chapter 2, I analyzed the prosecute-or-pardon conundrum, and throughout this book I have asserted that the problem is not so much with whether or not there should be prosecutions of war crimes. That is every society's choice, although I have indicated that pardons should be an exceptional response, not the standard one. The more important question, from the perspective of this book, is that of *who* judges presumed war criminals.

The third prescriptive conclusion of this book is that using international war crimes trials as a frontline approach to preventing or deterring genocide is a failing policy. Courts and tribunals are inherently reactive, and while they have their place in a world in which we cannot wish evil away, the responsible use of force will be a far more credible way to stop genocide. Certainly, the nature of the international society impedes political will to do so. But it is clear that it is the forum of cooperation offered by international institutions (an essential aspect of international society) like the United Nations that has made possible the recent adoption of the principle of the responsibility to protect civilian populations from genocide, crimes against humanity, and war crimes at its World Summit in 2005.[17]

Thus, the overall challenge for states is to internalize norms that abhor and prosecute violations of international humanitarian law. That is the best solution, one that makes international standards applicable across the board *within* sovereign states based on agreements reached in the context of an international society in which members recognize common values even as they pursue their legitimate self-interest in other matters. This, as we have seen from this survey of the "rise and fall" of global justice, is the policy option that is guaranteed to endure. To seek solutions in a consistently supranational policy approach will raise questions of legitimacy that have undermined what is either a *political* position or, at best, the altruistic intentions of its proponents.

Notes

CHAPTER 1

1. See "In Larger Freedom: Towards Development, Security and Human Rights for All," Report of the Secretary-General, UN Doc. A/59/2005, March 21, 2005, pp. 41–43.

2. "A Collision in East Asia," *The Economist*, April 16, 2005.

3. "Japan Must Come Clean on Its Past," *Gulf News* (Editorial), April 7, 2005.

4. "A Collision in East Asia."

5. See Michael Walzer, *Just and Unjust Wars* (New York: Basic Books, 1977).

6. The status of nuclear weapons in international humanitarian law remains ambiguous. See the Advisory Opinion of the International Court of Justice on the Legality of Threat or Use of Nuclear Weapons, July 8, 1996, www.icj-cij.org. Accessed on March 25, 2006.

7. See Human Rights Watch, "Making Sense of the Guantanamo Bay Tribunals," August 16, 2004, www.hrw.org. Accessed on March 25, 2006.

8. Yves Beigbeder, *Judging War Criminals: The Politics of International Justice* (London: Macmillan Press, 1999), p. 4.

9. Ibid.

10. Ibid.

11. See Plato, *Republic* (Hertfordshire, UK: Wordsworth, 1997), p. 38. This is part of an extended argument between the philosophers Glaucon, Thrasymachus, and Socrates on the nature and origin of justice.

12. Hedley Bull, *The Anarchical Society: A Study of Order in World Politics* (New York: Palgrave, 1977), p. 76.

13. Ibid.

14. Judith Shklar, *Legalism: Law, Morals and Political Trials* (Cambridge, MA: Harvard University Press, 1986). See also Gary Jonathan Bass, *Stay the Hand of Vengeance: The Politics of International War Crimes Tribunals* (Princeton: Princeton University Press, 2000), p. 7.

15. Bull, *Anarchical Society*, p. 80.

16. Shane Brighton, "Milosevic on Trial: The Dilemmas of Political Justice," www.bbc.co.uk/history/war/milosevic_trial. Accessed on 10 January 2006.

17. Ibid.

18. See Advisory Opinion of the International Court of Justice on the Legality of Threat or Use of Nuclear Weapons, July 8, 1996.

19. Bull, *Anarchical Society*, p. 8.

20. Bass, *Stay the Hand of Vengeance*, pp. 16–36.

21. Hidemi Suganami, "Alexander Wendt and the English School," *Journal of International Affairs and Development* 4(4): 403–423, 2001.

22. Bull, *Anarchical Society*.

23. Robert H. Jackson, *The Global Covenant: Human Conduct in a World of States* (Oxford: Oxford University Press, 2000), p. 83.

24. Ibid.

25. See also Christopher Rudolph, "Constructing an Atrocities Regime," *International Organization* 55(3): 656, Summer 2001.

26. See Michael P. Scharf and William A. Schabas, *Slobodan Milosevic on Trial: A Companion* (New York: Continuum, 2002), p. 44.

27. See Bass, *Stay the Hand of Vengeance*, p. 87, for a discussion of the differences of view between France and Great Britain on this matter—French law allowed it; British law did not.

28. Frédéric Mégret, "The Politics of International Criminal Justice," *European Journal of International Law*, 13: 5, 2002.

29. Ibid.

30. Ibid.

31. Ibid.

32. Bass, *Stay the Hand of Vengeance*, Introduction, Note 108.

33. Peter Wilson, "The English School and the Sociology of International Law: Strengths and Limitations," Paper presented at the Annual British International Studies Association Conference, University of Birmingham, December 15–17, 2003.

34. Ibid.

35. David Forsythe, "Politics and the International Tribunal for the Former Yugoslavia," in Roger Clark and Madeleine Sann, *The Prosecution of International Crimes: A Critical Study of the International Tribunal for the Former Yugoslavia* (New Brunswick: Transaction Publishers, 1996), p. 185.

36. Werner Levi, *Law and Politics in the International Society* (Beverly Hills, CA: Sage Publications, 1976, p. 31, quoted in Forsythe, "Politics and the International Tribunal for the Former Yugoslavia."

37. See Terry Nardin, "Legal Positivism as a Theory" in Mapel and Nardin, *International Society* (Princeton: Princeton University Press, 1999), p. 29.

38. See Jack Goldsmith and Eric Posner, *The Limits of International Law* (New York: Oxford University Press, 2005).

39. Ibid., p. 31.

40. Gerry Simpson, *Great Powers and Outlaw States: Unequal Sovereigns in the International Legal Order* (Cambridge: Cambridge University Press, 2004.)

41. See Celia W. Dugger, "Donor Nations to Focus on Growing States," *New York Times*, April 24, 2006. This article reports a decision by the International Monetary Fund and the World Bank to increase the voting powers of a number of newly emerging influential market economies such as China, South Korea, Mexico, and Turkey—a clear recognition of how international law can adjust to new realities. The article states: "More fairly reflecting the size of national economies through increased voting shares is important to retaining the institution's legitimacy as it advises governments on their economic policies, officials at the fund and analysts said."

42. Michael Glennon, "Why the Security Council Failed," *Foreign Affairs*, 29–30, May/June 2003.

43. Rudolph, "Constructing an Atrocities Regime," 656.

44. Adam Watson, "International Relations and the Practice of Hegemony," Lecture at the University of Westminster, June 5, 2002.

45. Rudolph, "Constructing an Atrocities Regime," 681. See also John Hagan, *Justice in the Balkans: Prosecuting War Crimes in The Hague Tribunal* (Chicago: University of Chicago Press, 2003), p. 106.

46. A phrase used by Martti Koskenniemi, "The Place of Law in Collective Security," *Michigan Journal of International Law*, 17(471), quoted by George J. Andreopoulos, "Violations of Human Rights and Humanitarian Law and Threats to International Peace and Security," in Ramesh Thakur and Peter Malcontent, *From Sovereign Impunity to International Accountability: The Search for Justice in a World of States* (Tokyo: United Nations University Press, 2004), p. 80.

47. Andreopoulos, ibid.

48. Shashi Tharoor, "Globalization and the Human Imagination," *World Policy Journal*, XXI(1), Summer 2004.

CHAPTER 2

1. I use the word "pardons" in a broad sense to describe not only formal pardons for offenses, but also policy decisions not to prosecute persons who, prima facie, may be guilty of violations of international humanitarian law.

2. Ramesh Thakur, "Politics vs. Justice at The Hague," *International Herald Tribune*, August 15, 2002.

3. Henry Kissinger, *A World Restored: Metternich, Castlereagh, and the Problems of Peace, 1812–1822* (Boston: Houghton Mifflin, 1973), p. 138.

4. Testimony of Professor Jeremy Rabkin, Hearings on International Justice, Committee on International Relations, United States House of Representatives, February 28, 2002.

5. Ibid.

6. See Kingsley Chiedu Moghalu, "Peace Through Justice," *Washington Post*, July 6, 1999.

7. Article 10 of the Statute of the Special Court for Sierra Leone provides: "An amnesty granted to any person falling within the jurisdiction of the Special Court in respect of the crimes referred to in Articles 2 to 4 of the present Statute shall not be a

bar to prosecution." The crimes referred to are crimes against humanity, Violations of Article 3 common to the Geneva Conventions and of Additional Protocol II, and other serious violations of international humanitarian law. See Statute of the Special Court for Sierra Leone, UN Doc. S/2000/915.

8. Gary Jonathan Bass, *Stay the Hand of Vengeance: The Politics of International War Crimes Tribunals* (Princeton: Princeton University Press, 2000), chap. 3. This section owes much to Bass's detailed history of the subject. Unlike Bass, however, I have sought in this chapter to analyze the connection between these historical events and the development of some important norms of international humanitarian law. Another useful work is James F. Willis, *Prologue to Nuremberg: The Politics and Diplomacy of Punishing War Criminals of the First World War* (Westport, CT: Greenwood, 1982).

9. See Ruth Henig, *Versailles and After: 1919–1933* (London: Routledge, 1995).

10. James Atkinson, "The Treaty of Versailles and its Consequences," unpublished paper, 2002.

11. Bass, *Stay the Hand of Vengeance*, p. 73.

12. Ibid., p. 74.

13. Ibid., pp. 77–87.

14. Ibid., quoting A.M. Luckau, *The German Delegation at the Paris Peace Conference* (New York: Columbia University Press, 1941), p. 112.

15. See "Seeds of Evil: The Rise of Hitler," www.schoolshistory.org.uk.

16. Ibid.

17. James F. Willis, *Prologue*, pp. 177–178.

18. Bass, *Stay the Hand of Vengeance*, p. 60.

19. Nicholas Wood, "Milosevic's Name on the Ballot Signals Serbian Nationalism," *The New York Times*, December 27, 2003. See also Misha Glenny, "The Prosecutor Muddies Serbian Waters," *International Herald Tribune*, February 17, 2004. Not surprisingly, economic malaise as a factor in the nationalist backlash to war crimes prosecutions was as well active in Germany's Weimar Republic between World Wars I and II.

20. Bass, *Stay the Hand of Vengeance*, p. 80.

21. Ibid.

22. Ibid., p. 81.

23. Ibid., p. 67.

24. Ibid.

25. Proceedings of the Imperial War Cabinet, November 28, 1918, as quoted in Bass, *Stay the Hand of Vengeance*, pp. 69–70.

26. Bass, *Stay the Hand of Vengeance*, p. 103.

27. See Article 5(1)(d) of the Rome Statute, UN Doc. A/CONF.183/9 of July 17, 1998, and corrected by procès-verbaux of November 10, 1998. Article 5(2) provides that the Court's jurisdiction over the crime of aggression will become effective once a provision is adopted in accordance with articles 121 and 123 defining the crime and setting out the relevant conditions for the exercise of jurisdiction. Article 123: "Seven years after the entry into force of this Statute the Secretary-General of the United Nations shall convene a Review Conference to consider amendments to this Statute. Such review may include, but is not limited to, the list of crimes contained in Article 5."

28. Woodrow Wilson, Speech to the United States Congress, February 11, 1918, in *The Papers of Woodrow Wilson*, Arthur S. Link et al., (ed.) (Princeton: Princeton University Press, 1984), 46: 320.

29. Bass, *Stay the Hand of Vengeance*, p. 103.

30. Ibid.

31. Ibid.

32. Ibid.

33. Ibid.

34. See Dorothy V. Jones, *Toward a Just World: The Critical Years in the Search for International Justice* (Chicago: University of Chicago Press, 2002).

35. Benjamin B. Ferencz, "The Evolution of International Criminal Law: A Bird's Eye View of the Past Century," in *Humanitäres Völkerrecht* (Baden-Baden: Nomos Verlagsgesellschaft, 2001), p. 355.

36. Ibid.

37. Ibid., p. 9.

38. The unsuccessful attempts by the Allied States to prosecute the German Kaiser Wilhelm following World War I, and similar attempts to prosecute the individuals believed to be responsible for the massacres of Armenians in Turkey in 1915 were the most notable examples.

39. George Schwarzenberger, *International Law as Applied by International Courts and Tribunals*, 465(10), 1968 (quoting John Knebel Capellini, Basil Diary, 1473–1476).

40. Ibid.

41. See *The Judgment of Nuremberg, 1946: The International Military Tribunal for the Trial of German Major War Criminals* (London: The Stationery Office, 1999), p. xvii.

42. See the London Charter of the International Military Tribunal at Nuremberg, August 8, 1945. The London Charter was signed by the four Allied Powers. It was subsequently endorsed by nineteen other governments: Greece, Denmark, Yugoslavia, the Netherlands, Czechoslovakia, Poland, Belgium, Ethiopia, Australia, Honduras, Norway, Panama, Luxembourg, Haiti, New Zealand, India, Venezuela, Uruguay, and Panama. The Charter for the International Military Tribunal for the Far East was subsequently issued by United States General Douglas MacArthur.

43. For an excellent account of the human drama of the Nuremberg trials see Joseph E. Persico, *Nuremberg: Infamy on Trial* (New York: Penguin Books, 1994), pp. 61–62.

44. Ibid., p. 78.

45. See Ann Tusa and John Tusa, *The Nuremberg Trial* (New York: Cooper Square Press, 1983), chap. 2.

46. Ibid., p. 63.

47. Ibid., p. 21. The Declaration was adopted at St. James in London by the representatives of nine European countries that had been occupied by German forces. It stated: "international solidarity is necessary to avoid the repression of these acts of violence simply by acts of vengeance on the part of the general population and in order to satisfy the sense of justice of the civilized world."

48. Ibid., chap. 4.

49. *The Judgement of Nuremberg.*

50. See Tusa, *The Nuremberg Trial*, pp. 494–503, for more detailed biographies of the Nazi defendants.

51. See Office of United States Chief of Counsel for Prosecution of Axis Criminality, *Nazi Conspiracy and Aggression: Opinion and Judgement* (Washington: United States Government Printing Office, 1947), pp. 189–190.

52. Persico, *Nuremberg*, p. 83.

53. Barry Gewen, "What Is a War Crimes?", *The American Interest*, Summer 2006, p. 144.

54. *The Judgement of Nuremberg*, p. 80.

55. Quoted in Ann Tusa and John Tusa, *The Nuremberg Trial*, p. 155.

56. While the Rules of Procedure and Evidence of the ICTY allowed for a transfer of cases from that international tribunal to a national court in certain circumstances, that of the ICTR did not. This situation, which led to a clumsy situation with political dimensions in one of the cases handled by the ICTR, created a "one-way street" situation where the Tribunal had the first call on any suspect but had no discretionary room to hand such a suspect over to a national court should its prosecutor decide to drop charges. The Rules of Procedure of the Tribunal were later amended to rectify this anomaly.

57. See Persico, *Nuremberg*, p. 33.

58. Ibid.

59. *Judgment of Nuremberg*, p. 82.

60. Ibid.

61. The 1923 draft Treaty of Mutual Assistance sponsored by the League of Nations, and the preamble to the League of Nations 1924 Protocol for the Pacific Settlement of International Disputes ("Geneva Protocol").

62. Drexel Strecher, Interview with Court TV (United States) on the Nuremberg trials, 1995, www.courttv.com.

63. Van der Aa, Proceedings of the XIth International Penal and Penitentiary Congress, quoted in Dorothy Jones, *Toward a Just World* (Chicago: University of Chicago Press, 2002), pp. 154–155.

64. Ibid.

65. Ibid.

66. Persico, *Nuremberg*, pp. 35–36.

67. There are several elements that reflect the continental civil law system in the Statutes and Rules of Procedure of the ICTY and the ICTR, but these legal documents are essentially reflective of a common law approach. Moreover, it is no surprise that, given the influence of the United States in the Security Council, these statutes were drafted by, or with strong input from, lawyers in the U.S. Department of State.

68. Persico, *Nuremberg*, p. 34.

69. Ibid.

70. Persico, *Nuremberg*, p. 442.

71. Ibid.

72. Moghalu, *Rwanda's Genocide: The Politics of Global Justice* (New York: Palgrave Macmillan, 2005).

73. Gewen, "What Is a War Crime?" p. 138.

74. Numerous other trials were held at various military tribunals established by the victorious Allied Powers, with "conventional atrocities" or "crimes against

humanity" classified as "Class B" crimes, and the planning, ordering, authorization, and failure to prevent such atrocities categorized as "Class C" crimes. John Dower, *Embracing Defeat: Japan in the Wake of World War II* (New York: W.W. Norton & Company, 1999).

75. Tim Maga, *Judgment at Tokyo: The Japanese War Crimes Trials* (Lexington, KY: The University of Kentucky Press, 2001), p. 3.

76. Dower, *Embracing Defeat*, chap. 15.

77. See B.V.A. Röling and Antonio Cassese, *The Tokyo Trial and Beyond* (Cambridge: Polity Press, 1993).

78. Dower, *Embracing Defeat*, p. 459.

79. Yves Beigbeder, *Judging War Criminals: The Politics of International Justice* (London: Macmillan Press, 1999), p. 57.

80. Dower, *Embracing Defeat*, p. 461.

81. Ibid., pp. 451, 453.

82. For an analysis of the politics of historical truth in the context of international criminal justice, see Martti Koskenniemi, "Between Impunity and Show Trials," *Max Planck Yearbook of United Nations Law*, Vol. 6, 2002, pp. 1–35.

83. Ibid., p. 21.

84. Telford Taylor, *The Anatomy of the Nuremberg Trials. A Personal Memoir*, 1992, p. 555, quoted in Koskenniemi.

85. Dower, *Embracing Defeat*, p. 324.

86. Beigbeder, *Judging War Criminals*, p. 57.

87. Ibid.

88. Dower, *Embracing Defeat*, p. 325.

89. Ibid.

90. Ibid.

91. Beigbeder, *Judging War Criminals*, p. 57.

92. Dower, *Embracing Defeat*, p. 325.

93. Ibid., p. 326.

94. For example, Interview with Yoshiko Saito, April 14, 2004.

95. Sterling Seagrave and Peggy Seagrave, *The Yamoto Dynasty: The Secret History of Japan's Imperial Family* (New York: Broadway Books, 2000).

96. Maga, *Judgment at Tokyo*, pp. 86–87.

97. See Yutaka Arai, "Revisionist Views on War Crimes by Japanese Prompt Fears for Nation's Democracy," *Financial Times* (Letter to the Editor), February 26–27, 2005, responding to an interview by Yuko Tojo, granddaughter of Hideki Tojo in the same newspaper. See "Let Japan's Sleeping Gods of War Lie," Lunch with the FT, *Financial Times*, February 19–20, 2005.

98. Beigbeder, *Judging War Criminals*, p. 75.

99. Ibid., pp. 66–75.

100. Haruko Taya Cook and Theodore F. Cook, *Japan at War, An Oral History* (New York: The New Press, 1992), quoted in Beigbeder, *Judging War Criminals*, pp. 66–67.

101. Ibid.

102. Ibid., p. 51.

103. Ibid., p. 68.

104. Ibid.

105. Roling and Cassese, *The Tokyo Trial and Beyond*, p. 84.

106. Advisory Opinion of the International Court of Justice on the Legality of the Use or Threat of Nuclear Weapons, 1996.

107. Beigbeder, *Judging War Criminals*, p. 72.

108. See, for example, Hal Gold, *Unit 731: Testimony* (Boston, MA: Tuttle Publishers, 2004).

CHAPTER 3

1. Michael P. Scharf and William A. Schabas, *Slobodan Milosevic on Trial: A Companion* (New York: Continuum, 2002), p. 13.

2. Ibid., p. 14.

3. See Misha Glenny, *The Balkans: Nationalism, War and the Great Powers, 1804-1999* (New York: Penguin, 1999), chap. 1. This history accounts for the contemporary support, or at least sympathy, that Serbs have received from Russia in the politics of accountability for war crimes in the Balkans.

4. Gary Jonathan Bass, *Stay the Hand of Vengeance: The Politics of War Crimes Tribunals* (Princeton: Princeton University Press, 2000), p. 209.

5. Scharf and Schabas, *Slobodan Milosevic on Trial*.

6. See Chris Stephen, *Judgment Day: The Trial of Slobodan Milosevic* (London: Atlantic Books, 2004), p. 37.

7. See International Criminal Tribunal for the former Yugoslavia, *The Path to The Hague: Selected Documents on the Origins of the ICTY* (The Hague: 2001), p. 11.

8. Ibid., pp. 47–49.

9. Ibid., p. 61.

10. See Bass, *Stay the Hand of Vengeance*, p. 211.

11. Ibid.

12. See M. Cherif Bassiouni, "The Commission of Experts Established Pursuant to Security Council Resolution 780: Investigating Violations of International Humanitarian Law in the Former Yugoslavia," in Roger S. Clark and Madeleine Sann (eds.), *The Prosecution of International Crimes: A Critical Study of the International Tribunal for the Former Yugoslavia* (London: Transaction Publishers, 1996), p. 69. See in particular note 25 on the same page.

13. Statement of Lawrence Eagleburger, U.S. Secretary of State, "The Need to Respond to War Crimes in the Former Yugoslavia." See *The Path to The Hague*, pp. 67–69.

14. See, for example, Bass, *Stay the Hand of Vengeance*, p. 214.

15. See Letter of Mr. Lawrence Eagleburger to Antonio Cassese (the first President of the International Criminal Tribunal for the former Yugoslavia), dated May 8, 1996, in *The Path to The Hague*, p. 89.

16. Letter from the Secretary-General to the President of the Security Council, February 9, 1993, UN Doc. S/25274 (1993), transmitting the *Interim Report of the Commission of Experts Established Pursuant to Security Council Resolution 780 (1992)*.

17. UN Doc. S/RES/808 (1993).

18. Ibid.

19. See Rachel Kerr, *The International Criminal Tribunal for the Former Yugoslavia: An Exercise in Law, Politics, and Diplomacy* (Oxford: Oxford University Press, 2004).

20. John Hagan, *Justice in the Balkans: Prosecuting War Crimes in the Hague Tribunal* (Chicago: University of Chicago Press, 2003), p. 38.

21. Ibid.

22. Bass, *Stay the Hand of Vengeance*, p. 217

23. See Stanley Meisler, "Jury Still Out on Bosnian War Crimes Tribunal Created by U.N." *Los Angeles Times*, December 25, 1993, p. A5.

24. Bass, *Stay the Hand of Vengeance*, p. 219.

25. Stephen, *Judgment Day*, p. 106.

26. See Hagan, *Justice in the Balkans*, p. 81.

27. See Richard Holbrooke, *To End a War* (New York: Modern Library, 1999).

28. Stephen, *Judgment Day*, pp. 135–136.

29. See Kerr, *The International Criminal Tribunal for the Former Yugoslavia*, p. 192.

30. UN Doc. S/RES/1199 (1998), September 23, 1998.

31. Stephen, *Judgment Day*, pp. 158–160.

32. Ibid.

33. "Report Looks at Claims against NATO," Associated Press, January 4, 2000.

34. Ibid.

35. See Henry Kissinger, "The Pitfalls of Universal Jurisdiction: Risking Judicial Tyranny," *Foreign Affairs*, July/August, 2001.

36. Alexander Cockburn and Jeffrey St. Clair (eds.), "Yugoslavia a Year Later: Turning a Blind Eye to NATO War Crimes," www.counterpunch.com, May 22, 2000.

37. Ibid.

38. Jerome Socolovsky, "White House Blasts Kosovo Inquiry," Associated Press, January 4, 2000.

39. "Credibility and Legitimacy of International Criminal Tribunals in the Wake of Milosevic's Death," *Harvard International Review*, http:/hir.harvard.edu/articles/print.phparticle=1402 accessed June 6, 2002.

40. Steven Lee Myers, "Kosovo Inquiry Confirms US Fears of War Crimes Court," *The New York Times*, January 3, 2000.

41. Cockburn and Clair, op. cit.

42. See David Forsythe, "Politics and the International Tribunal for the Former Yugoslavia" in Roger S. Clark and Madeleine Sann, *The Prosecution of International Crimes: A Critical Study of the International Tribunal for the Former Yugoslavia* (London: Transaction Publishers, 1996), p. 201. See also *United States v Yamashita* (1945), UN War Crimes Commission, Law Reports of Trials of War Criminals 4: 1 (1947), and *United States v Calley*, 48 C.M.R. 19 (U.S. C.M.A. 1973).

43. Forsythe, Ibid.

44. Ibid.

45. Stephen, *Judgment Day*, pp. 158–160.

46. See "Serbia: Court Finds Milosevic Behind Rival's Murder," *New York Times*, June 30, 2006.

47. Ibid., p. 160.

48. Statement by President Clinton at the Elysée Palace in Paris, June 17, 1999, quoted in Bass, *Stay the Hand of Vengeance*, p. 274.

49. Stephen, *Judgment Day*, p. 163.

50. Kingsley Chiedu Moghalu, *Rwanda's Genocide: The Politics of Global Justice* (New York: Palgrave Macmillan, 2005), p. 45.

51. Scharf and Schabas, *Slobodan Milosevic on Trial*, p. 37.

52. Ibid.

53. See *The Prosecutor v Slobodan Milosevic*, Second Amended Indictment, October 23, 2002, Case No. 11-02-54-T (Croatia Indictment).

54. Ibid.

55. Ibid.

56. *Prosecutor v Slobodan Milosevic*, Amended Indictment, November 22, 2002, Case No. IT-02-54-T (Bosnia Indictment).

57. See *Prosecutor v Slobodan Milosevic, Milan Milutinovic, Nicola Sainovic, Drajoljub Ojdanic, and Vlajko Stojiljkovic*, Second Amended Indictment, October 16, 2001, Case No. IT-99-37-PT (Kosovo Indictment).

58. Ibid.

59. Stephen, *Judgment Day*, p. 167.

60. Joseph Lelyveld, "The Defendant," *The New Yorker*, May 27, 2002.

61. Scharf and Schabas, *Slobodan Milosevic on Trial*, pp. 129–130.

62. See Judith Armatta, "Justice, Not a Political Platform, for Milosevic," *International Herald Tribune*, October 8, 2004.

63. Joseph Lelyveld, "The Defendant."

64. "Justice on Trial," *The Economist*, February 28, 2004.

65. Article 14 (3), International Covenant on Civil and Political Rights.

66. See Marlise Simons, "Wily Milosevic Keeps Hague Judges Guessing," *International Herald Tribune*, September 22, 2004.

67. Ibid.

68. "Hague Imposes Defense Lawyer on Yugoslavia's Milosevic," HINA (Croatian News Agency), September 2, 2004.

69. See *Slobodan Milosevic v Prosecutor*, Decision on Interlocutory Appeal of the Trial Chamber's Decision on the Assignment of Defence Counsel, Case No. IT-02-54-AR 73.7, November 1, 2004.

70. See Moghalu, *Rwanda's Genocide* (New York: Palgrave Macmillan, 2005).

71. See Nina H.B. Jørgensen, "The Right of the Accused to Self-Representation before International Criminal Tribunals," *American Journal of International Law*, October 2004, pp. 711–726.

72. See Armatta, "Justice, Not a Political Platform."

73. "Milosevic to begin War-Crimes Defense, *International Herald Tribune*, July 5, 2004.

74. Ibid. See also "Milosevic 'Fit Enough' For Trial," *The Nation*, July 8, 2004, Bangkok edition.

75. Nikki Tait, "Mountain Still to Climb in Milosevic Court Case," *Financial Times*, July 5, 2004.

76. Victor Sebestyen, "Rough Justice at The Hague," *The Spectator*, July 17, 2004.

77. See Misha Glenny, "The Prosecutor Muddies Serbian Waters," *International Herald Tribune*, February 17, 2004.

78. Nicholas Wood, "Pro-Western Reformer Carries Day in Serbia," *International Herald Tribune*, June 29, 2004.

79. See Laura Silber, "Serbian Voters Bring Some Good Tidings," *International Herald Tribune*, July 7, 2004.

80. Nicholas Wood, "Pro-Western Reformer Carries Day in Serbia."

81. Ibid.

82. Ibid.

83. See Gary Jonathan Bass, "Milosevic in The Hague," *Foreign Affairs*, May/June 2003, p. 93.

84. Kingsley Chiedu Moghalu, "Milosevic and Political Justice in the Balkans," *New Perspectives Quarterly*, 23(1), Winter 2006.

85. See "Milosevic Medical Plea Rejected," BBC News, February 24, 2006, http://news.bbc.co.uk.

86. Elisabeth Rosenthal, "Report Details Stormy Relationship Between Milosevic and Court-Appointed Medical Team," *New York Times*, June 5, 2006.

87. Ibid.

88. "The Death of Milosevic," *International Herald Tribune*, editorial, March 15, 2006.

89. Andrew Purvis, "Justice Denied," *Time*, March 20, 2006.

90. Ibid.

91. Somini Sengupta, "African Held for War Crimes Dies in Custody of a Tribunal," *New York Times*, July 31, 2003.

92. Purvis, "Justice Denied."

93. Timothy William Waters, "Why Insist on the Surrender of Ratko Mladic?" *New York Times*, May 12, 2006.

94. Milan Panic, "Milosevic's Death Cleanses Serbian National Pride," *New Perspectives Quarterly*, 23: 1, Winter 2006.

95. Kingsley Chiedu Moghalu, "Peace through Justice: Rwanda's Precedent for the Milosevic Trial, *Washington Post*, July 6, 1999.

96. See Bass, "Milosevic in the Hague," p. 87

97. Ibid.

98. Ibid.

99. See Daryl A. Mundis, "The Judicial Effects of the 'Completion Strategies' on the Ad Hoc International Criminal Tribunals," *American Journal of International Law*, 99: 1, January 2005, pp. 142–158. See also Moghalu, *Rwanda's Genocide*, chap. 6.

100. See Moghalu, *Rwanda's Genocide*, pp. 95–96.

101. See Marlise Simons, "Court Looks for Ways to Speed Milosevic trial," *New York Times*, July 28, 2004.

102. Tait, "Trying Times: After Two Years and 300 Witnesses, Harsh Lessons Emerge from the Prosecution of Slobodan Milosevic," February 19, 2004.

103. See Pierre-Richard Prosper, "War Crimes and State Responsibility for Justice", Remarks at Organization for Security and Cooperation in Europe (OSCE) Conference in Belgrade, June 15, 2002, available at http://belgrade.usembassy.gov/press/2002020615.html, accessed on July 28, 2006.

104. Simons, "Court Looks for Ways to Speed Milosevic Trial," *New York Times*, July 28, 2004.

105. Ibid.

106. Ibid.

107. See *Prosecutor v Ante Gotovina*, Indictment, May 21, 2001, Case No. IT-01-45-I, www.un.org/icty.

108. See Keith B. Richburg, "Kosovo's Prime Minister Quits after Being Indicted for War Crimes," *Washington Post*, March 9, 2005.

CHAPTER 4

1. Henry Kissinger, "The Pitfalls of Universal Jurisdiction," *Foreign Affairs*, July/August 2001.

2. See Christopher Hitchens, *The Trial of Henry Kissinger* (London: Verso Press, 2001).

3. Eduardo Gallardo, "Court Strips Chile's Pinochet of Immunity," Associated Press, May 28, 2004.

4. See Article 53 of the Vienna Convention on the Law of Treaties, 1969.

5. See Coleman Phillipson, *The International Law and Custom of Ancient Greece and Rome*, Vol. 2 (Salem, MA: Ayer, 1911). Hugo Grotius expanded on this theory in his classic work *De Jure Belli AC Pacis*, translated by Francis W. Kelsey (Oxford: Clarendon Press, 1925).

6. United Nations Convention on the Law of the Sea, October 7, 1982, UN Doc. A/CONF.62/122, Article 150, which reproduces Art. 19 of the 1958 Geneva Convention on the Law (Philadelphia, PA: University of Pennsylvania Press, 2004), 97–120.

7. For an illuminating discussion of universal jurisdiction see Alfred Rubin, *Ethics and Authority in International Law* (Cambridge: Cambridge University Press, 1997).

8. See Richard A. Falk, "Assessing the Pinochet Litigation: Wither Universal Jurisdiction?" in Stephen Macedo (ed.), *Universal Jurisdiction: National Courts and the Prosecution of Serious Crimes under International Law* (Philadelphia, PA: University of Pennsylvania Press, 2004), pp. 27–120.

9. See Malcolm Shaw, *International Law* (Cambridge: Cambridge University Press, 1997), pp. 462–469.

10. Ibid., p. 470.

11. M. Cherif Bassiouni, "The History of Universal Jurisdiction," in Macedo, *Universal Jurisdiction*.

12. *In re Piracy Jure Gentium*. See also Alfred Rubin, *The Law of Piracy* (Irvington on Hudson, NY: Transnational Publishers, 1998). But it should be noted that the genocides in Rwanda and the former Yugoslavia have led a number of European countries to bring perpetrators to justice through trials that have been based on universal jurisdiction. See Bassiouni, "The History of Universal Jurisdiction," note 101.

13. See Terry Nardin, "Legal Positivism as a Theory of International Society," in Mapel and Nardin, *International Society* (Princeton: Princeton University Press, 1999).

14. Bassiouni, "The History of Universal Jurisdiction," p. 51.

15. Ibid.

16. See Geneva Conventions of August 12, 1949 (International Committee of the Red Cross). Identical provisions are made in all the four Geneva Conventions.

17. Amnesty International, "Universal Jurisdiction: The Duty of States to Enact and Implement Legislation," chap. 4 (War Crimes: State Practice at the National Level, Al Index (or 53/004/2001), London, 2001), p. 1.

18. Ibid.

19. *Niyonteze v Public Prosecutor*, Tribunal Militaire de Cassation (Switzerland), April 27, 2001, www.vbs.admin.ch.

20. Luc Reydams, "International Decision: *Niyonteze v Public Prosecutor*," 96 *American Journal of International Law*, January 2002.

21. Amnesty International, "Universal Jurisdiction," chap. 2 (The History of Universal Jurisdiction), 25–26. Amnesty has clearly placed excessive emphasis on a scholarly article in this regard. It relies extensively on Willard Cowles, "Universality of Jurisdiction over War Crimes," *California Law Review*, 33: 177, 1945.

22. Ibid.

23. *The Hadamar Trial*, Judgment, Case No. 4, U.S. Mil. Commission—Wiesbaden, October 8–15, 1945, quoted in Amnesty, "Universal Jurisdiction," 28.

24. *In re Eisentrager*, judgment Case No. 84, U.S. Mil. Commission—Shanghai, October 3, 1946–1947, quoted in Amnesty, "Universal Jurisdiction."

25. Sandrock and three others (*The Almelo Trial*), Judgment, Case No. 3, Brit. Mil.Ct.—Almelo, November 24–26, 1945; Law Reports of Trials of War Criminals, 1, 1949.

26. See Article 7, Rome Statute of the International Criminal Court, UN Doc. A/CONF.183/9.

27. Robert Jennings and Arthur Watts, *Oppenheim's International Law* (9th edn.), 998 (London: Longman 1992).

28. *Prosecutor v Ntuyahaga*, Decision on the Prosecutor's Motion to Withdraw the Indictment, Case No. ICTR-98-40-T (Trial Chamber I, March 18, 1999). The Tribunal also noted the Tribunal does not have exclusive jurisdiction over crimes included in its mandate and that its criminal proceedings are complementary to those of national jurisdictions." Ibid.

29. *Prosecutor v Tadic*, Decision on the Defence Motion for Interlocutory Appeal on Jurisdiction, Case No. IT-94-1-AR72 (Appeals Chamber October 2, 1995), para. 58.

30. See Rosalyn Higgins, *Problems and Processes: International Law and How We Use It* (Oxford: Oxford University Press 1992). Higgins noted, rightly, in this writer's view, that "the fact that an act is a violation of international law does not of itself give rise to universal jurisdiction." Ibid.

31. Bassiouni, "The History of Universal Jurisdiction," p. 53.

32. Amnesty International, "Universal Jurisdiction," chap. 7, p. 6.

33. Ibid.

34. Ibid. See also Samantha Power, *A Problem from Hell: America and the Age of Genocide* (London: Flammingo, 2002), chap. 3–4 for a detailed account of Raphael Lemkin's lobbying for adoption of the Genocide Convention.

35. Ad Hoc Committee on Genocide, Report of the Committee and Draft Convention Drawn up by the Committee, UN Doc. E/794, May 24, 1948.

36. Power, *A Problem from Hell*, pp. 55–56.

37. William A. Schabas, *Genocide in International Law* (Cambridge: Cambridge University Press, 2000), pp. 548.

38. Case Concerning Application of the Convention on the Prevention and Punishment of the Crime of Genocide, (Bosnia and Herzegovina v Yugoslavia), Preliminary Objections, Judgment of July 11, 1996, International Court of Justice, para. 31.

39. See Kingsley Chiedu Moghalu, "Rwanda Panel's Legacy: They Can Run but Not Hide," *International Herald Tribune*, 30–31, November 1998.

40. Falk, "Assessing the Pinochet Litigation", in Macedo, *Universal Jurisdiction*.

41. Ibid., p. 97, 98.

42. See Craig S. Smith, "Aiming at Judicial Targets All over the World," *The New York Times*, October 18, 2003, for a profile of Judge Garzon and his related judicial activities.

43. *Regina v Bartle* and the Commissioner of Police for the Metropolis and others *Ex Parte Pinochet Ugarte*, All England Law Reports, vol. 1998 pt. 1, 97 (1999).

44. Ibid.

45. Falk, " Assessing the Pinochet Litigation."

46. Ibid.

47. Ibid.

48. Amnesty International, "Universal Jurisdiction," chap. 2.

49. Gallardo, "Court Strips Chile's Pinochet of Immunity."

50. Belgium: "Act Concerning the Punishment of Grave Breaches of International Humanitarian Law", *38 International Legal Materials* 918 (1999)

51. Ibid., Article 7.

52. A. Hays Butler, "The Growing Support for Universal Jurisdiction in National Legislation," in Macedo, p. 69.

53. Amnesty International, chap. 6, p. 8.

54. Ibid.

55. Quoted in Amnesty, Ibid.

56. Amnesty, chap. 6, p. 11.

57. Marlise Simmons, "Human Rights Cases begin to Flood to Belgian Courts," *The New York Times*, December 27, 2001.

58. See Simons, "Mother Superior Guilty in Rwanda Killings," June 9, 2001.

59. "Rwandans on Trial," *The New York Times* (Editorial), May 1, 2001.

60. Ibid.

61. Ibid.

62. Simons, "Human Rights Cases."

63. See Richard Bernstein, "Belgium Rethinks Its Prosecutional Zeal," *The New York Times*, April 1, 2003.

64. See Glenn Frankel, "Belgian War Crimes Law Undone by its Global Reach," *Washington Post*, September 30, 2003, and Bernstein, "Belgium Rethinks."

65. Bernstein, "Belgium Rethinks."

66. Ian Black and Ewen MacAkill, "US Threatens to Boycott Belgium over War Crimes Law," *The Guardian*, June 13, 2003.

67. Frankel, "Belgian War Crimes."

68. Ibid.

69. Human Rights Watch, "Belgium: Universal Jurisdiction Law Repealed," Press Statement, August 1, 2003.

70. Ibid.

71. International Court of Justice, Case Concerning the Arrest Warrant of April 11, 2000 (*Democratic Republic of Congo v Belgium*), Decision of February 14, 2002.

72. Ibid., p. 7.

73. Ibid., p. 20.

74. Ibid., p. 22.

75. Ibid.

76. Ibid., pp. 29–30.

77. See, for example, A.P. van der Mei, "Universal Jurisdiction in a Politically Divided World," in Evelyn A. Ankumah and Edward K. Kwakwa, eds., African Perspectives on Universal Jusrisdiction (Accra: Africa Legal Aid, 2005), pp. 29–55.

78. See Moghalu, "International Law and the New World Order," *The Guardian*, April 29, 1991, Nigeria edition.

79. The ad hoc international criminal tribunals were the first international court post-Nuremberg to try individuals for crimes of international humanitarian law as subjects of international law, thus bringing international law as applied by international courts into the sphere of mere mortals, while the ICJ remained the lofty guardian of international law as it applied to states and had no jurisdiction over individuals. Proposals made by some scholars after World War I to give the Permanent Court of International Justice, the ICJ's forerunner, jurisdiction over international crimes committed by individuals, were not adopted. See Jones, *Toward a Just World* (Chicago: University of Chicago Press, 2002), p. 198.

80. International Court of Justice, Case Concerning the Arrest Warrant—Separate Opinion of President Guillaume.

81. Ibid.

82. Ibid. These include the New York Convention against the Taking of Hostages of 1979, the Torture Convention of 1984, and the New York Convention for the Suppression of Terrorist Bombings of 1997, among several others.

83. Ibid.

84. Ibid.

85. ICJ, *Yerodia* Case, Separate Opinion of Judge Koroma.

86. Frankel, "Belgian War Crimes."

87. Princeton University Program in Law and Public Affairs: "The Princeton Principles on Universal Jurisdiction" (Princeton: 2001), www.princeton.edu.

88. Ibid., p. 49.

89. See Edward Kwakwa, "The Cairo-Arusha Principles on Universal Jurisdiction in Respect of Gross Human Rights Offences: Developing the Frontiers of the Principle of Universal Jurisdiction," *African Yearbook of International Law*, 2003, pp. 407–430, note 23.

90. Ibid.

91. See Mouhamed Kébé, "Universal Jurisdiction in Light of the Habré Case," in Evelyn Ankumah and Edward Kwakwa, eds., *African Perspectives on Universal Jurisdiction*.

92. Ibid.

93. See "Hissene Habré: Senegal's Albatross, Litmus Test for Africa, www. globalpolicy.org/intljustice.universal/2005/1128habré.htm. Accessed on July 29, 2006.

94. Lydia Polgreen, "African Union Tells Senegal to Try Ex-Dictator of Chad," *New York Times*, July 3, 2006.

95. Ibid.

96. *Public Prosecutor v Jorgic*, Oberslandesgericht Düsseldorf, September 26, 1997.

97. See "Federal High Court Makes Basic Ruling on Genocide," Press Release of the Federal High Court of Germany (English Translation), Nr. 39 of April 30, 1999, www.preventgenocide.org.

CHAPTER 5

1. Report of the Secretary-General on the Establishment of a Special Court for Sierra Leone, UN Doc. S/2000/915, para. 10, p. 3.

2. Ibid.

3. Letter from Dr. Ahmad Tejan Kabbah, President of the Republic of Sierra Leone to Mr. Kofi Annan, Secretary of the United Nations dated June 12, 2000.

4. Ibid.

5. "Framework for Special Court for Sierra Leone," document attached to President Kabbah's letter to the Secretary-General dated June 12, 2000.

6. Ibid.

7. For a thorough discussion of the legitimacy of the Security Council—created war crimes tribunals, see Kingsley Chiedu Moghalu, *Rwanda's Genocide: The Politics of Global Justice* (New York: Palgrave Macmillan, 2005), pp. 40–48.

8. Ibid., pp. 42–44.

9. Report of the Secretary-General on the Establishment of a Special Court for Sierra Leone.

10. Letter from the President of the Republic of Sierra Leone to the Secretary-General.

11. See Lansanna Gberie, Jarlawah Tonpoh, Efam Dovi, and Osei Boateng, "Charles Taylor: Why Me?" *New African*, May 2006, p. 12.

12. For a political–psychological profile of Charles Taylor's rise to power in Liberia see Bill Berkeley, *The Graves Are Not Yet Full: Race, Tribe and Power in the Heart of Africa* (New York: Basic Books, 2001) pp. 21–61.

13. See Gberie et al., "Charles Taylor," p. 13.

14. See *The Prosecutor v Charles Ghankay Taylor*, Decision on Immunity from Jurisdiction, Special Court for Sierra Leone, Case No. SCSL-2003-01-1, May 31, 2004. p. 3.

15. See Kingsley Chiedu Moghalu, "A Warlord's Date with Justice," *Mail & Guardian*, June 23, 2003, Johannesburg edition.

16. Somini Sengupta, "Besieged Liberian," *New York Times*, July 11, 2003.

17. "Africa's Most Wanted," *The Economist*, December 6, 2003.

18. Ibid.

19. See "An American Embassy in Tripoli," *New York Times* (Editorial), May 17, 2006.

20. *The Prosecutor v Charles Ghankay Taylor*, Indictment, Case No. SCS1-03-1.

21. Kabbah's government was restored in 1998 by the intervention of ECOMOG troops led by Nigeria.

22. *The Prosecutor v Charles Ghankay Taylor*, Indictment.

23. It should be noted here that Nigeria is nevertheless an influential member of the Management Committee of the Special Court for Sierra Leone, a group of the major donors that fund the Court. But this has more to do with maintaining its wider strategic influence as a regional superpower, given its heavy investment of financial resources and peacekeeping forces in Sierra Leone and Liberia in the 1990s, than with a single-minded commitment to legalism.

24. A. Bolaji Akinyemi, "The Taylor Saga: A Clash of Civilizations," *New African*, 20–23, May 2006.

25. Ibid.

26. Sengupta, "Besieged Liberian."

27. Ken Shulman, "The Butcher and the Ballot," *International Herald Tribune*, October 7, 2005. See also Madu Onuorah, "Obasanjo Protests Pressure to Release Taylor," *The Guardian*, July 5, 2005, Nigeria edition. And see "Hearing of the Africa Subcommittee of the House International Relations Committee; Subject: Confronting War Crimes in Africa," Federal News Service, June 24, 2004, and Oghogho Obayuwana, "Global Bar Chief Asks Nigeria to Hand Over to U.N. Tribunal," *The Guardian*, November 26, 2004.

28. Akinyemi, "The Taylor Saga."

29. *Prosecutor v Charles Ghankay Taylor*, Decision on Immunity from Jurisdiction, Case No. SCSL-2003-01-1, note 1, p. 2.

30. Ibid.

31. See Case Concerning Arrest Warrant of 11 April 2000 (*Democratic Republic of Congo v Belgium*) (2002) ICJ Reports, February 14, 2002.

32. *The Prosecutor v Charles Ghankay Taylor*, Decision on Immunity from Jurisdiction, pp. 5–6.

33. Ibid., p. 6.

34. Ibid., p. 7.

35. Ibid., p. 10.

36. Ibid., p. 11.

37. Ibid.

38. Ibid.

39. Ibid., pp. 11–12.

40. Ibid., p. 12.

41. Ibid., p. 16.

42. Ibid., p. 19.

43. Report of the Secretary-General in the Establishment of a Special Court for Sierra Leone, para. 9, p. 3.

44. Ibid., para. 10.

45. Decision on Immunity from Jurisdiction, p. 21.

46. General Assembly Resolution 177(ii), Formulation of the Principles Recognized in the Charter of the Nuremberg Tribunal and in the Judgement of the Tribunal.

47. Decision on Immunity from Jurisdiction, p. 25.

48. *Yerodia* case, para. 61 (emphasis added).

49. See Francis Okino and Kemi Oguntase, "Akinyemi Faults Charges against Taylor, Defends Asylum," *The Guardian*, February 27, 2004.

50. Decision on Immunity form Jurisdiction, p. 25.

51. See Sengupta, "Besieged Liberian."

52. See "Special Court for Sierra Leone Holds Talks in Liberia about Charles Taylor," www.un.org/news, July 16, 2004.

53. See Charles Ozoemena and Ise-Oluwa Ige, "Government Moves to Extradite Charles Taylor," *Vanguard*, March 9, 2006.

54. See Jon Lee Anderson, "After the Warlords," *The New Yorker*, 58–65, March 27, 2006.

55. Ibid., p. 62.

56. Ibid.

57. Gberie et al., "Charles Taylor."

58. Ibid., p. 63.

59. See Madu Onuorah, "Presidency Gets Liberia's Request for Taylor's Extradition," *The Guardian*, March 18, 2006.

60. See Warren Hoge, "Liberia Wants Exile Handed Over," *International Herald Tribune*, March 18, 2006.

61. Onuorah, "Presidency Gets Liberia's Request."

62. Ibid.

63. Ibid.

64. See Gberie et al., "Charles Taylor."

65. Akinyemi, "The Taylor Saga."

66. Ibid.

67. Hoge, "Liberia Wants Exile Handed Over."

68. Lydia Polgreen, "Nigeria Says Ex-President of Liberia Has Disappeared," *New York Times*, March 2, 2006.

69. Ibid.

70. See Laolu Akande, "Ex-President's Arrest Vindicate Nigeria, Says Obasanjo," *The Guardian*, March 30, 2006.

71. Lydia Polgreen, "Liberian Seized to Stand Trial on War Crimes," *New York Times*, March 30, 2006.

72. See Laolu Akande, "Ex-President's Arrest Vindicates Nigeria, says Obasanjo."

73. See "A Close Escape," *The Economist*, April 1, 2006, p. 27.

74. Baffour Ankomah, "A Pound of Flesh, But In Whose Interest?" *New African*, 8–9, May 2006.

75. Gberie et al., "Charles Taylor."

76. Akinyemi, "The Taylor Saga."

77. Ibid.

78. *Prosecutor v Charles Ghankay Taylor*, Amended Indictment, Case No. SCSL-2003-01-1.

79. Lydia Polgreen, "Liberian Seized to Stand Trial on War Crimes."

80. See "Liberia Needs No War Crimes Court," *The Analyst*, editorial, April 11, 2006, Monrovia edition.

81. Ibid.

82. See Lydia Polgreen and Marlise Simons, "Sierra Leone Asks to Move Liberian's Trial," *New York Times*, March 31, 2006. See also "Special Court President Request Charles Taylor to Be Tried in The Hague," Special Court for Sierra Leone Press Release, March 30, 2006.

83. "Special Court President Requests Charles Taylor to Be Tried in The Hague."

84. See Hoge, "Britain Backs Request to Move Liberian's Trial to the Hague," *New York Times*, April 1, 2006.

85. See "Security Council Approves Trial Transfer of Former Liberian President Charles Taylor to Netherlands," UN Doc. SC/8755, June 16, 2006.

86. See "A Big Man in a Small Cell," *The Economist*, April 8, 2006, p. 46.

87. Thalif Deen, "Global Hunt for Jailhouse for ex-Liberian President," *Terraviva UN Journal*, Inter Press Service, April 17, 2006. See also "Denmark: No Cell for Charles Taylor," *New York Times*, April 26, 2006.

88. "A Big Man in a Small Cell."

89. "UK Agrees To Jail Taylor", BBC News, http://newsvote.bbc.co.uk, June 15, 2006.

90. Polgreen and Simons, "Sierra Leone Asks to Move Liberian's Trial."

91. See John E. Leigh, "Bring It All Back Home," *New York Times*, April 17, 2006.

92. Ibid.

93. Polgreen, "Liberian Seized to Stand Trial on War Crimes."

CHAPTER 6

1. Leila Nadya Sadat, "The Evolution of the ICC: From The Hague to Rome and Back Again," in Sara B. Sewall and Carl Kaysen, *The United States and the International Criminal Court: National Security and International Law* (New York: Rowman & Littlefield, 2000), p. 37. See also Marc Weller, "Undoing the Global Constitution: UN Security Council Action on the International Criminal Court," *International Affairs* 78: 4,2002, p. 695.

2. Ibid.

3. See Michael J. Struett, "The Politics of Constructing an International Criminal Court," Paper prepared for presentation at the International Studies Association Annual Meeting, New Orleans, March 24, 2002, www.isanet.org.

4. Ibid.

5. Ibid.

6. Ibid., p. 27.

7. Leila Nadya Sadat and S. Richard Carden, "The New International Criminal Court: An Uneasy Revolution," *Georgetown Law Journal*, March 2000.

8. See Barbara Crossette, "A Reality: New Global Criminal Tribunal," *International Herald Tribune*, April 12, 2002.

9. Antonio Cassese, "From Nuremberg to Rome: From Ad Hoc International Military Tribunals to the International Criminal Court," in Antonio Cassesse et al. (eds.), *The Rome Statute of the International Criminal Court: A Commentary*, vol. 1 (Oxford: Oxford University Press, 2002), p. 18.

10. Sadat and Carden, "The New International Criminal Court."

11. Ibid.

12. See David W. Zeigler, *War, Peace and International Politics* (1997) referenced in Sadat and Carden, note 39. See also Robert P. George, "Natural Law and International Order," in David R. Mapel and Terry Nardin (eds.), *International Society: Diverse Ethical Perspectives* (Princeton: Princeton University Press, 1998), p. 61.

13. Spyros Economides, "The International Criminal Court," in Karen E. Smith and Margot Light, *Ethics and Foreign Policy*, p. 122.

14. Article 17(1), Rome Statute of the International Criminal Court (hereafter Rome Statute), www.icc-cpi.int.

15. Article 17(1), Rome Statute.

16. See Paper on Some Policy Issues before the Office of the Prosecutor," September 2003, www.icc-cpi.int.

17. See Address by Judge Philippe Kirsch, President of the ICC, to the Third Session of the Assembly of State Parties to the Rome Statute of the International Criminal Court, The Hague, September 6, 2004, www.icc-cpi.int.

18. Article 17, Rome Statute.

19. Sadat and Carden, "The New International Criminal Court."

20. A senior official of the ICC (identity withheld at the official's request), interview with the author, The Hague, September 13, 2004 (on file with the author).

21. Ibid.

22. Article 15, Rome Statute.

23. Ibid.

24. Article 14, Rome Statute.

25. Article 13, Rome Statute.

26. Article 16, Rome Statute.

27. Yves Beigbeder, *Judging War Criminals: The Politics of International Justice* (New York: St. Martin's Press, 1999), p. 192.

28. David Wippman, "The International Criminal Court," in Christian Reus-Smit, *The Politics of International Law*, p. 162.

29. Jenia Iontcheva Turner, "Nationalizing International Criminal Law: The International Criminal Court as a Roving Mixed Court," *Stanford International Law Journal*, January 2005.

30. See Kingsley Chiedu Moghalu, "Image and Reality of War Crimes Justice: External Perceptions of the International Criminal Tribunal for Rwanda," *Fletcher Forum of World Affairs*, 26, Fall 2002.

31. Turner, op. cit.

32. U.S. President Clinton, defending the NATO bombing of Yugoslavia, quoted in Robert Jackson, *The Global Covenant: Human Conduct in a World of States* (Oxford: Oxford University Press, 2000), 281. President Bush has frequently invoked the rhetoric of spreading "liberty and democracy" to justify the invasion of Iraq in 2003.

33. See Jackson, 170. The other traditions are international responsibility, humanitarian responsibility, and responsibility for the global commons.

34. Ibid., p. 171.

35. Ibid.

36. Jason Ralph, "Between Cosmopolitan and American Democracy: Understanding U.S. Opposition to the International Criminal Court," *International Relations* 17(2) 196–197, 2003.

37. For an illuminating journalistic account of the final days of the negotiations in Rome from a U.S. perspective see Lawrence Weschler, "Exceptional Cases in Rome: The United States and the Struggle for an ICC," in Sewall and Kaysen, *International Criminal Court* (Lanham: Rowman & Littlefield Publishers, 2000).

38. Ibid., p. 107.

39. Australia, Egypt, Israel, Japan, Jordan, Argentina, Republic of Korea, New Zealand, and Taiwan.

40. See "Contempt of Court," editorial, *International Herald Tribune*, April 12, 2002.

41. See "International Criminal Court: Letter to UN Secretary-General Kofi Annan," U.S. Department of State Press Statement by Richard Boucher, Spokesman, Washington, DC, May 6, 2002, reproducing the text of the U.S. letter, signed by Under Secretary of State for Arms Control and International Security John Bolton. See also "U.S. Congress Passes Anti-ICC Hague Invasion Act," Coalition for the International Criminal Court Press Release, New York, July 26, 2002, www.iccnow.org.

42. "International Criminal Court: For US or Against US?" *The Economist*, November 22, 2003.

43. Ibid.

44. See U.K. Parliament, Lords Hansard's text for November 19, 2002, www.parliament.uk.

45. Ibid.

46. Interview with Pierre-Richard Prosper, United States Ambassador at Large for War Crimes Issues, in Washington, DC, June 30, 2004 (on file with author).

47. Draft resolution S/2002/1420. See also "U.S. Defiant on War Crimes Court," www.cnn.com, July 1, 2002.

48. European Parliament Resolution on the Draft American Service members Protection Act (ASPA), P5_TA-Prov (2002) 0367: Consequences for Transatlantic Relations of Law on the Protection of US Personnel, July 4, 2002.

49. Kai Ambos, "International Criminal Law Has Lost Its Innocence," *German Law Journal*. 3(10), October 1, 2002.

50. See Colum Lynch, "Annan Opposes Exempting U.S. from Court," *Washington Post*, June 18, 2004.

51. Ibid.

52. Lynch, "China May Veto Resolution on Criminal Court," May 29, 2004.

53. Ibid.

54. Rome Statute, Article 12.

55. "Wary US Eye on UN Court," editorial, *Christian Science Monitor*, June 25, 2004.

56. Ibid.

57. See Rome Statute, Art. 12. See also Gerhard Hafner, Kristen Boon, Anne Rübesame, and Jonathan Huston, "A Response to the American View as Presented by Ruth Wedgwood," *European Journal of International Law*, 10: 17, 1999.

58. Hafner et al., Ibid.

59. Ibid. See Also Weller, "Undoing the Global Constitution."

60. See Marc Grossman, "American Foreign Policy and the International Criminal Court," Remarks to the Center for Strategic and International Studies, Washington, DC, May 6, 2002, www.state.gov.

61. Weller, p. 702.

62. Paul W. Kahn, "American Hegemony and International Law: Speaking Law to Power: Popular Sovereignty, Human Rights and the New International Order," *Chicago Journal of International Law* 1(1): 3, 2000.

63. Weschler, "Exceptional Cases in Rome," *The United States and the International Criminal Court*, (Lanham: Rowman & Littlefield Publishers, 2000), p. 97.

64. Barbara Crossette, "Helms Vows to Make War on U.N. Court," *New York Times*, March 27, 1998.

65. See Ruth Wedgwood, "The International Criminal Court: An American View," *European Journal of International Law*, 10, 1999.

66. See Cdr. J.W. Crawford, III, "The Law of Noncombatant Immunity and the Targeting of National Electrical Power Systems," *The Fletcher Forum of World Affairs*, 212: 101–119, Summer/Fall 1997.

67. Ibid., p. 102.

68. Protocol I, Article 51(2).

69. Ibid., Article 51(5)(b).

70. "Letter of transmittal from President Ronald Reagan, Protocol II Additional to the 1949 Geneva Conventions, and Relating to the Protection of Victims of Non-International Armed Conflicts," Reprinted in *American Journal of International Law*, 81: 910, 1987.

71. Crawford, "The Law of Noncombatant Immunity," p. 107.

72. Ibid., note 39.

73. Ibid., note 41.

74. Ibid.

75. Sadat and Carden, "The New International Criminal Court," p. 26.

76. Rome Statute, Article 7(1)(f).

77. Ibid., Article 7(1)(k).

78. Ibid., Article 2(5), and Articles 121 and 123.

79. Ibid., Article 123.

80. Final Act of the United Nations Diplomatic Conference of Plenipotentiaries on the Establishment of an International Criminal Court, July 17, 1998, Resolution E, UN Doc. A/Conf 183/10.

81. Jules Deschênes, "Toward International Criminal Justice," in Roger S. Clark and Madeleine Sann (eds.), *The Prosecution of International Crimes* (London: Transaction Publishers, 1996), p. 32. See also Convention for the Prevention and Punishment of Terrorism, opened for signature November 16, 1937, reprinted in *International Legislation*, 7: 862 (Manley O. Hudson et al., 1941); Convention for the Creation of an International Criminal Court, opened for signature November 16, 1937, reprinted in *International Legislation*, 7: 878. This convention received not a single ratification.

82. Ruth Wedgwood, "The Constitution and the ICC" in Sewall and Kaysen (eds.), *International Criminal Court*, p. 125. These crimes include: International Convention for the Suppression of Terrorist Bombings, G.A. Res 52/164 (December 15, 1997); International Convention against the Taking of Hostages (December 17, 1979), G.A. Res 34/146 Convention for the Suppression of

Unlawful Seizure of Aircraft, United Nations Treaty Series, 860: 105, December 16, 1970; Convention for the Suppression of Unlawful Acts against the Safety of Civil Aviation (Montreal Convention), September 23, 1971; 974 U.N.T.S.177; and Convention on the Prevention and Punishment against Internationally Protected Persons, Including Diplomatic Agents, 1035 U.N.T.S. 167, December 14, 1973.

83. Henry A. Kissinger, "America's Assignment," *Newsweek*, November 8, 2004.

84. Sadat and Carden, "The New International Criminal Court," p. 25.

85. *Reservations to the Convention on the Prevention and Punishment of the Crime of Genocide*, Advisory Opinion of May 28, 1951, www.ic-cij.org., March 20, 2005.

86. See Wippman, "The International Criminal Court."

87. Benjamin B. Ferencz, "Can Aggression Be Deterred by Law?" *Pace International Law Review*, 350–351, Fall 1999.

88. Grant M. Dawson, "Defining Substantive Crimes within the Subject Matter Jurisdiction of the International Criminal Court: What is the Crime of Aggression?" *New York Law School Journal of International and Comparative Law*, 19, 2000.

89. Charter of the International Military Tribunal, Article 6.

90. Ferencz, "Can Aggression be Deterred by Law?" p. 345.

91. Ibid., p. 3.

92. Ibid., p. 346.

93. UN Doc. A/9890 (1974).

94. Ibid.

95. See Linda Jane Springrose, "Aggression as a Core Crime in the Rome Statute Establishing an International Criminal Court," *Saint Louis-Warsaw Transatlantic Law Journal*, 5, 1999.

96. Dawson, op.cit.

97. Dawson, 10.

98. Springrose, 6.

99. Michael Walzer, *Just and Unjust Wars* (New York: Basic Books, 1977), p. 62.

100. Ibid., pp. 58–63.

101. Ibid., pp. 80–81.

102. Ibid., p. 81.

103. Noah Weisbord, "When Peace and Justice Clash," *International Herald Tribune*, April 29, 2005.

104. See Mahnoush H. Arsanjani and W. Michael Reisman, "The Law-in-Action of the International Criminal Court," *American Journal of International Law*, 99(2): 394, April 2005.

105. Ibid., p. 395.

106. See Payam Akhavan, "The Lord's Resistance Army Case: Uganda's Submission of the First Referral to the International Criminal Court,, *American Journal of International Law*, 99(2): 403–421, April 2005.

107. Sudan is not a party to the Rome Statute of the International Criminal Court, but the Security Council can refer cases to the Court, including involving nationals of nonstate parties. See Chapter 9 for a detailed discussion of the ICC.

108. Lynch, "U.S. Urges War Crimes Tribunal for Darfur Atrocities," January 28, 2005.

109. Warren Hoge, "UN Votes to Send Any Sudan War Crime Suspects to World Court," *The New York Times*, April 1, 2005.

110. See UN Press Release SC/8351, March 31, 2005, www.un.org/News/docs/2005/sc8351.doc.htm.

111. See Hans-Peter Kaul, "Developments at the International Criminal Court: Construction Site for More Justice", *American Journal of International Law*, 99(2): 380–381, April 2005.

112. See Warren Hoge, "U.N. Council Imposes Sanctions on 4 Men in Darfur War Crimes," *New York Times*, April 26, 2006.

113. See Wippman, "The International Criminal Court," p. 155.

114. See "China's Oil Ties to Sudan Force It to Oppose Sanctions," *Sudan Tribune*, October 20, 2004. See also Nicholas D. Kristof, "China and Sudan, Blood and Oil," *New York Times*, April 23, 2006.

115. See address by Luis Moreno Ocampo, Prosecutor of the International Criminal Court, to the United Nations Security Council, New York, December 13, 2005.

116. Madeline Morris, "Complementarity and Conflict: States, Victims and the ICC" in Sewall and Kaysen, *International Criminal Court*, p. 196.

CHAPTER 7

1. See International Criminal Tribunal for the former Yugoslavia, *The Path to The Hague: Selected Documents on the Origins of the ICTY*, p. 9.

2. Ibid.

3. Ibid

4. See Philippe Sands, *Lawless World: America and the Making and Breaking of Global Rules* (London: Penguin, 2005), chap. 8.

5. Ibid., p. 185.

6. Ibid., p. 187.

7. See Letter from Jack Straw, British foreign secretary, to Rt. Hon. Donald Anderson MP, titled "Iraq: Legal Position Concerning the Use of Force" dated March 17, 2003, transmitting the legal opinion of Lord Goldsmith, the British attorney general.

8. Note of Professor Pellet on the Responsibility of Saddam Hussein, April 16, 1991 (translated from French), in *The Path to The Hague*, p. 19.

9. Ibid.

10. "Bush: Saddam Should Face Death Penalty," CNN interview, December 16, 2003, http://www.cnn.com.

11. "Annan Opposes Death Penalty," *Boston Globe*, December 16, 2003.

12. See Kingsley Chiedu Moghalu, *Rwanda's Genocide: The Politics of Global Justice* (New York: Palgrave Macmillan, 2005), pp. 39–40.

13. Ibid., p. 31.

14. For a philosophical and legal argument in favor of the death penalty for the specific crime of genocide, see Jens David Ohlin, "Applying the Death Penalty to Crimes of Genocide," *American Journal of International Law*, 99(4): 747–777, October 2005.

15. Moghalu, "A Road Map for Saddam's Trial," *Global Viewpoint*, January 27, 2004, www.digitalnpq.org.

16. See Moghalu, *Rwanda's Genocide*, in particular Chapter 8 and the conclusion chapter. See also Ralph Zacklin, "The Failings of International Criminal Tribunals," *Journal of International Criminal Justice*, 2: 541–545, 2004.

17. See David Tolbert, "The International Criminal Tribunal for the Former Yugoslavia: Unforeseen Successes and Foreseeable Shortcomings," *The Fletcher Forum of World Affairs*, 26(2): 7–19, Summer/Fall 2002.

18. Gary J. Bass, "Milosevic in The Hague," *Foreign Affairs*, May/June 2003, p. 86.

19. Statute of the Iraqi Special Tribunal, Article 10.

20. Ibid., Article 1.

21. Ibid., Article 28.

22. Ibid., Article 7.

23. Ibid.

24. See Rod Nordland and Babak Dehghanpisheh, "Judgment Days," *Newsweek*, July 12, 2004.

25. See John Burns and Ian Fisher, "A Defiant Saddam Rejects Charges," *International Herald Tribune*, July 2, 2004.

26. See Marlise Simons, "Iraqis Not Ready for Trials; U.N. to Withhold Training," *New York Times*, October 22, 2004.

27. Ibid.

28. Ibid.

29. See Michael A. Newton, "Justice Abandoned," *International Herald Tribune*, November 25, 2004.

30. Simons, "Iraqis Not Ready for Trials."

31. "Undignified, But Not A Farce," *The Economist*, February 18, 2006.

32. Steve Negus, " Saddam Case Not Ready for Trial Until Next Year," *Financial Times*, September 25–26, 2004.

33. "Undignified, But Not a Farce."

34. Mark S. Ellis, "Next, The Trial of Saddam," *International Herald Tribune*, April 9–10, 2005.

35. John Simpson, "Saddam's Trial Is Not a Farce," BBC News, December 23, 2005, http://news.bbc.co.uk.

36. Ibid.

37. See Paul von Zielbauer, "With Hussein Still Boycotting Trial, A Relative Denies Guilt and MAKES Speeches to the Judge," *New York Times*, July 26, 2006.

38. See Dan Murphy, "An Iraqi Judge Even Saddam Respects," *Christian Science Monitor*, May 18, 2006.

39. John F. Burns and Dexter Filkins, "Iraqis Fight Over Control of the Trial of Saddam," *International Herald Tribune*, September 25–26, 2004.

40. "Iraq Issue Arrest Warrant for Chalabi," Associated Press, August 8, 2004.

41. Burns and Filkins, "Iraqis Fight over Control of Trial of Saddam."

42. Ibid.

43. Ibid.

44. Moghalu, "Saddam's Trial as Politics and Strategy," *Global Viewpoint*, July 13, 2004, www.digitalnpq.org.

45. Olaoluwa Olusanya, "The Statute of the Iraqi Special Tribunal for Crimes against Humanity—Progressive or Retrogressive?" *German Law Journal* 5(7): 859–878, 2004.

46. See Jess Bravin, "U.S. Seeks Timetable to Close U.N. War Crimes Tribunal," *Wall Street Journal*, March 1–3, 2002.

47. Ibid.

48. Olusanya, "The Statute of Iraqi Special Tribunal," p. 875.

49. Ibid. See also Statute of the Iraqi Special Tribunal, Article 14(c).

50. Olusanya, "The Statute of the Iraqi Special Tribunal."

51. Ibid.

52. "Does It Have to Be War?" *The Economist*, March 4, 2006.

53. See Paul von Zielbauer, "For Hussein, A Long, Raucous Trial Ends in His Absence," *New York Times*, July 28, 2006.

54. "The Saddam Hussein Trials," *New York Times*, editorial, April 10, 2006.

55. Ibid.

56. See Simon Sebag Montefiore, "A Disciple of Stalin in the Dock," *International Herald Tribune*, July 3–4, 2004.

CHAPTER 8

1. Beth Simmons, "Is Sovereignty Still Relevant?" *American Journal of International Law*, 94: 227, January 2000.

2. Richard N. Haas, "Pondering Primacy," *Georgetown Journal of International Affairs*, 94, Summer/Fall 2003, where he states: "It is just a fact—neither necessarily good nor bad—that there are things that governments cannot control," but notes at the same time that "governments are not powerless, and they can still do a lot to shape what goes in and out of their borders."

3. See Anne-Marie Slaughter, *The New World Order* (Princeton: Princeton University Press, 2005). See also Slaughter, "Sovereignty and Power in a Networked World," *Stanford Journal of International Law*, 40: 283, 2004.

4. Wheeler, 1992, cited in Barry Buzan, *From International to World Society: English School Theory and the Social Structure of Globalization* (Cambridge: Cambridge University Press, 2004).

5. See Patti Waldmeir, "The Vanishing Borders of Justice," *Financial Times*, July 5, 2004, which discusses the impact of globalization of law on the United States Supreme Court.

6. See "China, the United States and Unocal: The Triumph of Politics over Oil Bargaining," www.globalcomment.com, August 10, 2005. See also "U.S. Urged Not to Meddle with CNOOC's Takeover of UNOCAL," Statement by the Embassy of the People's Republic of China in the United States, July 6, 2005, www.china-embassy.org. Accessed May 10, 2006; and David Barboza and Andrew Ross Sorkin, "Chinese Oil Giant in Takeover Bid for U.S. Corporation," *New York Times*, June 23, 2005.

7. Jonathan Weisman and Bradley Graham, "Dubai Firm to Sell U.S. Port Operations," *Washington Post*, March 10, 2006.

8. See Kingsley Chiedu Moghalu, *Rwanda's Genocide: The Politics of Global Justice* (New York: Palgrave Macmillan, 2005).

9. Ibid., p. 100 and chap. 6.

10. Supreme Court of the United States: *Hamdan v Rumsfeld, Secretary of Defense, et al* (Decided June 29, 2006), www.spuremecourtus.gov/opinions.05pdf, accessed July 31, 2006.

11. Adam Litpak, "Scholars Agree That Congress Could Reject Conventions, but Not That It Should,," *New York Times*, July 15, 2006.

12. Ibid.

13. Rachel Kerr, *The International Criminal Tribunal for the Former Yugoslavia: An Exercise in Law, Politics, and Diplomacy* (Oxford: Oxford University Press, 2004), p. 208.

14. Ibid.

15. "My Judge Is a Party Animal," *The Economist*, January 1, 2005, p. 37.

16. Edwin Madunagu, "Dialectics of Law and Politics," *The Guardian*, May 4, 2006, Nigeria edition.

17. See "2005 World Summit Outcome," UN Doc. A/60/L.1, para. 138–140.

Selected Resources

Ankumah, Evelyn and Kwakwa, Edward, eds., *African Perspectives on International Criminal Justice* (Accra, Ghana: Africa Legal Aid, 2005).

Bass, Gary, *Stay the Hand of Vengeance: The Politics of War Crimes Tribunals* (Princeton, NJ: Princeton University Press, 2000).

Beigbeder, Yves, *Judging War Criminals: The Politics of International Justice* (London: Macmillan Press, 1999).

Berkeley, Bill, *The Graves Are Not Yet Full: Race, Tribe and Power in the Heart of Africa* (New York: Basic Books, 2001).

Broomhall, Bruce, *International Justice & the International Criminal Court: Beyond Sovereignty and the Rule of Law* (New York: Oxford University Press, 2003).

Brown, Chris, *Sovereignty, Rights and Justice: International Political Theory Today* (Cambridge: Polity, 2002).

Bull, Hedley, *The Anarchical Society: A Study of Order in World Politics* (Basingstoke, UK: Palgrave Macmillan, 1977).

Buzan, Barry, *From International to World Society? English School Theory and the Social Structure of Globalization* (Cambridge: Cambridge University Press, 2004).

Byers, Michael and Nolte, Georg, eds., *United States Hegemony and the Foundations of International Law* (Cambridge: Cambridge University Press, 2003).

Clark, Roger and Sann, Madeleine, eds., *The Prosecution of International Crimes: A Critical Study of the International Tribunal for the Former Yugoslavia* (New Brunswick, NJ: Transaction Publishers, 1996).

Dower, John, *Embracing Defeat: Japan in the Wake of World War II* (New York: W.W. Norton, 1999).

Foot, Rosemary, Gaddis, John Lewis and Hurrell, Andrew, eds., *Order and Justice in International Relations* (Oxford: Oxford University Press, 2003).

Glenny, Misha, *The Balkans: Nationalism, War and the Great Powers, 1804–1999* (London: Penguin Books, 1999).

Gold, Hal, *Unit 731: Testimony* (Boston, MA: Tuttle Publishers, 2004).

Hagan, John, *Justice in the Balkans: Prosecuting War Crimes in The Hague Tribunal* (Chicago, IL: University of Chicago Press, 2003).

Higgins, Rosemary, *Problems and Processes: International Law and How We Use It* (Oxford: Oxford University Press, 1992).

Hill, Christopher, *The Changing Politics of Foreign Policy* (Basingstoke, UK: Palgrave Macmillan, 2003).

Holbrooke, Richard, *To End a War* (New York: Modern Library, 1999).

Jackson, Robert: *The Global Covenant: Human Conduct in a World of States* (Oxford: Oxford University Press, 2000).

Jennings, Robert and Watts, Arthur, *Oppenheim's International Law* (London: Longman, 1992).

Jones, Dorothy, *Toward a Just World: The Critical Years in the Search for International Justice* (Chicago, IL: University of Chicago Press, 2002).

Jones, Dorothy, *Code of Peace: Ethics and Security in the World of the Warlord States* (Chicago, IL: University of Chicago Press, 1991).

Kerr, Rachel, *The International Criminal Tribunal for the Former Yugoslavia: An Exercise in Law, Politics and Diplomacy* (Oxford: Oxford University Press, 2004).

Macedo, Stephen, ed., *Universal Jurisdiction: National Courts and the Prosecution of Serious Crimes Under International Law* (Philadelphia: University of Pennsylvania Press, 2004).

Maga, Tim, *Judgment at Tokyo: The Japanese War Crimes Trials* (Lexington: University Press of Kentucky, 2001).

Maogoto, Jackson, *War Crimes and Realpolitik: International Justice from World War I to the 21st Century* (Boulder, CO: Lynne Rienner, 2004).

Mapel, David and Nardin, Terry, *International Society: Diverse Ethical Perspectives* (Princeton: Princeton University Press, 1998).

McGoldrick, Dominic, Rowe, Peter and Donnelly, Eric, *The Permanent International Criminal Court: Legal and Policy Issues* (Oxford: Hart Publishing, 2004).

Moghalu, Kingsley, *Rwanda's Genocide: The Politics of Global Justice* (New York: Palgrave Macmillan, 2005).

Morgenthau, Hans, *Politics among Nations: The Struggle for Power and Peace* (Boston, MA: McGraw Hill, 1993).

Nardin, Terry and Mapel, David, eds., *Traditions of International Ethics* (Cambridge: Cambridge University Press, 1992).

Persico, Joseph, *Nuremberg: Infamy on Trial* (New York: Penguin, 1994).

Reus-Smit, Christian, *The Politics of International Law* (Cambridge: Cambridge University Press, 2004).

Rubin, Alfred, *Ethics and Authority in International Law* (Cambridge: Cambridge University Press, 1997).

Rubin, Alfred, *The Law of Piracy* (Irvington on Hudson, NY: Transnational Publishers, 1998).

Sands, Philippe, *Lawless World: America and the Making and Breaking of Global Rules* (London: Penguin, 2005).

Schabas, William, *An Introduction to the International Criminal Court* (Cambridge: Cambridge University Press, 2004).

Scharf, Michael and Schabas, William, *Slobodan Milosevic on Trial: A Companion* (New York: Continuum Publishers, 2002).

Sewall, Sarah and Kaysen, Carl, *The United States and the International Criminal Court: National Security and International Law* (Lanham: Rowman & Littlefield, 2000).

Shaw, Malcolm, *International Law* (Cambridge: Cambridge University Press, 2003).

Shklar, Judith, *Legalism: Law, Morals and Political Trials* (Cambridge, MA: Harvard University Press, 1986).

Simpson, Gerry, *Great Powers and Outlaw States: Unequal Sovereigns in the International Legal Order* (Cambridge: Cambridge University Press, 2004).

Smith, Karen and Light, Margo, *Ethics and Foreign Policy* (Cambridge: Cambridge University Press, 2001).

Stephen, Chris, *Judgment Day: The Trial of Slobodan Milosevic* (London: Atlantic Books, 2004).

Stover, Eric and Weinstein, Harvey, eds., *My Neighbor, My Enemy: Justice and Community in the Aftermath of Mass Atrocity* (Cambridge: Cambridge University Press, 2004).

Thakur, Ramesh and Malcontent, Peter, *From Sovereign Impunity to International Accountability: The Search for Justice in a World of States* (Tokyo: United Nations University Press, 2004).

The Stationery Office, *The Judgment at Nuremberg* (London, 1999).

Tusa, Ann and Tusa, John, *The Nuremberg Trial* (New York: Cooper Square Press, 1983).

Walzer, Michael, *Just and Unjust Wars* (New York: Basic Books, 1977).

Willis, James, *Prologue to Nuremberg: The Politics and Diplomacy of Punishing War Criminals of the First World War* (Westport, CT: Greenwood Press, 1982).

Index